Twilight and History

Twilight and History

Edited by

NANCY R. REAGIN

John Wiley & Sons, Inc.

This book is printed on acid-free paper. ♾

Published by John Wiley & Sons, Inc., Hoboken, New Jersey
Published simultaneously in Canada

Design by Forty-five Degree Design, LLC

Library of Congress Cataloging-in-Publication Data:

Twilight and history / edited by Nancy R. Reagin.
p. cm.
Includes index.
ISBN 978-0-470-58178-0 (pbk: alk. paper)
1. Meyer, Stephenie, 1973– Twilight saga series. 2. Young adult fiction, American—History and criticism. I. Reagin, Nancy Ruth, 1960–
PS3613.E979Z887 2010
813'.6–dc22

2009049267

Printed in the United States of America

10 9 8 7 6 5 4 3 2 1

For Seth, who first persuaded me to read Twilight

Contents

Acknowledgments: For Those Who Turned Us **ix**
Twilight's Timeline **xi**

Introduction: Frozen in Time **1**
Nancy R. Reagin

PART ONE
Your Basic Human-Vampire-Werewolf/Shape-shifter Triangle: Bella, Edward, and Jacob

1 "An Old-Fashioned Gentleman"? Edward's Imaginary History **7**
Kate Cochran

2 Biting Bella: Treaty Negotiation, Quileute History, and Why "Team Jacob" Is Doomed to Lose **26**
Judith Leggatt and Kristin Burnett

3 CinderBella: Twilight, Fairy Tales, and the Twenty-First-Century American Dream **47**
Sara Buttsworth

4 Courting Edward Cullen: Courtship Rituals and Marital Expectations in Edward's Youth **70**
Catherine Coker

PART TWO
Some Family History: The Cullen Coven

5 Jasper Hale, the Oldest Living Confederate Veteran 89
Elizabeth Baird Hardy

6 Smoky Mountain Twilight: The Appalachian Roots of Emmett McCarty Cullen and His Family 106
Elizabeth Baird Hardy

7 Better Turned Than "Cured"? Alice and the Asylum 127
Grace Loiacono and Laura Loiacono

8 Carlisle Cullen and the Witch Hunts of Puritan London 145
Janice Liedl

9 A Subtle and Dangerous Gift: Jasper Hale and the Specter of the American Civil War 163
Andrea Robertson Cremer

10 Like Other American Families, Only Not: The Cullens and the "Ideal" Family in American History 182
Kyra Glass von der Osten

PART THREE
A World of Vampires: The Volturi and Beyond

11 The Sort of People Who Hired Michelangelo as Their Decorator: The Volturi as Renaissance Rulers 207
Birgit Wiedl

12 "Where Do the Cullens Fit In?": Vampires in European Folklore, Science, and Fiction 227
Eveline Brugger

13 Getting Younger Every Decade: Being a Teen Vampire during the Twentieth Century 245
Kat Burkhart

The Forks High School Faculty 263

Index: Alice Foresaw All of This 267

Acknowledgments

For Those Who Turned Us

It was fandom that turned me first, and to which this book is most indebted. Being involved in literary fandoms taught me the pleasures of exploring an imaginary world and the fun of uncovering the history within and behind each world-building exercise.

Eric Nelson and Connie Santisteban at Wiley drew me into their "vegetarian" coven, proposing this book and seeing it though its development with unfailing support and good humor. Lisa Burstiner and Alexa Selph contributed greatly to the book's readability and backstopped me on the details of the story world.

I myself turned the contributors, and I thank each of them for bringing her expertise and imagination to this book. And we are all indebted to Stephenie Meyer, whose world drew us in and who gave us all so much to write about.

Twilight's Timeline

HUMAN HISTORY	TWILIGHT SAGA HISTORY*
	ca. 1000 B.C. (B.C.E.) Aro, Caius, Marcus, and their wives found the Volturi
551 B.C. (B.C.E.) Birth of Confucius	
ca. 500 Italian city of Volterra is founded	
ca. 400 Birth of Gautama Buddha, founder of Buddhism	
384 Birth of Aristotle	
ca. 30 A.D. (C.E.) Jesus of Nazareth crucified	
ca. 312 Emperor Constantine converts to Christianity	
453 Defeat and death of Attilla the Hun	
	ca. 500 A.D. (C.E.) Volturi-Romanian War
632 Death of Muhammad, prophet of Islam	
	ca. 1000 Kate, Tanya, and Irina born, turned by their "mother"; Plague of the Immortal Children; Births of Carmen and Elezar, in Spain
1095 First Crusade preached at Clermont	
1347 Black Plague reaches Europe	
1436 Johannes Gutenberg develops the printing press	

*Most of the dates for Twilight events are taken from the four volumes of the Twilight Saga. Some dates were taken from the personal correspondence of Stephenie Meyer and the creators of the Twilight Lexicon as incorporated in their timeline, available at www.twilightlexicon.com/?page_id=9. One date was taken from the Twilight Saga Wiki, available at http://twilightsaga.wikia.com/wiki/Twilight_Saga_Wiki.

Twilight's Timeline *(continued)*

HUMAN HISTORY	TWILIGHT SAGA HISTORY
1492 Christopher Columbus reaches the New World, beginning European conquest	
ca. 1502 Beginning of Atlantic slave trade	
1517 Martin Luther launches Protestant Reformation	
1640–1649 English Civil War	**1642 or 1643** Carlisle Cullen born
1657 Birth of Solimena, the Italian artist who is said to have painted Carlisle and the Volturi	
	ca. 1665/6 Carlisle Cullen is turned into a vampire
ca. 1700 An earthquake and tsunami strike the territories of the Quileute Nation, resulting in a great flood, recorded in their myths	
	ca. 1720 Carlisle travels to Italy, meets the Volturi
ca. 1750 Beginning of the Industrial Revolution	
1789 Beginning of the French Revolution	
1810–1821 Mexican War of Independence	
	early 1800s Benito creates army of newborns, launcl ing wars in Mexico and elsewhere
1836 Samuel Colt patents his revolver	
	1844 Jasper Whitlock born
1848 Karl Marx and Friedrich Engels publish the *Communist Manifesto*	
1856 The Quileute Nation signs the Treaty of Olympia with the U.S. government	**ca. 1856** Nahuel born in South America

HUMAN HISTORY	TWILIGHT SAGA HISTORY
1861–1865 U.S. Civil War	**1861** Jasper Whitlock enlists in the Confederate Army, quickly rising to the rank of major
	1862 Jasper Whitlock is turned
ca. 1870 Rubber extraction boom begins in Brazil, transforming the Amazon basin	
ca. 1875 Alexander Graham Bell develops the telephone	
1889 Quileutes granted their traditional settlement as a reservation, at the mouth of the Quillayute River on the Pacific coast in Washington State	
	1895 Esme Platt Evenson born
1897 Bram Stoker's *Dracula* published	
	1901 Edward Masen born Mary "Alice" Brandon born
1914–1918 World War I; U.S. joins war in 1917	
	1915 Emmett McCarty born Rosalie Hale born
1918 Spanish influenza pandemic kills millions	**1918** Edward falls ill with influenza, is turned by Carlisle
	1920 Alice committed to asylum by her family
	1920s Alice is turned
	1921 Esme is turned by Carlisle
1928 Alexander Fleming discovers penicillin	
1929 Beginning of Great Depression	

Twilight's Timeline *(continued)*

HUMAN HISTORY	TWILIGHT SAGA HISTORY
	1933 Rosalie is turned by Carlisle
	1935 Emmett is turned by Carlisle
	ca. 1936 Carlisle and the Cullens move to Forks, Washington, for the first time, and make treaty with the Quileute Nation
1939–1945 World War II	
	1948 Alice finds Jasper Whitlock
1949 Chinese Revolution	
	ca. 1950 Alice and Jasper find Carlisle and join the Cullen Coven
1960 Birth control pill becomes available	
ca. 1980 Rapid development of the Internet	
	1986 Leah Clearwater born Sam Uley born
	1987 Bella Swan born
	1990 Jacob Black born
1991 Collapse of the Soviet Union, end of Cold War	
	1992 Seth Clearwater born
	2003 The Cullens move to Forks
	2005 Bella Swan moves to Forks, meets Edward Cullen, and reconnects with Jacob Black

Introduction
Frozen in Time

Nancy R. Reagin

Do you realize what century this is?" Bella Swan asks Edward Cullen in *Eclipse*, frustrated that he insists on observing the "rules" of his own youth when it comes to courtship. It's a good question: again and again in the Twilight Saga, the vampire characters act in ways that show that while they may know—on an intellectual level—what century it is, they don't always care. Each of them was frozen in time at the moment of being turned into a vampire. "You think of me as a . . . living stone—hard and cold," Edward tells Bella. "That's true. We are set the way we are, and it is very rare for us to experience a real change." (*Eclipse*, 500.) Each of these characters has a unique personal history, which forms the unchanging core of his or her identity.

Stephenie Meyer's Twilight Saga has become a pop culture phenomenon, and not only because of Edward's inhumanly angelic face and perfect, marble body. The Italian novelist and literary critic Umberto Eco observed that films and novels that attract large numbers of enthusiastic fans tend to be those that "provide a completely furnished world," so that its fans can quote characters and discuss the story world's details as if they were part of their own reality.[1] *Twilight* certainly matches this description: we can lose ourselves in a world where shape-shifting wolves defend unsuspecting humans against ravenous bands of newborn vampires. And while its love triangle of vampire-human-werewolf/shape-shifter pulls us in deep, Twilight's alternate universe is both like and unlike our own. It's a world-building exercise that's been thought out down to the last detail, including a body of imagined lore and myth for both the Quileutes and the vampires (which Bella explores on her universe's Internet) unlike any we've seen elsewhere: vampires who sparkle rather than dissolve when exposed to sunlight and werewolves who can change form at a moment's notice, liberated from the moon's cycle.

But part of Twilight's attraction is its rich use of historical events to create a detailed backstory for many characters. Each of the vampires comes from a particular time and place, frozen in age and mentality at the moment he or she was turned. Each of them moves through the decades and centuries, carrying the values and experiences of generations long dead, even (among the Volturi) from cultures thousands of years in the past. Their history becomes part of who they are now, today.

Jasper Hale is and always will be a Confederate veteran: what did he experience during the Civil War, and how did that shape him? Carlisle Cullen was raised among English Puritans and witch-hunters and witnessed not only the Enlightenment of the eighteenth century but also most of our nation's history. How did the political and religious struggles of his youth lead to his ethical vampiric "vegetarianism"? What did Alice Cullen experience in her dark asylum cell, so terrible that even being turned was a welcome escape? How are the Volturi like other powerful ruling families in Italian history? And what *were* those early-twentieth-century rules regarding courtship and marriage, which Edward insists on following?

Bella sees herself as modern, but even she is the product of a particular time and place. A century from now, she will seem old-fashioned to the humans around her, too. You don't have to be Alice to foresee *that* development. Carlisle has probably seen it many times before: time and change pass around and over many newborn vampires, leaving them "frozen" and unchanging, with a worldview different from that of the modern humans they live among. Edward knows it will happen to Bella, too, and he answers a question of hers from this standpoint, which she finds annoying: "A hundred years from now, when you've gained enough perspective to really appreciate the answer, I will explain it to you." (*Eclipse*, 513.)

But this cuts both ways. Enough time has passed since the Cullens' "deaths" that *we* are the ones who have "gained enough perspective" to see the Cullen coven, the Quileutes, the Volturi, and their world through a new lens: that of history. If we place them against the backdrop of their original historical cultures, Twilight's characters stand out in sharp relief, and many details are freshly illuminated. They sparkle and glitter when we shine this new light upon them, and we fall in love with Twilight's world all over again. But now, we understand them even better.

All Twilight Saga references are from the following American editions published by Little Brown and Co.: *Twilight* (2005), *New Moon* (2006), *Eclipse* (2007), *Breaking Dawn* (2008). References to *Midnight Sun* are from www.stepheniemeyer.com/pdf/midnightsun_partial_draft4.pdf.

Notes

1. Umberto Eco, *Travels in Hyper Reality: Essays* (San Diego: Harcourt Brace Jovanovich, 1986), 197.

PART ONE

Your Basic Human-Vampire-Werewolf/Shape-shifter Triangle

Bella, Edward, and Jacob

"An Old-Fashioned Gentleman"?

Edward's Imaginary History

Kate Cochran

Edward Cullen is the ideal man: "Interesting . . . and brilliant . . . and mysterious . . . and perfect . . . and beautiful . . . and possibly able to lift full-sized vans with one hand," as Bella Swan notes. (*Twilight*, 79.) His barely restrained passion, the result of the war between his utter devotion to one woman and his animalistic desire to consume her, is reined in by his moral conscience and colored by the mystery of his aloofness; the fact that his century-old soul is housed in a physically superior seventeen-year-old body is only one aspect of his attractiveness. Both the key to the Twilight Saga's appeal and arguably its most compelling figure, Edward's character also reflects the imaginative way that history is invoked in the four books.

The known details of Edward's personal history are few. He was turned in 1918 at the age of seventeen after being stricken during the Spanish flu epidemic and before shipping off to fight in World War I. But instead of manifesting the mores of the Lost Generation that came of age during the 1920s or even of an indeterminate past, Edward instead embodies the old-fashioned qualities of the nineteenth-century Byronic heroes from Bella's favorite romantic novels. Edward is compared to *Pride and Prejudice*'s Darcy, *Jane Eyre*'s Rochester, and *Wuthering Heights*'s Heathcliff, becoming a general Victorian "gentleman" figure.[1] In an interview, Stephenie Meyer said, "Edward is the most popular [character], and I think it's because he's an old-fashioned gentleman in some ways, and in other ways he's a very modern, sort of tortured soul, although I guess, you know, you go back to Byron and it's all there."[2] An examination of Edward's literary ancestors shows that the Twilight Saga is informed by Meyer's sense of literary history more than by documented historical fact. The perfect man therefore represents Bella's (and Meyer's) fictional heroes, come to life.

Imaginary History: How Literature and History Play Together

"Imaginary history" refers to the different ways that history and literature borrow from each other. For historians, the term can refer to the creation of subjective history or to the use of fictional story to convey historical facts. Gavriel Rosenfeld's article "Why Do We Ask 'What If?': Reflections on the Function of Alternate History" examines how some historians use subjective history, specifically wondering how history would have been different if the "other side" had won World War II, the Civil War, and the American Revolution. Rosenfeld asserts that the value of "allohistorical speculation" lies in "its ability to shed light upon the evolution of historical memory"; that is, when we wonder about what could have happened, we are commenting on what we choose to remember.[3] Other historians employ the phrase "imaginary history" to describe how they use literary devices and styles to communicate history. As Linda Orr explains, in "The Revenge of Literature: A History of History," before the mid-nineteenth century, historians frequently used fictional story to document history, although more recently they have sought to distance the field of history from that of literature. Orr examines the basic concerns of historiography in issues such as realism, bias, source analysis, and linguistic "truth." She observes, however, that "the more history presses toward science, the more literature, or a has-been history, is produced,"[4] showing that even when the two disciplines attempt to diverge, they remain inextricably linked.

"Imaginary history," however, can also indicate the construction of an imaginary past, as it does in the Twilight Saga. Meyer uses history as one means of setting her vampire characters apart, which jibes with George Garrett's definition of "imaginary history." In "Dreaming with Adam: Notes on Imaginary History," Garrett explains that novelists craft the impressionistic world of imaginary history by simply removing the details of the present day: "We therefore work backwards, stripping away the things we know well, to reach the past where they were neither known nor imagined," leaving the impression of an unspecified historical setting.[5] Thus, instead of giving details from each vampire's actual historical background (for example, information about Carlisle Cullen's life in seventeenth-century England), Meyer more often merely indicates that they are not of the twenty-first century. For instance, when Bella remarks on Edward's speech—"I could never quite mimic the flow of his perfect, formal articulation. It was something that could only be picked up in an earlier century"—she does not specify which "earlier century" Edward sounds like. (*New Moon*, 9.)

Meyer's version of imaginary history is linked to feelings of nostalgia, particularly when her unidentified past is merely the present with its more unsavory aspects stripped away. We think of nostalgia as a fondness or yearning for aspects of the past now lost—aspects from both from the communal past and a personal past. For instance, one might feel nostalgic for one's childhood (personal) or for a historical era (communal). There is a sense of murkiness and unreality in these visions of the past; however, the most powerful feelings of nostalgia arise from the remembering or desire for what never really was, a "past" that seems both safe and easily understood due to its simplicity and reliance on shared values.

Bella envisions such a past for Edward as she muses about their engagement: "I saw the same odd vision of Edward and me on a porch swing, wearing clothes from another kind of world. A world where it would surprise no one if I wore his ring on my finger. A simpler place, where love was defined in simpler ways. One plus one equals two." (*Eclipse*, 325.) She refers to her own nostalgia for Edward's past as "*Anne of Green Gables* flashbacks," showing that for Bella, Edward's past is the same kind of imaginary history that Meyer employs: one based in literature. (*Eclipse*, 277.)

The Lost Generation: Edward's Historical Moment

But how does Edward account for his own history? In the saga, little is disclosed about Edward's past. The most revealing comment he offers comes during his attempt to persuade Bella to agree to marry him: "In my world, I was already a man. I wasn't looking for love—no, I was far too eager to be a soldier for that; I thought of nothing but the idealized glory of the war that they were selling prospective draftees then." (*Eclipse*, 276–277.) Edward identifies his desire to fight in World War I as the most defining characteristic of his past. However, his memory of the war raises some questions about historical inconsistencies.

Edward notes that "they were selling" an "idealized glory of the war"; certainly, wartime propaganda abounded during World War I: Sean Dennis Cashman explains that "American propaganda of 1917 [referred to World War I as] the Great Crusade."[6] Much of the American propaganda of the time depicted Germans as bloodthirsty brutes feasting on innocents and destroying democracy.[7] Edward mentions that the propaganda was directed at "prospective draftees." In fact, President Woodrow Wilson's May 1917 draft bill mandated registration for all men between the ages of twenty-one and thirty years old; the draftees who were to serve were selected by lottery drawings. Cashman notes that "the three drafts altogether drew 23,908,576 men in the United States. However, only 6,373,414 went into service," partly because of many draftees' quickie marriages and conscientious objections.[8] Edward was turned in 1918, after the drafts had already taken place; therefore, he must have enlisted. In addition, he was only seventeen years old in 1918, so he must have misrepresented his age when he signed up, claiming to be older so that he'd be accepted.

More important than the misleading implication that Edward was a prospective draftee in 1918, however, is how out of step he was with the opinions popularly held by other members of his generation. World War I is generally acknowledged to have been profoundly disillusioning, breeding "irony, protest, and disgust" because of the horrors of war, the perversion of technology, the falsity of propaganda, and the alienation of civilian populations.[9] The authors who came of age during this era came to be known as the Lost Generation, a term coined by Gertrude Stein and memorialized in Ernest Hemingway's *A Moveable Feast* (1964). Malcolm Cowley, himself identified as a member of the Lost Generation, examines John Dos Passos, William Faulkner, F. Scott Fitzgerald, Ernest Hemingway, and Thomas Wolfe in "The Generation That Wasn't Lost," writing that these authors "had more experiences in common than any other generation of writers in American history. All of them were shaken loose from their moorings by the First World War, even if they were too young to serve in the Army . . . these writers had no home except in the past, no fixed standards, and, in many cases, no sense of direction."[10] Since Stephenie Meyer employs imaginary history in the form of literary references to illustrate Edward's background, it would make sense for her to invoke this era and these authors and their characters, as the context that forms the backdrop for his human life.

Each of the five authors, with the exception of Wolfe, crafted novels that reflected the terrible effects of World War I. For instance, Dos Passos's *1919* (1932), part of his U.S.A. trilogy, contains the concluding tale "The Body of an American," which tells the story of a fallen soldier of World War I. Faulkner's *Soldier's Pay* (1925) recounts the return of a wounded soldier to his home in Georgia; Hemingway's expatriate Jake Barnes in *The Sun Also Rises*

(1926) tries to come to terms with his emasculating war wound. And Nick Carraway, the narrator of Fitzgerald's *The Great Gatsby* (1925), represents the postwar disillusionment of his generation as his already tenuous optimism is shaken by his experiences in West Egg, New York. As Cowley notes of the Lost Generation authors, "At first they rebelled against the hypocrisy of their elders and against the gentility of American letters. Next they rebelled against the noble phrases that justified the slaughter of millions in the First World War."[11] While Edward's enlistment in World War I mirrors those of Dos Passos, Faulkner, Hemingway, and Fitzgerald, and his bitter remembrance of his enthusiasm to fight is similar to their characters' disillusionment, his temperament is not truly reflective of the rebellion of the Lost Generation. Instead, Edward's "old-fashionedness" more closely recalls the qualities of a Victorian gentleman.

The Victorian Gentleman: A Secular Saint

Edward's most notable characteristics—emotional and physical restraint, a strong moral conscience, fierce family loyalty, and wide-ranging accomplishments—align with popular notions of the Victorian gentleman. James Eli Adams observes that the Victorian gentleman was often portrayed as a man whose "moral ideal" constituted a kind of "secular sainthood."[12] Although it may seem incongruous to liken a vampire to a saint, Edward's self-denial and determination to protect Bella, particularly from himself, justify the comparison. Edward's restraint is most obvious when it comes to his physical relationship with Bella: "He started to pull away—that was his automatic response whenever he decided things had gone too far, his reflex reaction whenever he most wanted to keep going. Edward had spent most of his life rejecting any kind of physical gratification." (*Breaking Dawn*, 25.) While Edward tells her he desires her, he takes great care not to allow their kisses to become erotic. When Bella's father, Charlie, confronts Bella about sex, she tells him, "Edward is very old-fashioned. You have nothing to worry about." (*Eclipse*, 59.) In fact, it is Bella who has "nothing to worry about"; Edward is utterly in control of their sexual relationship.

Bella tries to convince Edward to have sex—"'Do you get the feeling that everything is backward?' he laughed in my ear. 'Traditionally, shouldn't you be arguing my side, and I yours?'" (*Eclipse*, 451)—but he insists that their shared chastity is vital. He says, "My virtue is all I have left," since he has broken so many other moral laws and wants to ensure that even though Bella is determined to become a vampire, he will not be responsible for keeping her out of heaven. (*Eclipse*, 452.) Therefore, he insists on marriage before they consummate their relationship. When Edward asks Charlie for permission to marry Bella, he says, "We're going away to Dartmouth together in the fall, Charlie . . . I'd like to do that, well, the right way. It's how I was raised." (*Breaking Dawn*, 16).[13] Ultimately, Bella overcomes her profound ambivalence about marrying Edward, at least in part because she so desperately wants to have sex with him, which emphasizes the difference in their moral beliefs.

Edward's diverse accomplishments are consistent with the pursuits of an idealized Victorian gentleman. He composes music and plays the piano, speaks several languages, is very well read, has attended medical school twice, and even makes a mean omelet. Edward attributes his skills to his lonely nights: "There's a reason why I'm the best musician in the family, why—besides Carlisle—I've read the most books, studied the most sciences, become fluent in the most languages . . . Emmett would have you believe that I'm such a know-it-all because of the mind reading, but the truth is that I've just had a *lot* of free time." (*Breaking Dawn*, 485.) Interestingly, then, Edward's chastity is largely responsible for both his sexual restraint and his numerous accomplishments.

In keeping with the Victorian gentleman's "steadfastness and virility," Edward tries to protect Bella from all forms of danger, including the danger that he might be overcome with bloodlust and bite her.[14] His protectiveness leads him to warn her frequently: "It's not only your company I crave! Never forget *that*. Never forget I am more dangerous to you than I am to anyone else."

(*Twilight*, 266.) He is equally vigilant about other forms of danger—Bella's preternatural clumsiness, the vengeance of the nomadic vampires James and Victoria, the threat of the Volturi, Tyler Crowley's out-of-control van, the would-be rapists in Port Angeles—leading him to call Bella a "danger magnet," although he blames himself for most of those perilous situations. Edward says, "I infuriate myself . . . The way I can't seem to keep from putting you in danger. My very existence puts you at risk. Sometimes I truly hate myself. I should be stronger." (*Twilight*, 365–366.) That self-hatred also places him squarely within the tradition of the Byronic hero.

The Byronic Hero: Darcy, Rochester, and Heathcliff

The Byronic hero, based on both the persona and the fictional characters of author George Gordon (Lord Byron), is a brooding, mysterious man who is intelligent, sophisticated, educated, magnetic, charismatic, socially and sexually dominant though detached from human society, moody, and prone to bouts of temper.[15] He often has a troubled past and is riddled with self-destructive secrets. His lover Lady Caroline Lamb was famously quoted describing Byron as "mad, bad, and dangerous to know"; recent examples of this type include the cartoon hero Batman, Dr. Gregory House from television's *House, M.D.*, the late actor James Dean, and rap artist 50 Cent. The Byronic hero is sometimes called an antihero because of his negative qualities; indeed, Sandra M. Gilbert and Susan Gubar compare him to a bewitching monster like Milton's Satan: "He is in most ways the incarnation of worldly male sexuality, fierce, powerful, experienced, simultaneously brutal and seductive, devilish enough to overwhelm the body and yet enough a fallen angel to charm the soul."[16] The Byronic hero's mystery, moodiness, and sensuality call to mind Bella's reaction to Edward in their meadow: "I sat without moving, more frightened of him than I had ever been. I'd never seen him so completely freed of that carefully cultivated façade. He'd never been less human . . . or more beautiful. Face ashen, eyes wide, I sat like a bird locked in the eyes of a snake." (*Twilight*, 264.)

At several points in the saga, Bella notes that Edward's beauty is terrifying. In keeping with Gilbert and Gubar's comparison of the Byronic hero to Satan, Bella not only describes being captivated as if she were "locked in the eyes of a snake," but she also equates him with an angel, albeit a forbidding one. When she tries to get him to explain how he saved her from Tyler's van, Bella thinks, "I was in danger of being distracted by his livid, glorious face. It was like trying to stare down a destroying angel." (*Twilight*, 65.) Later, when Alice Cullen brings Nahuel to end the confrontation with the Volturi, Bella again compares Edward to a fearsome angel: "His face glowed with an expression of triumph that I didn't understand—it was the expression an angel of destruction might wear while the world burned. Beautiful and terrifying." (*Breaking Dawn*, 730.) Edward, then, manifests a kind of supernatural pull, both in his disquieting beauty and in his formidable power.

But the Byronic hero is not simply wildly seductive and strong, he is also tormented. He remains painfully aware of his own flaws even as he despises them in others; his introspection often leads him to black moods and self-destructive behavior. Edward's penchant for self-flagellation clearly identifies him with the Byronic hero's torment. Nowhere is this more evident than in his desperate attempt to commit suicide in *New Moon*, after he thinks Bella has killed herself out of despair over his leaving her. Upon their return to Forks, Bella confronts him about his misplaced guilt: "You can't let this . . . this *guilt* . . . rule your life. You can't take responsibility for the things that happen to me here. None of it is your fault, it's just part of how life *is* for me. I know it's your . . . your nature to shoulder the blame for everything, but you really can't let that make you go to such extremes!" (*New Moon*, 507.) While Edward never again attempts to die to compensate for his guilt, his tendency toward reflection and self-criticism remain constant.

Some of the most famous Byronic heroes in English literature are like Edward: Darcy, Rochester, and Heathcliff. Not only are *Pride and Prejudice* and *Wuthering Heights* explicitly mentioned in the saga, but there are also overt and covert literary references made to these authors, texts, and characters. For instance, when Bella flips through her Austen compilation, she sees both "Edward Ferrars" from *Sense and Sensibility* and "Edmund Bertram" from *Mansfield Park*, leading her to wonder, "Weren't there any other names available in the late eighteenth century?" (*Twilight*, 148.) Although not explicitly mentioned in the saga, it is noteworthy that two characters in *Wuthering Heights* are named Edgar and Isabella Linton. In *Jane Eyre*, Rochester's first name is Edward, and his wife Bertha's maiden name is Mason; Edward Cullen's original name was Edward Masen. More significant than these references, however, are the Byronic parallels among Edward, Darcy, Rochester, and Heathcliff.

Darcy: First Impressions

Fitzwilliam Darcy of Jane Austen's *Pride and Prejudice* (1813) is moody, cold, superior, and judgmental. He is an object of fascination for the heroine, Elizabeth Bennet, because she feels an attraction to him despite his aloofness. Some of his appeal is revealed via his friendship with Mr. Bingley, whose naive enthusiasm bespeaks a kindness, tolerance, and love of fun on the part of Darcy. His actions when Lydia and Wickham elope, in addition to his past behavior in his relationship with Wickham, recommend him as honorable, caring, and thoughtful; he also seems entirely immune to the flattery and flirtation of Caroline Bingley. These characteristics may be even more attractive since they are at least initially masked by his strong reserve. Moreover, the fact that his positive qualities hide behind aloofness reveal his closely guarded passionate nature, a certain lure for Elizabeth.

The original title of *Pride and Prejudice* was *First Impressions*, which is quite fitting, considering that Darcy and Elizabeth's misperceptions commence from their first meeting. When Darcy arrives at the ball in Hertfordshire, he is immediately admired: "Mr. Darcy soon drew the attention of the room by his fine, tall person, handsome features, noble mien; and the report which was in general circulation within five minutes after his entrance, of his having ten thousand a year."[17] He soon loses the good opinion of the locals, however, because of his coldness: "[H]e was looked at with great admiration for about half the evening, till his manners gave a disgust which turned the tide of his popularity; for he was discovered to be proud, to be above his company, and above being pleased; and not all his large estate in Derbyshire could then save him from having a most forbidding, disagreeable countenance."[18] Like Darcy, Edward makes a strong first impression in the cafeteria. Bella is immediately astounded by the Cullens' beauty, but when she asks about Edward, Jessica Stanley says, "He's gorgeous, of course, but don't waste your time. He doesn't date. Apparently none of the girls here are good-looking enough for him." (*Twilight*, 22.) Both Darcy and Edward, then, are set apart by their emotional distance.

Darcy offends Elizabeth at the ball. When it is suggested that he ask her to dance, he says (and she overhears), "She is tolerable; but not handsome enough to tempt *me*; and I am in no humour at present to give consequence to young ladies who are slighted by other men."[19] His haughty rejection of her is reminiscent of Edward's expression when Bella is seated next to him in class: "I peeked up at him one more time, and regretted it. He was glaring down at me again, his black eyes full of revulsion. As I flinched away from him, shrinking against my chair, the phrase *if looks could kill* suddenly ran through my mind." (*Twilight*, 24.) Of course, Edward is reacting to the overwhelming scent of Bella's blood; similarly, Darcy finds himself attracted to Elizabeth: "But no sooner had he made it clear to himself and his friends that she had hardly a good feature in her face, than he began to find it was rendered uncommonly intelligent by the beautiful expression of her dark eyes. To this discovery succeeded some others equally mortifying."[20] Like all good Byronic heroes, Edward and Darcy feel self-disgust, though it seems to manifest as disgust for their love objects.

Perhaps because of their seeming disgust, combined with the superiority of both Darcy and Edward in terms of social standing, physical attractiveness, and income, neither Bella nor Elizabeth can believe that they are desired. For instance, Elizabeth is disquieted by "how frequently Mr. Darcy's eyes were fixed on her. She hardly knew how to suppose that she could be an object of admiration to so great a man. . . . She could only imagine however at last, that she drew his notice because there was something about her more wrong and reprehensible, according to his ideas of right, than in any other person present."[21] In the meadow, Bella despairs: "He was too perfect. . . . There was no way this godlike creature could be meant for me." (*Twilight*, 256.) When Edward and Darcy declare themselves, however, it is phrased like surrender, showing just how profoundly Elizabeth and Bella are desired. Darcy says, "In vain have I struggled. It will not do. My feelings will not be repressed. You must allow me to tell you how ardently I admire and love you."[22] Edward tells Bella, "I'm tired of trying to stay away from you," and "You are the most important thing to me now. The most important thing to me ever." (*Twilight*, 85, 273).

Rochester: Reader, I Married Him

Edward Rochester, the hero of Charlotte Brontë's *Jane Eyre* (1847), feels no guilt for wooing Jane, even though he is already secretly married. Although, after Jane learns of the existence of Rochester's first wife, the mad Bertha Mason, who is kept imprisoned in the attic at Thornfield Hall, Rochester says, "I am little better than a devil at this moment," he still wants Jane to stay with him as his mistress.[23] At the end of the novel, however, when Jane returns to find Rochester blinded and maimed from the fire that consumed Bertha and the house, he finally expresses some sense of guilt that he is no longer physically worthy of Jane: "I am no better than the old lightning-struck chestnut-tree in Thornfield orchard. . . . And what right would that ruin have to bid a budding woodbine cover its decay with freshness?"[24] Those guilt feelings are remarkably short-lived, and he and Jane are married immediately. Rather than being tormented by guilt, then, like many Byronic heroes, Rochester primarily suffers from the effects of his dark secret, which renders him mysterious and frightening. At times Jane describes him as proud, sardonic, moody, morose, imperious; indeed, Mrs. Fairfax says Rochester has "painful thoughts."[25] Just as Edward tends to brood, most often about how his vampirism endangers Bella, so, too, is Rochester melancholy, though he does not believe that he is to blame for his dark secret.

After Briggs interrupts Jane and Rochester's wedding, Rochester explains the circumstances of his marriage to Bertha Mason: that he was hoodwinked into marrying a half-mad, drunken woman five years his senior who soon disgraced him in their Caribbean home; that her continued existence kept him from finding love or companionship, despite the fact that he keeps her shut up in the attic; that he feels "hampered, burdened, cursed."[26] Certainly Rochester's isolation (though interrupted with a few mistresses) is reminiscent of Edward's ninety years without a mate: they both feel doomed to solitude. Alice tells Bella, "It's been almost a century that Edward's been alone. Now he's found you. You can't see the changes that we see, we who have been with him for so long. Do you think any of us want to look into his eyes for the next hundred years if he loses you?" (*Twilight*, 410–411.) More telling is the equation between the madwoman Bertha and Edward's vampirism: the Byronic heroes' dark secrets. When Jane tells Rochester about her vision of the woman with the "fiery eye," "lurid visage," and "gaunt head" who tears her wedding veil, she says it reminded her "of the foul German spectre—the Vampyre."[27] But Jane's descriptions of Rochester at their first, aborted wedding bear a strong resemblance to Edward's physicality. She notes his "flaming and flashing eyes," his "pale, firm, massive front" like "quarried marble," his face like "colourless rock," and "His eye, as I have often said, was a black eye: it had now a tawny, nay a bloody light in its gloom," all of which correspond to Edward's vampire physique.[28]

Perhaps the most interesting way in which Rochester resembles Edward is in his attempt to control the woman he loves. Citing their advanced ages, both Edward and Rochester often take charge of Bella and Jane. While Edward has ninety years on Bella, and the advantage of mental telepathy and knowledge of the vampire world, Rochester says, "I claim only such superiority as must result from twenty years' difference in age and a century's advance in experience."[29] Gilbert and Gubar refer to "Rochester's loving tyranny";[30] Edward himself invokes that word when he warns Bella, prior to the impending vampire nomad visit, "I'm going to be a little . . . overbearingly protective over the next few days—or weeks—and I wouldn't want you to think I'm naturally a tyrant." (*Twilight*, 328.) But some might argue that Edward *is* tyrannical: he asks Alice to kidnap Bella for the weekend in *Eclipse*; he wants to force Bella to have an abortion in *Breaking Dawn*; he removes himself from her life in *New Moon* for her own good. In addition, throughout the series Edward sometimes treats Bella as if she were a baby, carrying her in his arms, swaddling her in blankets, singing her to sleep with a lullaby. Rather than being seen as tyrannical, then, Edward can be viewed as paternalistic, acting as though he were her parent rather than her boyfriend. That will to dominate is surely one of the hallmarks of the Byronic hero, as well as of the Victorian gentleman.

Finally, Edward and Rochester are similar in their regard for their love objects as the panacea for the loneliness and torment that result from their dark secrets. For instance, both men are surprised by their compulsion to confide in the objects of their affection. Rochester says, "Strange that I should choose you for the confidant in all this . . . [but] you, with your gravity, considerateness, and caution, were made to be the recipient of secrets."[31] And Edward states, "I was prepared to feel relieved. Having you know about everything, not needing to keep secrets from you. But I didn't expect to feel more than that. I *like* it. It makes me . . . happy." (*Twilight*, 344.) There is relief for the Byronic hero as he unburdens his soul of terrible secrets; the absolute honesty that he shares with his love forges their unbreakable connection.

Heathcliff: I Cannot Live without My Soul

In contrast to Darcy's overbearing ego and Rochester's moody paternalism, Heathcliff, from Emily Brontë's *Wuthering Heights* (1847), is not bound by the rules of "polite society" and is therefore utterly free to acknowledge his naked devotion to Cathy. Identified from the beginning as exotic and savage, a foundling brought to the Heights by Mr. Earnshaw, Heathcliff embodies the ferocity and animalism of the Byronic hero. Mr. Linton calls him "a strange acquisition my late neighbour made in his journey to Liverpool—a little Lascar, or an American or Spanish castaway," while Nelly romanticizes his mysterious past: "You're fit for a prince in disguise. Who knows, but your father was Emperor of China, and your mother an Indian queen."[32] The exoticism that Mr. Linton and Nelly ascribe to Heathcliff is Victorian shorthand for savagery, since in their minds it would stand in contrast to the "civility" of Imperial Britain. And, though Heathcliff returns to the Heights as an adult, having acquired his fortune and eventually buying out Hindley Earnshaw, Nelly still notices: "A half-civilized ferocity lurked yet in the depressed brows and eyes full of black fire, but it was subdued; and his manner was even dignified, quite divested of roughness though too stern for grace."[33] Heathcliff, it seems, cannot overcome his innate wildness.

Heathcliff's wildness sometimes manifests as brutality. Abused by Hindley and abandoned by Cathy after Mr. Earnshaw's death, Heathcliff becomes cruel and even monstrous, as when he kills Isabella Linton's lapdog after Isabella elopes with him, or taunts Linton, Catherine, and Hareton. Edward's "monstrosity" is his vampirism, against which he battles daily. While Edward never displays the unrestrained cruelty of Heathcliff, he does admit to what he calls "a typical bout of rebellious adolescence" in which he hunts and kills humans who intend to commit evil acts, like murder. (*Twilight*, 342.) He says, however, that "as time went on, I began to see the monster in my eyes. I couldn't escape the debt of so much human life taken, no matter how justified," so he returned to Esme and Carlisle and life as a "vegetarian." (*Twilight*, 343.) And, regardless of how humane the vampire vegetarian lifestyle might be, Edward possesses the barbarous power required to kill James, Victoria, and anyone else who would seek to harm Bella.

The flip side of the Byronic hero's savagery, then, is his passionate attachment to his love. As children, Heathcliff and Cathy are inseparable, seemingly sharing the same soul as they run wild over the moors. Their perfect happiness is ruined when Cathy convalesces at Thrushcross Grange and falls under the influence of the overcultured Lintons; she determines to marry Edgar Linton, although she still insists to Nelly: "I *am* Heathcliff—he's always, always in my mind—not as a pleasure, any more than I am always a pleasure to myself—but as my own being."[34] It is when Cathy is dying that Heathcliff reveals the depth of his ardor; when he rushes to Cathy's sickroom, Nelly reports that "he gnashed at me, and foamed like a mad dog, and gathered her to him with greedy jealousy," braying, "Be with me always—take any form—drive me mad! Only *do* not leave me in this abyss, where I cannot find you! oh, God! it is unutterable! I *cannot* live without my life! I *cannot* live without my soul!"[35]

Edward actually quotes that final line, after Bella quotes Cathy's lament to him: "If all else perished, and he remained, I should still continue to be; and if all else remained, and he were annihilated, the universe would turn to a mighty stranger." (*Eclipse*, 611.) In fact, *Wuthering Heights* is the only one of Bella's novels mentioned in each of the Twilight Saga's four books, with the exception of *New Moon*: an odd omission, since one could argue that the plotline of *New Moon* more closely mirrors *Wuthering Heights* than the other books do. Like *Wuthering Heights, New Moon* opens with Edward and Bella's carefree happiness, though the English moors are replaced with the meadow outside Forks. When Edward abandons Bella, she is emotionally destroyed and recklessly acts out, riding motorcycles and cliff-diving. However, she still races to his version of a vampire's deathbed, in Volterra, driven by their love. And when Edward returns to her, he exclaims, "As if there were any way that *I* could exist without needing *you*!" (*New Moon*, 510.) Bella, however, sees her situation in *Eclipse* as being similar to the plot of *Wuthering Heights*, since she is torn between Jacob and Edward, just as Cathy is between Edgar and Heathcliff.

In fact, Edward begins to identify with Heathcliff during *Eclipse*. Although at first he denigrates Heathcliff and Cathy as "ghastly people who ruin each other's lives," he later notes, "The more time I spend with you, the more human emotions seem comprehensible to me. I'm discovering that I can sympathize with Heathcliff in ways I didn't think possible before." (*Eclipse*, 28, 265.) Indeed, Heathcliff is likened to a vampire by Nelly when he roams the moors alone at night, and when Edward rereads Bella's copy of *Wuthering Heights*, the book is left open to the page that shows Heathcliff describing his rival Edgar Linton in almost vampiric terms: "Had he been in my place, and I in his, though I hated him with a hatred that turned my life to gall, I never would have raised a hand against him. . . . I never would have banished him from her society, as long as she desired his. The moment her regard ceased, I would have torn his heart out, and drank his blood!"[36] Edward, however, says he sympathizes with Heathcliff because he is coming to understand human emotions; instead of Heathcliff's drive to become more civilized, Edward is overcoming his Byronic savagery by trying to become more human.[37]

Imagining Edward's History through Literature

This chapter began with the observation that Stephenie Meyer incorporates imaginary history into her Twilight Saga as a way to describe her vampire characters. According to George Garrett, "to write imaginary history is to celebrate the human imagination," that is, "the possibility of imagining lives and spirits of other human beings, living or dead."[38] For Meyer, these imaginings come from her own sense of literary history, and her reading list is similar to Bella's: "I kept my eyes down on the reading list the teacher had given me. It was fairly basic: Brontë, Shakespeare, Chaucer, Faulkner. I'd already read everything. That was comforting . . . and boring." (*Twilight*, 15.) The classic literature that Meyer invokes—like *Pride and Prejudice*, *Jane Eyre*, and *Wuthering Heights*—would be at home on any high school syllabus.

Far from being boring, though, Meyer's imaginary history, created through literary references, fashions the perfect man. In an interview in *Newsweek*, Meyer was asked, "Edward is so perfect—you've ruined regular men for a lot of teens. Do you feel bad?"

to which she responded, "Oh, a little bit, I guess. I just wanted to write for myself, a fantasy. And that's what Edward is."[39] For Meyer, as well as multitudes of Twilight fans, the fantasy of the perfect man is cobbled together from various Byronic heroes. Even though Edward was "born" much later, and would have come of age during the 1920s, his "true" history can be found in nineteenth-century Victorian novels.

Notes

1. Although the Victorian era is designated as 1837 to 1901, the span of Queen Victoria's reign, and *Pride and Prejudice* was first published in 1813, this chapter examines the similarities between Austen's work and the Brontës' novels in terms of their male protagonists. It is arguable that Darcy exhibits as many traditional "Victorian" qualities as the more Romantic Rochester and Heathcliff, if not more. In fact, although *Wuthering Heights* was published in 1847 (as was *Jane Eyre*), it is set in the late 1700s to early 1800s.

2. "Conversation with Stephenie Meyer," *Twilight: Three-Disc Deluxe Edition*, DVD (directed by Catherine Hardwicke, Summit Entertainment, 2008).

3. Gavriel Rosenfeld, "Why Do We Ask 'What If?' Reflections on the Function of Alternate History," *History and Theory* 41, no. 4 (Dec. 2002): 91, 93.

4. Linda Orr, "The Revenge of Literature: A History of History," *New Literary History* 18, no. 1 (Autumn 1986): 6.

5. George Garrett, "Dreaming with Adam: Notes on Imaginary History," *New Literary History* 1, no. 3 (Spring 1970): 417–418. Garrett's version of "imaginary history" resembles Mikhail Bahktin's "historical inversion," which describes how the cultural ideals lacking in the present are attributed to the past, from *The Dialogic Imagination: Four Essays*, ed. Michael Holquist, trans. Caryl Emerson and Michael Holquist (Austin: Univ. of Texas Press, 1981), 147.

6. Sean Dennis Cashman, *America in the Age of the Titans: The Progressive Era and World War I* (New York: New York Univ. Press, 1988), 460.

7. See, for instance, Joseph Carter's *1918: Year of Crisis, Year of Change* (Englewood Cliffs, NJ: Prentice-Hall, Inc., 1968), which notes that World War I propaganda "had to appeal to the basic (and often basest) emotions of the masses—curiosity, preoccupation with violence and sex, greed, and finally, but not least, patriotism" (22). Some excellent examples of these posters can be found in Peter Paret, Beth Irwin Lewis, and Paul Paret, *Persuasive Images: Posters of War and Revolution from the Hoover Institution Archives* (Princeton; NJ: Princeton Univ. Press, 1992).

8. Cashman, *America in the Age of the Titans*, 488.

9. Ibid., 425.

10. Malcolm Cowley, "The Generation That Wasn't Lost," *College English* 5, no. 5 (February 1944): 233.

11. Ibid., 237.

12. James Eli Adams, *Dandies and Desert Saints: Styles of Victorian Masculinity* (Ithaca, NY: Cornell Univ. Press, 1995), 42.

13. Edward's statement here causes Bella to reflect: "He wasn't exaggerating; they'd been big on old-fashioned morals during World War I." (*Breaking Dawn*, 16.) However, in

keeping with Garrett's observation about imaginary history, Bella doesn't indicate exactly what those "old-fashioned morals" are, aside from the reluctance to cohabitate and/or have sex outside the bounds of matrimony. Perhaps the one way in which Bella is identified with the twenty-first century is her desire to engage in premarital sex; otherwise, she seems like a throwback to an earlier era, as well, with her domesticity, bookishness, shyness, kindness, and proclivity for self-sacrifice.

14. Daniela Garofalo, *Manly Leaders in Nineteenth-Century British Literature* (Albany: State Univ. of New York Press, 2008), 21.

15. Not coincidentally, Lord Byron's friend and physician John Polidori wrote one of the first narratives in English about vampires, "The Vampyre" (1819). Supposedly Polidori wrote the tale during a stormy country house weekend in 1816 when Percy Bysshe Shelley encouraged him, Byron, and Mary Shelley to compose scary stories. That weekend, Mary Shelley began what later became *Frankenstein, or, the Modern Prometheus* (1818).

16. Sandra M. Gilbert and Susan Gubar, *The Madwoman in the Attic: The Woman Writer and the Nineteenth-Century Literary Imagination*, 2nd ed. (New Haven, CT: Yale Univ. Press, 2000), 206.

17. Jane Austen, *Pride and Prejudice* (Oxford: Oxford Univ. Press, 1998), 7.

18. Ibid., 8.

19. Ibid., 9.

20. Ibid., 19.

21. Ibid., 44.

22. Ibid., 168.

23. Charlotte Brontë, *Jane Eyre* (New York: W.W. Norton, 1987), 256.

24. Ibid., 391.

25. Ibid., 112.

26. Ibid., 120.

27. Ibid., 250.

28. Ibid., 253, 254, 255, 256.

29. Ibid., 117.

30. Gilbert and Gubar, *Madwoman in the Attic*, 357.

31. Charlotte Brontë, *Jane Eyre*, 126.

32. Emily Brontë, *Wuthering Heights* (Oxford: Clarendon Press, 1976), 62, 72.

33. Ibid., 118.

34. Ibid., 102.

35. Ibid., 197, 204.

36. Ibid., 181.

37. Edward says of vampires, "The others—the majority of our kind who are quite content with our lot—they, too, wonder at how we live. But you see, just because we've been . . . dealt a certain hand . . . it doesn't mean that we can't choose to rise above—to conquer the boundaries of a destiny that none of us wanted. To try to retain whatever essential humanity we can." (*Twilight*, 307.) It is true that the Cullens' vegetarianism and pretense at a normal life show their commitment to retain their humanity; Edward actively attempts to recover his humanity throughout the course of his relationship with the human Bella, in part by remembering small details like opening the car door for her.

38. Garrett, "Dreaming with Adam," 15.

39. Susan Elgin, "The Secret Life of Vampires," *Newsweek*, August 4, 2008, 63.

Biting Bella

Treaty Negotiation, Quileute History, and Why "Team Jacob" Is Doomed to Lose

Judith Leggatt and Kristin Burnett

Treaties, the terms of treaties, and the renegotiation of treaties are central to Stephenie Meyer's Twilight series. Meyer's story takes place in Forks, Washington, twelve miles away from the Quileute reservation and their settlement of La Push. The Quileute people figure prominently in Meyer's story. Indeed, the treaty negotiated between the Quileute people, including shape-shifters who turn into wolves when their land is threatened, and the Cullens, "vegetarian" vampires who feed on animals rather than people, is essential to the story because it stands in the way of Edward's turning Bella into a vampire and thus fully consummating their relationship. The treaty demarcates Native land from vampire land and stipulates that the Quileute people will keep the Cullens' identity a secret and not interfere with their activities, so long as the Cullens do not trespass on Quileute land, and *never* bite a human. The Quileute character

Jacob Black, who is Bella Swan's second love interest, emphatically insists on a strict interpretation of the treaty in order to keep Bella human and, thus, his hope of romance with her alive. The last three novels of the tetralogy center on the difficult negotiations that occur between the two groups.

In this chapter, we examine how the series depicts the history of Native-newcomer relations, both through the erotic triangle of Bella, Edward, and Jacob and through the treaty between the vampires and werewolves. The uneasy peace that exists between the Cullens and the Quileute Nation in the first book of the series parallels similar treaties made between Native Americans and the settler governments of North America, including the Treaty of Olympia, signed between the Quileute Nation and the United States of America in 1856. The negotiation of the supernatural treaty and the drastic changes that were forced upon the Quileute people because of it not only parallel the specific historical relationships between the Quileutes and American settlers, but also reflect the larger framework of Native/non-Native relations, both legal and cultural, across North America.

The supernatural treaty in *Twilight* is a literary parallel to the historic Treaty of Olympia, and the saga offers a lens through which to examine that treaty, its historical significance, and the present-day implications and understandings of such an agreement. The manner in which the historical and contemporary Quileute experienced the treaty differs dramatically from the Quileute in Meyer's novel. That the treaty between the Cullens and the Quileute people is respected by both parties forms a stark contrast to the history of treaties in the United States. The failure of federal and state governments to observe the principles of the treaties they negotiated in good faith is a constant refrain in American history. Nevertheless, there remains one important similarity between the historical and fictional treaties: both result in the transfer of land ownership. In the Twilight Saga, Bella represents the land, Jacob embodies the Quileute people, and Edward Cullen stands in for the newcomers.

That Bella becomes a vampire and marries Edward, and that Jacob must come to terms with Bella's choice and is compelled to transfer his affections to the offspring of a union he so opposed, symbolizes the fact that assimilation and accommodation were always considered necessary for the Quileute people in order to survive their contact with non-Native people. Jacob tells Bella, "I was the natural path your life would have taken . . . If the world was the way it was supposed to be, if there were no monsters and no magic." (*Eclipse*, 599.) Just as Edward, who in the natural course of things would have died before Bella was born, throws the path of Jacob and Bella's relationship off course before it can begin, so too does the conquest of North America lead to the relegation and relocation of Native people to reservations that are much smaller than, and often far removed from, their traditional land. While Meyer presents a positive, if stereotypical, image of the Quileute people and of the treaty process as a means of coexistence, the conflicts in the novels, and their resolution through the renegotiation of the treaties and through the creation of a mixed-species family, all lead to a shift in power away from the Quileute people to the newcomers.

Treaties and the Shaping of Indigenous Identity

Treaties have often shaped relations between the United States and Native American peoples. From 1778 to 1868, when the last such treaty was signed in the United States, there were 368 treaties ratified by the federal government.[1] The early treaties were agreements of "peace and friendship," recognizing territorial boundaries and acknowledging the sovereignty and autonomy of Native American nations. Initially, the U.S. government entered into such contracts with Native peoples out of necessity; it was not in a position to wage war, and treaties became the least disruptive means of gaining peace and ensuring settlement. In these early decades, the United States recognized the rights of Native people as nations and dealt with them as such; in 1832 the Supreme Court redefined the status of Native American tribes as domestic dependent nations.[2] This ruling was rarely put into practice, however, and the original intent of the treaties remains a matter of debate.

As the non-Native population grew and available agricultural land became scarce, the treaty system came under increasing pressure in the United States. The tremendous growth of White western settlement and the resistance of Native peoples to such expansion was not resolved by the treaties. In fact, violence and anger between Native and non-Native peoples grew throughout the nineteenth century. Moreover, the United States negotiated treaties more and more from a position of overwhelming strength, and thus increasingly operated on the assumption that treaty rights were something bestowed on Native people out of newcomer generosity. In fact, in both history and the Twilight novels, both parties wished to avoid fighting and were willing to make concessions to keep the peace.

In *Eclipse*, both parties' oral histories acknowledge that the superior might of the vampires made the treaty unnecessary for them at that time, an assumption also made by the U.S. negotiators of the treaties in the latter half of the nineteenth century; in history, this assumption ultimately led to the demise of the treaty system. The imbalance of power relations fundamentally altered the goals and objectives of the treaties. Although both sides sought to negotiate the best possible circumstances for themselves, Native people were seen by the U.S. negotiators as an impediment to progress and settlement, and treaties became a means of imposing European American culture on Native societies, rather than the product of diplomatic negotiations between sovereign nations. Neither the Cullens nor the U.S. government gave up anything in the treaty process; the Cullens were already "vegetarian," so their lives were not altered to accommodate the Quileute, and the settler government acquired vast tracts of Native land without resorting to costly military solutions.

As a result, when the treaties of the Northwest Pacific Coast came about at the end of the United States' treaty-making era, they dealt more with stealing land, paternalism, and assimilation than with peace and friendship.[3] From 1854 to 1855, the first governor of the Washington Territory and superintendent of Indian affairs, Isaac I. Stevens, negotiated ten treaties with the Native people residing in Puget Sound, Neah Bay, Walla Walla, and the confluence of the Judith and Missouri rivers in present-day Montana.[4] These treaties set into motion the United States' Indian policy in the region. Aboriginal people were reduced to living on small reservations where the U.S. government hoped that they would be made into farmers, educated, "civilized" according to European American culture and values, and eventually assimilated into the dominant society.

In 1855 the Quileute people of present-day northeast Washington signed the Quinault river Treaty with the government of the Washington Territory. The following year the Quileute signed the Treaty of Olympia with the United States. The Quileute agreed to "cede, relinquish, and convey to the United States all their right, title, and interest in and to the lands and country occupied by them."[5] In exchange the Quileute were, in 1889, granted a reservation made up of their traditional settlement in the southwest corner of Clallam County at the mouth of the Quillayute River on the Pacific Coast of Washington State. They also retained the right to gather, hunt, and fish in their "usual and accustomed grounds and stations."[6]

According to the treaty, the Quileute reservation was and is the exclusive property of the Quileute Nation. Like many other Native Americans, the Quileute have struggled from the beginning to protect their land from the encroachment of non-Native settlers and resource development. The Quileute people have been forced to turn to the courts and direct action in order to guarantee and protect the rights they negotiated under the treaty with the federal government over a century ago, much as the Quileute characters in the Twilight books had to transform into wolves to protect their land from vampires. While the historical Quileute had to accept and use the settlers' legal system—a system foreign to their way of being—in order to fight for their rights, the fictional Quileute change their nature in a more literal way, becoming supernatural creatures in order to combat a supernatural threat. The connection between supernatural and more everyday protection is made clear by the fact that Sam's pack is interested in keeping the land safe, and not just from vampires. Jacob tells Bella about an outsider who was in

La Push "selling meth to kids, and Sam Uley and his *disciples* ran him off our land. They're all about *our land*, and *tribe pride*." (*New Moon*, 173.) Vampires symbolize the many historical and contemporary social and economic problems that arose in Native communities as a result of colonization, and the shape-shifting Quileute try to protect their people from those problems.

The world created in the novels shows more respect for the treaties than there ever has been historically. Not only are the Quileute and the Cullens always conscious of the terms of the treaty, but they also value the treaty enough to be flexible, and they do not use violations of the letter of the treaty as excuses to abrogate the treaty, even after seventy years. For instance, when Jacob tells Bella that his people believe that the Cullens are vampires, a secret Jacob would not have revealed if he believed the story to be true, the Cullens do not consider the treaty void. Nor do the Quileute believe that Edward violates the treaty when he turns Bella into a vampire, because it was done according to her wishes. Thus, Sam concedes that the "spirit of the treaty remains. They are not a danger to our people, nor are they a danger to the people of Forks. Bella Swan made an informed choice, and we are not going to punish our former allies for her choice." (*Breaking Dawn*, 162.) The respect and flexibility that both sides show for the treaty at first seems to offer a more positive model for Native-newcomer relations, as opposed to the lack of good faith in the historical treaty-making process that has plagued Native North Americans throughout the nineteenth and twentieth centuries. Unfortunately, both the fictional and the nonfictional process have the same results: change and assimilation.

Treaties in general are a controversial topic in the United States. Many non-Aboriginal people see treaties as unjust documents that privilege Native people at the expense of non-Natives.[7] The longevity and significance of the treaties is not an accident and is the result of a great deal of effort on the part of Native people to force the dominant society to acknowledge the promises made by the federal government more than a century ago. Just as the power of the treaty between the Quileute people and the Cullens lies not in any written document but in the way the treaty is stored in the direct memories of both parties, so too does the durability of the Pacific Northwest Treaties, and treaties throughout the United States more generally, lie in the preservation of treaties not only in U.S. law, but more importantly, in the memories of the people who negotiated them and who regard the treaties as enduring compacts between nations.[8] As legal historian Alexandra Harmon notes, history "reminds us that present needs, conceptions of the past, and malleable memories may complicate or even sabotage our efforts to learn what actually happened years ago. In short, it tests our capacity to grasp history's complexity, accept its paradoxes, and understand the past on its own terms."[9] Similarly, Sam argues, "Times have changed since our ancestors made that treaty," and both Sam and Jacob negotiate new understandings with the Cullens based on their differing views about the history and spirit of the treaty. (*Breaking Dawn*, 161.) In both history and the Twilight novels, treaties have taken on a life of their own, and the meanings of treaties have been fashioned and refashioned to fit the current circumstances and needs of the people who perceive themselves to have a vested interest in the land, its people, and its resources. The renegotiations of the treaty in the novels are indicative of the breaking and reworking of treaties that have taken place throughout the history of the United States.

In order to understand how the treaty in the novels shapes land rights and the identity of the Quileute werewolves, it is necessary to understand the ways in which treaty policy in the United States marked changing understandings of Native peoples among both settlers and, more dangerously, the Native peoples themselves. One important element of the assimilation process put into place by the treaties was the effort on the part of the federal government and its agents to transform the Quileute people's political system. The federal government's Indian policy demanded that the Quileute of La Push establish an elected governing council. Altering the political system of Native people was intended to force them to adopt European American culture and values that were grounded in principles of individualism and capitalism. The efforts of federal

Indian Agents and missionaries to impose such changes were not always successful, and hereditary chiefs continued to have a ceremonial role in Quileute society.[10] This role complemented, rather than competed with, the elected council. Similarly, the Quileute political structure in Meyer's novels includes an elected council but also acknowledges a hereditary chief: Billy Black.

Once the presence of the vampires triggers the transformation of the Quileute youth into wolves, Sam, as the alpha of the pack, technically becomes "chief of the whole tribe," despite the fact that Jacob is descended from Ephraim. At first Jacob refuses the hereditary position of chief, in part because he does not agree with hereditary positions; however, when Sam abuses his role as alpha and turns the other wolves into slaves, Jacob breaks from the group and becomes the reluctant leader of a second pack.

While Sam follows the traditional Quileute understanding of the role of alpha, Jacob's pursuit of alternative resolutions is characteristic of a more Western democratic approach. Significantly, Article 11 of the Treaty of Olympia states that the Quileute "agree to free all slaves now held by them, and not to purchase or acquire others hereafter."[11] Thus, Sam's assumed role as chief is undercut by his failure to live up to the terms of the historic treaty. At first this split seems to leave Jacob and his pack homeless while Sam and his pack maintain the protection of the reservation. This situation does not last long, and Jacob is quickly made the leader of the Quileute nation when the vampires choose Jacob, their closer ally, to assume the role of mediator between the two groups, effectively undermining Sam's power to enforce the treaty and protect the land, and thus, the werewolves' reason for being. When Edward wants to change Bella into a vampire in order to save her life, he asks Jacob, as "Ephraim's heir" to "deviate from what we agreed to in our treaty." (*Breaking Dawn*, 342.) It is with this renegotiation of the treaty with the vampires that Jacob takes on the role of leader of his nation. Jacob agrees as "Ephraim's heir, [the vampires] have [his] permission, [his] word, that this will not violate the treaty. The others will just have to blame me. You were right—they can't deny that it's my right to agree to this." (*Breaking Dawn*, 345.)

The historical treaty process often created new leaders. Settlers chose to negotiate with whoever would cooperate with them and serve their interests, no matter how the nation itself regarded those individuals.[12] For example, when a Quileute named Tommy Payne "petitioned the [U.S.] Commissioner of Indian Affairs to recognize him as chief," in 1915, the federal government's Neah Bay Indian Agent argued against his petition and suggested that "if anyone were to be appointed chief, he should be an Indian who spoke, read and wrote English."[13] Most likely, Payne was not someone the Indian Agent saw as easy to deal with. In fact, in 1931 Payne was working with the Quileute council to protest treaty violations and even called himself Chief.[14] Regardless of the validity of Payne's claim to represent the Quileute, the fact that Indian Affairs had the ultimate power to appoint a chief shows how the colonial system had changed and come to control the political makeup of the nation. Although band members may have continued to recognize the authority of certain hereditary chiefs, the ability of these chiefs to work with the government was increasingly constrained by the state's refusal to acknowledge or deal with them.

After the initial changes in the makeup of nations as a result of settlement on reservations, Native Americans on the Pacific Northwest Coast in the post–World War II period increasingly turned to treaties as a means to address political, social, and economic inequities and create alternative identities for themselves within American society.[15] Native Americans now began to present themselves as the "earliest recipients of solemn U.S. promises."[16] In turn, courts upheld these promises and the contention of Native Americans that the United States was duty-bound and legally obligated to fulfill the promises made in the treaties. In order to assert these rights, however, Native American people had to lay claim to a particular tribal identity, because the courts acknowledged the rights only of federally recognized groups.[17] Being Native American was not enough; U.S. law and policy required Native Americans to take on a dual legal persona—both as an individual who is Indian and also as a member of a specific tribe.[18] Thus, the struggles of Native Americans to preserve their culture and communities have become intimately tied to the preservation of treaties and reservations. In fact, reservations, land, nature, the environment, and treaties are concepts that have come to embody "Indianness" in North American society today. Indeed, the dominant society has developed a set of stereotypes about Native peoples' inherent character that reduces them to an association with nature and the land.

The idea of changing one's identity in order to survive takes on physical form in Meyer's novels, where Jacob and the Quileute turn into wolves in order to defend the land from the encroachment of the vampires, but at the same time, the presence of the vampires changes their identity: "It's the reason we exist—because they do." (*New Moon*, 309.) Ironically, in order to defend themselves, the Quileute people must mutate into a form completely different from the one they previously had, even though Quileute legend describes how they were originally transformed into people from wolves.[19] The self-construction of "the Indian" that arises as a defensive measure is clearly evident in Meyer's novels. The Quileute people are repeatedly associated with the land, and their wolf form makes them a part of the natural world of the Olympic Peninsula. Bella's father, Charlie, accepts Billy's argument that Sam and the other Quileute "know the forest better than" the White people of Forks. (*New Moon*, 80.)

Jacob argues that cultural survival is based in part on the wolf form: "What I am was born in me. It's a part of who I am, who my family is, who we all are as a tribe—it's the reason why we're still here." (*Eclipse*, 111.) Here, Jacob imagines and defines his people in opposition to the vampires, whom he sees as unnatural. Meyer repeatedly casts the werewolves and vampires as polar opposites. Most obviously, where vampires are literally cold, werewolves are hot. These dichotomies often evoke more negative stereotypes of "the Indian." Where the Cullens have learned to control their emotions and their natural impulse to drink human blood, the werewolves are a danger to those they love, a danger made clear by the scars Emily bears from Sam's attack. This danger is emphasized repeatedly in the love triangle of Bella, Edward, and Jacob. Edward constantly tries to keep Bella safe, even buying her a car with "missile-proof glass and four thousand pounds of body armor," while Jacob allows her to be reckless and teaches her to ride a motorcycle. (*Breaking Dawn*, 7.) Where Edward constantly maintains control in the relationship and puts limits on the sexual contact that Bella wants, Jacob twice forces himself on Bella, first through his physical strength, and then through trickery. Negative stereotypes of Native people as reckless and passionate and of Native men as sexual predators, all perpetuated in literature and movies, become a compelling reason for Bella to choose Edward over Jacob.[20]

Another marker of Native identity that has been used in the court system and the interpretation of treaty rights is the importance of oral tradition to Native Americans. As with most Native Americans, the history of the Quileute lies more in the oral stories of the people than in the written accounts of newcomers. As Chris Morganroth III points out, "When Quileute narratives are brought together, we find a clear chronology of tribal history, which preserves the details of the Quileute people's relationship to the world around them."[21] It is easy for the contemporary Western rationalist to dismiss many of the oral histories as myth, but there are scientific data that support the veracity of these tales. For example, Meyer twice refers to the story of the great flood, which the Quileute people survived by tying their canoes to trees; this is an actual story told by the Quileute, and recent geological work by Ruth Ludwin suggests that it refers to a cataclysmic earthquake and tsunami that occurred in 1700.[22] Similarly, many of the first encounters with Europeans were with victims of shipwrecks, and often recorded only through the oral histories of the Quileute people.[23]

Meyer also draws upon Native American traditions of oral history in order make her story more compelling and perhaps give it a degree of realism and truth. Like contact with Europeans, the early encounters between the Quileute and the "cold ones" are part of an oral tradition and are remembered from generation to generation and recalled by tribal elders when the situation demands it. In *Eclipse*, Billy recounts the story of Quileute origins, their shape-shifting ancestors, their early conflicts with vampires, and the treaty with the Cullens. Jacob explains to Bella the importance of these stories as history: "It's Quil's first time, and he hasn't heard the stories yet. Well he's *heard* them, but this will be the first time he knows they're true. That tends to make a guy pay closer attention." (*Eclipse*, 243.) While there are no such legends in the Quileute tradition, beyond the creation story, the function of these stories in the Twilight Saga as history that has been mistaken for myth demonstrates the importance of oral history to the Quileute people and its application to present-day circumstances.

Rogue Entities and the Challenge of the Treaties

The treaty between the Quileute nation and the United States was not respected by all settlers. The story of Dan Pullen, who wanted to settle the Quileute village and who originally gave it the name "La Push," a bastardization of the French "La Bouche" after the river mouth, provides a representative example of problems faced by Native people. Pullen was one of the first settlers in Quileute territory, arriving in 1872. He chose to settle in the already established Quileute community at the mouth of the Quillayute River, "figuring he could drive them out or that the government would move them to a different reservation."[24] In 1882 he had a violent dispute over land with a Quileute spiritual leader, Doctor Obi. The government records of the time indicate that Obi, who had a history of resisting White encroachment, had destroyed a section of fence around Pullen's property and then attacked him with a club when Pullen attempted to talk. Obi's daughter tells a different story. She claims that Pullen had attempted to force Obi off his land so that he could stake a claim; Pullen had already stolen other Quileute land. When Obi refused to move, Pullen attacked him.[25]

In an unusual turn of events, the federal government thwarted Pullen's desire to settle the land occupied by the Quileute people. In February 1889, the government granted the community of La Push to the Quileute, who had occupied it for generations; in September of the same year, Dan Pullen set fire to the twenty-six houses that made up La Push when most band members were off pursuing seasonal gathering activities in Puget Sound. In doing so, he destroyed all the Quileute people's remaining regalia, masks, and other items that had been preserved from before White settlement.[26] Pullen leveled the site, planted grass, erected a barbed-wire fence, and threatened to shoot any Quileute who attempted to rebuild their houses. The Quileute people were forced to build their houses on the beach, which placed them in constant danger from high tides, storms, and spring floods. Pullen was eventually denied title to the land, told to leave in 1893, and finally evicted in 1898, almost twenty years after he tried to lay claim to the area.[27]

Just as Pullen refused to honor the treaty and relied on loopholes within the system in his attempt to dispossess the Quileute of their remaining land, so too do the nonvegetarian vampires, such as Laurent, Victoria, and the Volturi, cause tensions in the treaty between the Quileute and the Cullens. Victoria, especially, takes advantage of the uneasy relations between the Quileute people and the Cullens in order to evade capture and set them against each other. When she is pursued by both groups, Victoria uses the boundary between vampire and Quileute territory to escape "as if she were reading it from a map." (*Eclipse*, 86.) Her strategy forces Emmet Cullen to stray over the boundary line, provoking a violent reaction from Paul, and the two groups break off the chase to confront each other, allowing Victoria to escape, at least temporarily.

Ironically, in both the imaginary text and history, the behavior of rogue entities forces the two parties of the treaty to work together in order to maintain peace. In both cases, by taking the side of the Quileute against other European Americans, or vampires, the settlers strengthen their own position by presenting themselves as a necessary and benevolent mediating force. In 1885, W. L. Powell, the Indian Agent of Neah Bay, wrote to the commissioner of Indian affairs about Dan Pullen: "He gives any amount of trouble and we can never have peace among the Indians until he is removed. . . . It is a wonder to me that they have not killed this man, and if all I hear about him is true, I think they would be justified in doing so."[28] Local federal Indian Agents worked to establish and maintain the reservation at La Push, rather than have the Quileute people removed to the nearby Quinault Reservation, and to make certain that Pullen was denied the rights to any reservation land. The work of these Indian Agents, who sided with the Quileute people over the White settlers in spite of the fact that they themselves were also White, parallels the manner in which the Cullens respect their treaty with the werewolves over their bonds with other vampires. Carlisle Cullen refuses to allow Irina to take out the werewolves in exchange for her coven's help with the newborn army, and he tells Victoria, "You provided us with a common enemy. You allied us." (*Eclipse*, 547.) Later, the Volturi attempt to cast the treaty between the werewolves and Cullens as treason and incompatible with vampire law.

While the intentions of both the Neah Bay Indian Agents and the Cullens are noble, their generosity is ultimately self-serving, because it obligates the Quileute to outsiders. This theme is present both historically and in Meyer's works. According to the newcomers, the nonfictional Quileute people were supposed to be grateful that they were left with one square mile of land that they had already settled and were supposed to feel indebted to the generosity of the Bureau of Indian Affairs. In Meyer's novels, the werewolves are forced to tolerate the hunting practices of the Cullens' other guests. Even though the murders occur across state lines, it goes against the werewolves' nature to tolerate vampires who kill humans anywhere. The Cullens ultimately give up nothing for their increased familiarity with the werewolves, and instead, the Cullens acquire Bella and her child, a creature of both worlds.

Rialto Beach and the Erotic Triangle: Contemporary Treaty Conflicts

Treaty rights and the title to land were not fully settled when the original treaties were signed. Land issues remain a real concern for the Quileute people today. In the fall of 2005 the Quileute decided to take direct action in order to end a forty-year boundary dispute with Washington State. By closing access to the Second Beach at

Olympic National Park, the Quileute hoped to force the government to address their northern boundary issues at Rialto Beach, where Olympic National Park infringes on Quileute land. The roots of the current conflict began in 1910, when a storm shifted the mouth of the Quillayute River, which marked the border of the reservation, effectively cutting off eight acres of Quileute land on Rialto Beach.[29] Although legal precedent suggests that the border should remain where the river flowed when the reservation was established, the eight acres were given by the federal government to Olympic National Park in 1953; park authorities then built a parking lot and washrooms on the land. Disputes over the land simmered during the second half of the twentieth century and came to a head in 2005, when two Quileute people who were collecting firewood on the disputed area were arrested and charged. Although the charges were later dropped, this incident, together with an increased awareness of the dangers of tsunamis in the area (over half the reservation is on a floodplain), led the Quileute people to take more drastic action. They denied access to Second Beach by closing the parking lot and trail, both of which are Quileute territory, in order to bring the other party to the table. The band was willing to grant permanent access to Second Beach and the eight disputed acres of Rialto Beach in exchange for 789 acres of land above potential tsunami zones. The park's counteroffer was 274 acres of parkland.[30] The Quileute Nation and Olympic National Park reached a tentative settlement in late July 2009.[31] The issue was still ongoing when Meyer was writing.

Although the Quileute characters in Meyer's novels never mention this or any other ongoing boundary dispute with American government agencies, the dangers posed by a potential tsunami, leading to the renegotiation of the reservation boundaries, are akin to the dangers that lead both to increased tensions and later to a better understanding between the werewolves and the vampires. While the existence of Bella and Edward's half-vampire child leads Sam to declare that the treaty is void, because he sees her as a danger, the threats posed by Laurent, Victoria, the newborn army, and the Volturi create stronger bonds between the werewolves and the Cullens. For example, the danger of the newborn army leads Sam, through Jacob, to "rearranging some boundaries, so we can catch anyone who gets too near Forks." (*Eclipse*, 212.) As the series progresses, the threats increase, and the werewolves move from not being a factor in *Twilight*, to fighting a common enemy separately in *New Moon*, to fighting with the Cullens in one battle in *Eclipse*, to becoming formal allies in *Breaking Dawn*, under Jacob's leadership.

While the Rialto Beach dispute and the threat of tsunamis are the most important aspects of the ongoing negotiations between the Quileute and the settler governments, the single most important factor affecting the treaty between the werewolves and the Cullens is the relationship between Bella and Edward, and her desire for him to change her into a vampire. Such an action would violate the clause of the treaty that stipulates that the Cullens must never bite a human, either for food or to turn that human into a vampire. Since Bella *wants* to be turned into a vampire, the spirit of the treaty would not be broken, but the situation is complicated by the relationship between Bella and Jacob, who would like her to stay human and take him as a partner. While romantic relationships were never a part of the historical treaties, the relationship between Natives, newcomers, and the land was often conceived of metaphorically as a romantic one. Kim Anderson notes that "in both western and Indigenous frameworks, Native women have historically been equated with the land."[32] The land, first conceived of as a rich queen, quickly became associated with the figure of the "Indian Princess," a symbol of "virgin land, open for consumption" and waiting for the "European male wishing to lay claim to the 'new' territory."[33] For this reason, the story of John Smith and Pocahontas is a founding myth of America. In the Twilight series, however, Native women do not represent the land, a construction hit home by the fact that Leah Clearwater, the most prominent Quileute female in the series, fears that she might be sterile.

While Bella is definitely not a Native woman—the books constantly emphasize her extremely pale skin, once in explicit contrast to Jacob's "russet" tones—she represents the land in the Twilight novels. She describes herself first as real estate ("I was an empty shell. Like a vacant house—condemned—for months I'd been utterly uninhabitable. Now I was a little improved." [*New Moon*, 216]), and then as an entire country ("when it comes to all this *enemies* nonsense, I'm out. I am a neutral country. I am Switzerland. I refuse to be affected by territorial disputes between mythological creatures." [*Eclipse*, 143]). Despite her claim to be neutral, the specific and repeated references to her as land and the way in which Jacob and Edward explicitly pass her back and forth across the border line stipulated by the treaty indicate that she is tied to the land and to the treaty that divides it. In fact, it is her passing into a true marriage with Edward, when she becomes a vampire and changes her very nature, that breaks the original treaty but eventually leads to a new and stronger version of that treaty, one that softens the firm division between the two groups.

The moment that Bella becomes a vampire, breaking the terms of the original treaty, is the moment in which Jacob shifts his affections from Bella to her newborn daughter. In doing so, he becomes a member of the extended Cullen family and brings his pack with him. Sam's pack has to accept the new terms, not only because Jacob agreed to them, but also because "the most absolute of all the pack's laws was that no wolf ever kill the object of another wolf's imprinting." (*Breaking Dawn*, 456.) The conflation of the breaking of treaty terms with Jacob's transformation has disturbing parallels with "enfranchisement legislation" designed to break down the barriers between Native and settler communities, ostensibly to make them equals, but really to allow for the takeover of treaty land. One example of such legislation is the 1887 General Allotment Act, more commonly known as the Dawes Act, which broke up reservation land and divided it among individual Native men.[34] More and more during the late nineteenth and early twentieth centuries, the government saw the allotment of reservation land to individuals as the solution to the "Indian problem" and the best possible means of protecting Native people from land-hungry settlers.[35] The goal was to make Aboriginal people self-sustaining individuals who mirrored European American cultural practices and values. Similarly, the 1953 House Concurrent Resolution 108 ended federal supervision over many Native peoples and nations, making them full citizens of the United States, but at the same time terminating the rights that they had gained through treaties.[36] Historical "enfranchisement legislation" was ostensibly designed to give Native people equal status with settlers, but in fact it led to the loss of land and rights guaranteed by treaty.[37] In the Twilight Saga, Edward pressures Jacob into agreeing to change the terms of the treaty, and Bella, who represents the land, loses all romantic attachment to Jacob and now belongs wholly to Edward.

A simple reading of how the erotic triangle in the Twilight Saga plays out would suggest that the cold, rational, controlled, and pale Edward winning over the hot-blooded, emotional, impulsive, and russet-skinned Jacob is a signal that Native land will be taken over and Native people supplanted by European colonizers. The fact that the saga ends with Jacob's being brought into the family, through his controversial imprinting on Edward and Bella's newborn daughter, suggests something more complicated. The child, Renesmee, is linked to Jacob even before she is born; Alice Cullen cannot see the fetus or the werewolves, and the child's rapid growth reminds Bella of Jacob. Jacob argues that the imprinting makes Bella and Jacob part of the same family, the way Bella had always wanted, and, in fact, makes the truce between the Quileute and the Cullens "stronger than ever. Or more binding, depending on your viewpoint." (*Breaking Dawn*, 456.) Even as the novel depicts a shift in power away from the Quileute werewolves toward the European and European American vampires, the new mixed-species family that is created at the end of *Breaking Dawn* suggests ways in which Native culture and identity are appropriated by the colonizers to legitimize their claim to the land.[38] Renesmee, Edward and Bella's hybrid human-vampire daughter, has the same number of chromosomes as the Quileute shape-shifters, suggesting that the newcomers have become "native" to the land they now occupy. The gradual legitimization of the vampires' position in Forks through marriage and the renegotiation of treaties parallels the gradual encroachment of European settlers in the Pacific Northwest from the late nineteenth into the twenty-first century.

Notes

1. Francis Prucha, *American Indian Treaties: The History of a Political Anomaly* (Berkeley: Univ. of California Press, 1994), 1.

2. Ibid., 5.

3. Francis Prucha, *The Indians in American Society: From the Revolutionary War to the Present* (Berkeley: Univ. of California Press, 1985), 1–27.

4. Kent Richards, "The Stevens Treaties of 1854–1855," *Oregon Historical Quarterly* 106, no. 3 (Fall 2005), http://find.galegroup.com.ezproxy.lakeheadu.ca/gtx/retrieve.do?contentSet=IAC-Documents&resultListType=RESULT_LIST&qrySerId=Locale%28en%2CUS%2C%29%3AFQE%3D%28JN%2CNone%2C29%29%22Oregon+Historical+ Quarterly%22%3AAnd%3ALQE%3D%28DA%2CNone%2C8%2920050922%24&sgHit CountType=None&inPS=true&sort=DateDescend&searchType=PublicationSearch Form&tabID=T002&prodId=EAIM&searchId=R1¤tPosition=1&userGroupName=ocul_lakehead&docId=A137146591&docType=IAC.

5. United States Burean of Indian Affairs, "The Treaty of Olympia," www.quileutenation.org/index.cfm?page=treaty_of_olympia.html.

6. Ibid.

7. Alexandra Harmon, "Indian Treaty History: A Subject for Agile Minds," *Oregon Historical Quarterly* 106, no. 3 (Fall 2005), http://find.galegroup.com.ezproxy.lakeheadu.ca/gtx/retrieve.do?contentSet=IAC-Documents&resultListType=RESULT_LIST&qrySerId=Locale%28en%2CUS%2C%29%3AFQE%3D%28JN%2CNone%2C29%29%22Oregon+Historical+Quarterly%22%3AAnd%3ALQE%3D%28DA%2CNone%2C8%2920050922%24&sgHitCountType=None&inPS=true&sort=DateDescend&searchType=PublicationSearchForm&tabID=T002&prodId=AONE&searchId=R2¤tPosition=4&userGroupName=ocul_lakehead&docId=A137146594&docType=IAC.

8. Ibid.

9. Ibid.

10. Jay Powell and Vickie Jensen, *Quileute: An Introduction to the Indians of La Push* (Seattle: Univ. of Washington Press, 1976), 29.

11. United States Bureau of Indian Affairs, "The Treaty of Olympia," www.quileutenation.org/index.cfm?page=treaty_of_olympia.html.

12. Vine Deloria and Clifford Lytle, *American Indians, American Justice* (Austin: Univ. of Texas Press, 1983), 93–109.

13. George A. Pettitt, *The Quileute of La Push 1775–1945* (Berkeley: Univ. of California Press, 1950), 37.

14. Ibid., 39.

15. Alexandra Harmon, *Indians in the Making: Ethnic Relations and Indian Identities around Puget Sound* (Berkeley: Univ. of California Press, 1998), 218.

16. Ibid., 218.

17. Ibid., 243.

18. Ibid., 216.

19. Powell and Jensen, *Quileute*, 17.

20. Rayna Green, "The Pocahontas Perplex: Images of American Indian Women in American Culture," *Massachussetts Review* 16 (Autumn 1975): 698–714.

21. Chris Morganroth III and the Olympic Peninsula Intertribal Advisory Committee, "Quileute," in *Native Peoples of the Olympic Peninsula: Who We Are*, ed. Jacilee Wray (Norman: Univ. of Oklahoma Press, 2002), 135.

22. Ruth Ludwin et al., "Dating the 1700 Cascadia Earthquake: Great Coastal Earthquakes in Native Stories," *Seismological Research Letters* 76, no. 2 (March/April 2005): 140–148.

23. Pettitt, *The Quileute of La Push*, 21–23.

24. Iva Hosack Wahlgren, *Memories of a Quillayute and Sol Duc Country Pioneer* (Forks, WA: West End Pioneers Club, 1998), 21–22.

25. Pettitt, *The Quileute of La Push*, 24–25.

26. Powell and Jensen, *Quileute*, 41.

27. Pettitt, *The Quileute of La Push*, 27.

28. NA-NB, letter from W. L. Powell, November 23, 1885, Doc 28595. Cited in Pettitt, *The Quileute of La Push*, 27.

29. Christopher Dunagan, "Land Dispute Triggers Closing of Coastal Trail," *Wotanging Ikche—Lakota—Common News*, October 15, 2005.

30. Jessica Kowal, "La Push Journal: In a Bid for Higher Ground, a Tribe Raises the Stakes," *New York Times*, July 30, 2006.

31. Paige Dickerson, "Tribe, Park Reach Agreement on Land Swap," *Peninsula Daily News*, July 27, 2009.

32. Kim Anderson, *A Recognition of Being: Reconstructing Native Womanhood* (Toronto: Second Story Press, 2000), 100.

33.Ibid., 101.

34. United States Congress, *An Act to Provide for the Allotment of Lands in Severalty to Indians on the Various Reservations (General Allotment Act or Dawes Act), Statutes at Large* 24, 388–391, in *Documents of United States Indian Policy*, 2nd ed., ed. Francis Paul Prucha (Lincoln: Univ. of Nebraska Press, 1990), 171–174. The General Allotment Act authorized the president to order the survey of reservations, the creation of tribal allotment rolls, and the division of reservation lands into individual allotments. Native people born after the close of the allotment did not receive any land. Native Americans were not given land from the federal government; rather federal Indian Agents assigned allotments from land already owned by the tribe. According to the terms of the act, the federal government held allotments in trust for twenty-five years until it was determined that the individual in question was able to manage the land appropriately. Land not allotted to members of the tribe was sold off to White settlers, enabling the state to appropriate large tracts of Native land. The act was ultimately designed to free up Native land for White settlement and not to benefit Native Americans.

35. Brian Dippie, *The Vanishing American: White Attitudes and U.S. Indian Policy* (Middletown, CT: Wesleyan Univ. Press, 1982), 163.

36. United States Congress, *House Concurrent Resolution 108, Statutes at Large 67: B132. Documents of United States Indian Policy*, in *Documents of United States Indian Policy*, 2nd ed., ed. Francis Paul Prucha (Lincoln: Univ. of Nebraska Press, 1990), 233. According to historian Donald Fixico, termination was a policy designed to force Native Americans to integrate into European American society by depriving them of federal services guaranteed by treaties. For further information see Donald Fixico, *Termination*

and Relocation: Federal Indian Policy, 1945–1960 (Albuquerque: Univ. of New Mexico Press, 1986).

37. This phrase refers to a series of legal processes by which Native Americans were divested of their legal status and rights guaranteed under treaty law and various agreements signed with federal and state governments.

38. Caroll-Smith Rosenberg, "Captured Subjects/Savage Others: Violently Engendering the New American," *Gender & History* 5, no. 2 (Summer 1993): 177–195.

CinderBella

Twilight, Fairy Tales, and the Twenty-First-Century American Dream

Sara Buttsworth

Forget Princess, I want to be a Vampire!

—T-shirt slogan, 2009

Preface

Once upon a time there was a dark forest of deep green where magical creatures simultaneously offered succor and peril, sanctuary and slaughter. At the edge of this forest lived a girl with skin as white as snow, a luscious blush to her cheeks, dark hair that rippled down her back, and a smell more tempting than ripe apples. The girl, whose name meant "beauty," lived in exile with her father, for whom she kept house, cleaning and cooking with good will. She liked to read and had feet that would not dance and a mind that was silent to the probing of others. Bella and her father were not poor exactly, but they had little to spare. Peerless as she was, she had no real friends among her own kind. Instead, she fell in love with an outsider—a prince who had the face of an angel, beastly appetites, and skin that reflected sunlight better than any glass slipper. Bella did not always heed warnings never to stray from paths in the forest and was therefore lucky to be befriended by the wolves living there—guardians of the forest and the "provincial town" of Forks. The wolves cared not that Bella wore no hood of red, only that her blood continued to pump through her veins, lending its color to her pale cheeks—and that she did not become the handsome prince's next meal.

The Dreams of Lambs and Lions

The novels (and film adaptations) of the Twilight Saga operate in the dreamlike realm of the fairy tale, where horror and romance coexist. Bella's quest for eternal youth and a literal happily-forever-after follows a tradition that has often governed the behavior of young women in different ways through the centuries. This tradition has its roots in the storytelling of peasants around their hearths. The stories began to be much more formally didactic for the emerging middle classes when Charles Perrault and his contemporaries transformed oral folktales into their literary *contes des fées* ("fairy tales") for the glittering salons of Paris society in the seventeenth and eighteenth centuries. Once fixed on paper, folktales were later recast and redefined by the morality of the Brothers Grimm in the nineteenth century and were later broadcast worldwide by Disney studios throughout the twentieth and into the twenty-first centuries.[1]

The personal details of young women like Bella Swan have changed over the centuries, along with the cultural contexts of the stories in which they appear, displaying various skills, virtues, and levels of intellect. Throughout the twentieth century, particularly with the standardized morality and global reach of Disney films, heroines—even the feisty ones of the latter part of the period—have continued to be rewarded for, but never rescued from, their patience, passivity, and pallid beauty.

Stephenie Meyer's stories are a gripping read from beginning to end partly because of their fairy-tale appeal, which, far from being "timeless," is very much of *this* time. References to heroines and romantic couples (both doomed and happy) outside the folkloric realm abound in the Twilight novels: the writings of Shakespeare, Emily Brontë, and Jane Austen are Bella's staple entertainment. But Bella's story, with its stance on premarital sex, fidelity, self-sacrifice for a prolife attitude, and the questions it begs about how young women in a "postfeminist" age are supposed to be able to "have it all," make Meyer's work very much a fairy tale of the twenty-first century.

The Twilight novels make use of a number of important factors that have remained constant in fairy-tale texts. Perhaps the most important fairy-tale factor Meyer has employed is the transformative power of "survival tale[s] with hope."[2] As characters within fairy tales survive the challenges they meet, they are transformed and attain their hearts' desires. Meyer's heroine is no exception to the personal transformation that is undergone by so many fairy-tale protagonists. And it is no great leap to see Bella's story as a "survival tale with hope." So, in considering the Twilight Saga, it is not the resemblance to fairy tales that poses a quandary. Rather, the problem lies in deciding which fairy tale it resembles the most. Fragments of *Snow White*, *Cinderella*, *Beauty and the Beast*, and *Little Red Riding Hood* are *all* discernible throughout Meyer's work, so which story is it that binds this romance together?

The answer to this question is a story within a story. The fairy tale most apparent in these books is actually the American Dream—another story of "survival with hope" that has been handed down through the generations and adapted to changing cultural ideals and socioeconomic contexts. Bella comes from a lower-middle-class background. Her father, Charlie, is a small-town chief of police, and her mother, Renée, has a nondescript occupation (other than being Charlie's, and then Phil's, wife) and level of education that, foreshadowing her own child's early marriage and motherhood, seems to have been cut short by early marriage and pregnancy. Renée did not marry up in the same way that Bella does, and her neglected offspring certainly climbs up an entire socioeconomic beanstalk in marrying into the extremely wealthy Cullen family.

Bella may not have worn rags at the beginning of her story, but by its end she certainly has unfettered access to riches both materially and in terms of opportunities. And throughout the Twilight series, the American conviction that the United States is unique among nations, following different rules and pursuing a destiny different from that of other cultures (that is, the "exceptionalism" of the United States on the world stage), an idea that has been at the center of American Dream since the Puritans, is evident in its heroine, its vampires, and its werewolves, glittering as brightly as diamonds in the sun. What Bella's story illustrates above all else, however, is that the American Dream tradition for young women in the early twenty-first century remains a variant of *Cinderella*. With or without glass slippers, it is the right marriage that elevates one out of the dark cabin in the woods to the sunlit castle on the hill.

As surely as Old World stories tell of Jack's winning a king's ransom by way of a handful of magic beans, and Dick Whittington becoming lord mayor of London in reluctantly parting with his cat, the American Dream posits that upward mobility can be, and is, a reality. Anyone, according to this fairy tale, can grow up to be president—if he is a boy that is (and history suggests that those who have had any real hope of gaining access to this Dream have also been overwhelmingly white, the current U.S. president notwithstanding). What it means for a man to reach his goals has changed over time; Puritans tended to focus on community and being closer to God, for example, whereas by the mid-twentieth century the emphasis had shifted toward each person's freedom to develop an individual identity. The individual successes that have been the dream since the late nineteenth century have continued to dominate and tend to preclude any analysis of how class, race, or gender can be barriers to success.[3] But the possibility of transformation in a single person's life, rather than collective revolution, is the key to the fairy-tale kingdom of the American Dream. Many staple fairy tales of European origin feed into this utopian vision of individual, community, and national success—if the fool can marry the princess and become king, why not become president? The mythical success of the "everyman" is all around us.

But what if you are a girl: Can you become president or will you always just be someone else's queen? The Cinderella myth is alive and kicking up its glass slippers in a plethora of literary and cinematic texts produced in the late twentieth and early twenty-first centuries, to the extent that an entire "princess culture" has emerged.[4] The American Dream continues to be regularly invoked and reinvented, from popular fiction to popular film to the speeches and treatises of successive U.S. presidents, including Barack Obama (one of his books even has the American Dream in its title: *The Audacity of Hope: Thoughts on Reclaiming the American Dream*). Just how accessible is this goal for young women? The Twilight stories are very much a part of this nexus of myths as tales of upward mobility, standing at the crossroads between the Old World and the New. Peppered with direct and indirect fairy-tale references and a reverence for baseball, the ending that allows Bella to "have it all" consists of early marriage, dying young, and staying pretty.[5] Throughout Meyer's saga, Bella is in many ways as blank as her 1950 Walt Disney predecessor, and other than her delicious smell, it is that and her unselfishness (like Beauty's and Cinderella's before her) that attract Edward, her prince.

This chapter explores the Twilight novels in the context of fairy-tale tradition, including the American Dream, and the ways in which this tradition can shed light on just how tight the glass slipper is. The analysis is divided into two parts, the first on the American Dream, and the second on Cinderella stories—although obviously teasing these apart completely is not entirely possible, and fairy-tale references abound in both. The characters of Carlisle and Edward best illustrate some of the changes in the tradition of American Dream stories. And just as the Cullen male leaders best exemplify this tradition, the Quileutes represent those who have been, and continue to be, consistently excluded from it. The Cullen coven and Bella illustrate the ongoing importance of American culture's vision of itself as "different" from other nations, not only in their "cross-species" relationships and "puritan" diet, but in relation to the European vampire aristocracy, the Volturi.

The second part of the analysis focuses more on the female characters, especially Bella, Esme, and Rosalie, who are all heiresses to the legacies left behind by their fairy-tale predecessors—for the most part the heroines of twentieth-century cinematic tales. Both sections demonstrate the ways in which the Cullen family (of which Bella is really a part right from the beginning, almost as if she was "born to be a vampire" of the Cullen ilk), represents the different ideals of individual morality for men and women, individual success, social mobility, and the unique aspects of American culture that are the dreams any American Cinderella's heart might harbor. (*Breaking Dawn*, 524.)

Creatures of the Night: Defenders of the Dream

The transformative power of the fairy tale, and of fairy-tale heroes, is often one of turning established hierarchies on their heads. This fantasy is as crucial for the American Dream, where an individual can attain wealth and power regardless of his origins or structural or social obstacles, as it is for its fairy-tale siblings. The fool can be king for a day, for a lifetime, or for several, but the fool does not want to get rid of the social order that oppresses him. He merely wants to be on top of it. The hierarchies of society remain intact in the traditional folktale, but he who was at the bottom manages through hard work, perseverance, and sometimes dumb luck, to end up in a far loftier position than the one from which he started out.[6]

The Twilight Saga can also be seen as upending literary hierarchies in some ways, since vampires are not necessarily villains. Rather than the transgression, excess, and sexual deviance that have traditionally been keys to vampire stories, the Cullens and their friends represent chastity, morality, and restraint.[7] Interestingly, while the Cullens represent such a break with literary vampire traditions, they do not seek to overturn the vampire order. In the same way, to be opposed to their own great material wealth would jeopardize their ability to move through both vampire and human worlds (and other than perhaps Carlisle, none of the Cullens would ever really dream of questioning their right to fabulous riches). While they live outside many human systems of operation, they do use them to their advantage. Much as the Puritans represented a break from the "evils" of the Old World they fled as they sought utopia in the New, the Cullen family, headed by Carlisle, represents a break from the excesses and cruelties of Old World vampirism. The New World is still the place to make your fortune, however, and, through hard work, to gain access to a little piece of paradise in this world and the hereafter.

Long before Thomas Jefferson wrote "life, liberty and the pursuit of happiness" into the Declaration of Independence in 1776, before Abraham Lincoln ascended from a log cabin to the White House, and before Horatio Alger penned his popular fictions of rags-to-riches glory for those who worked hard and cared for others in the late 1860s, the Puritans arrived in the New World with their Spartan ways and their hopes of attaining a better life in the now and in heaven. Cultural historian Jim Cullen (not to be confused with Meyer's Cullens), in his book *The American Dream: A Short History of an Idea That Shaped a Nation*, stresses free will and individual choice as the key to the freedoms Americans have always held dear; he also examines how the Declaration had its roots in the hopes and fears of the Puritans who arrived in North America more than a century before.[8] The story and character of Carlisle, father of the Cullen coven, can be viewed alongside these ancestors of the Founding Fathers.

In describing Carlisle as having been born the son of a seventeenth-century Protestant preacher, Meyer invokes memories of the Puritans, the religious reform movement that inspired small groups to break away from the Anglican Church in Britain and seek freedom from persecution in the new colonies on the East Coast of North America. The characterization of Carlisle's father as a leader of witch hunts, which leads to the literal demonizing of his own son, roots the entire Cullen family history in a search for freedom from persecution as they pursue a different way of life. The Puritan nature of the Cullens, while not evident in the trappings of wealth with which they surround themselves, is instead expressed through something even more basic to their identities: how they sustain their bodies through diet. It is their diet and desire to treat humans as people rather than as "pets" or "snacks" that sets them apart from the Old World vampires—the Volturi and most of their followers.

In refusing to drink human blood, Carlisle sets an example that baffles the "nighttime patrons of the arts," Aro, Caius, and Marcus, who attempted to "cure his aversion to 'his natural food source' as they called it." (*Twilight*, 297.) It is unclear what these attempts entailed. However, the impressions of the Volturi created in *New Moon*, *Eclipse*, and *Breaking Dawn* convey the idea that had they stopped feeling so indulgent in Carlisle's direction, the Volturi would not have hesitated to use a number of forms of coercion and persecution to achieve conformity. So, feeling that there was no hope of continuing his "religion" of caring for others and not sucking the life out of them, Carlisle fled seventeenth-century Italy and began a lonely extended life that eventually found him transforming Edward on his deathbed three centuries later. Freedom from persecution, a "puritan" diet, and an ethic of caring that leads Carlisle to transform only those who are close to death (and who become a part of his "family" rather than followers in a retinue) are among the ways in which Meyer reflects the notion that Americans (even if they are vampires!) have a unique culture among the nations, which is crucial to the American Dream.[9] Through dint of hard work and self-sacrifice, Carlisle overcame his appetites to the extent that, rather than living apart from people, he could live among them and be a pillar of the various communities through which he moved. As he says while dealing with Bella's injured arm in the opening chapters of *New Moon*, "Like everything in life, I just had to decide what to do with what I was given." (*New Moon*, 35.)

Hard work and a strong moral center led Carlisle to a life of which he is proud. His diet means he maintains the ethics of Puritanism, but his profession and long life mean he can still achieve the luxuries that only great wealth can afford. Political scientist

Cal Jillson has claimed that like Puritans, for Quakers (a similar breakaway seventeenth-century sect), "[W]orking, saving and investing led to prosperity and enhanced one's role in the community because thriving was taken to be a visible sign that one was living in the light of the Lord's grace." But it was the very material success that followed their Protestant work ethic that inevitably undermined the communitarian emphasis of the early Puritan and Quaker communities: as they became wealthier, they often ceased to live as simply as their founders had.[10] There appears to be no such conflict for the New World vampires of the Cullen coven. Excess, in the vampire world it seems, is largely related to food.

The subtle differences between the characterizations of Edward and Carlisle move *Twilight*'s American Dream into the twentieth century in terms of values and aspirations. While Carlisle does represent individual success, he is also the founder of a community and completely bound to it. Where Carlisle's commitment to his little coven has much to do with faith, Edward's is based on love and loyalty—and his affections can waver, depending on which sibling he interacts with and whether or not their behavior accords with his own code of conduct.[11] He is much more of a loner than Carlisle, and this very much makes Edward a twentieth-century man.

Edward becomes a vampire in 1918 as Spanish influenza wreaks its havoc worldwide and kills more people than died in combat during the whole four years of World War I. Edward's pre-vampire life is sketchy, but he appears to have been from a well-off upper-middle-class family. Prior to contracting influenza, Edward was about to join the army (although he would mostly likely have missed out on World War I action, as the war was nearly over by this stage). Following his "transformation," Edward discovers a talent for mind reading and, with a minor rebellious detour, does his best to live up to Carlisle's example. Here we see a dream become a legacy passed down from one generation to the next. In Edward's case, and the case of the other vampires who are friends and allies of the Cullens, while they ultimately come together as a community, it is their personal independence that is to be defended at all costs.

Edward's many gifts are stressed throughout the four novels, including his capacity to read minds, his musical abilities, his determination, and his intellect, which helps him to earn a number of degrees in medical science. What separates, and perhaps elevates, Edward above his brothers and sisters is how he uses all of his extra time. For example, in *Breaking Dawn*, when Charlie is first introduced to the newly transformed Bella, we see a family no longer as interested in maintaining the need for the human charade of winding down for the evening: where Emmett and Rosalie are involved in constructing a massive house of cards, transient and trivial, Edward moves to the piano—a demonstration not only of skill but of talent. Edward is the only one of the Cullen children who demonstrates more than a fleeting interest in education and research, and his qualifications are far more worthy than the display of high school graduation caps in the *Twilight* film indicates. He does not need to sleep and therefore works on honing his particular skills and interests. It is this work ethic and the desire to use, rather than squander, the gifts he has that make him the perfect heir to Carlisle's legacies. It is not just his good looks that make him the prince of this American fairy tale: it is his morality, his intellect, and his unswerving commitment to his family's way of life that crown him in Bella's eyes.

Both Carlisle and Edward demonstrate through their chosen lifestyles the emphasis on a unique, individual destiny that is so important to the American Dream. However, other than diet, morality, and hard work, there is another element crucial to the national mythologies of the United States. To this end, I would like to make a slight detour here to discuss a minor character from *Breaking Dawn* who not only invokes the Founding Fathers and the spirit of the Wars of Independence, but who also exemplifies one of the ongoing themes of the twenty-first-century American Dream: individual freedoms. We meet Garrett as the Cullens begin to gather their friends and allies in preparation for the impending doom of a visit from the Volturi. One of the first things we hear him utter is, "The redcoats are coming, the redcoats are coming." (*Breaking Dawn*, 680.) Garrett takes us back to Paul Revere's famous midnight ride, one of the most mythologized events of the American Revolutionary War. In what has become known as the original national conflict for autonomy and freedom from old world dictatorship, the Revolutionary War is where and when Garrett became a vampire. And Garrett calls the Volturi out:

> "The Volturi care nothing for the death of the child. They seek the death of our free will. . . . So come, I say! Let's hear no more lying rationalizations. Be honest in your intents as we will be honest in ours. We will defend our freedom. You will or will not attack it. Choose now, and let these witnesses see the true issue debated here." [. . .]
>
> Aro smiled. "A very pretty speech, my revolutionary friend."
>
> Garrett remained poised for attack. "Revolutionary?" he growled. "Who am I revolting against, might I ask? Are you my king? Do you wish me to call you *master*, too, like your sycophantic guard?"
>
> "Peace Garrett," Aro said tolerantly. "I meant only to refer to your time of birth. Still a patriot, I see." (*Breaking Dawn*, 719.)

Garrett seeks to expose not only the Volturi's aristocratic pretensions, but also the Machiavellian power games with which they seek to direct all talent to their will and whims. Once again Meyer invokes an event that has become integral to American historical mythology. And because vampires are almost unkillable, Garrett's response places freedom from autocracy (and aristocracy) at the forefront of the stories of her individual vampires. Here, too, we see the idea of a unique American destiny at work. It is not only differences in diet that separate the Cullens and some of their friends from their Old World counterparts, but the value they place on individual talent and individual free will. No one is forced to join the Cullens' stand against the Volturi, and talents are not turned on friends except for training purposes. This forms a sharp contrast to the "guard" of the Volturi, who do indeed call Aro, Caius, and Marcus Master, and whose minds and talents are bent to their masters' will through the talents of vampires like Chelsea, who is able to alter how people feel about one another and weaken the bonds between them, and Jane, who can inflict excruciating pain from a distance with her mind.

In spite of different story arcs for female characters (see below), Meyer also puts distance between the Old and the New Worlds in their treatment of women. While there are females with active talents in the Volturi retinue, these "wives" are never mentioned by name and hover like prized yet useless possessions in the confrontation with the Cullens. The women of the Cullen family and friends all have their own names and their own talents—put to use in the defense of what they hold dear. So once again we see the New World vampires standing against those of the Old and demonstrating the power and value of free will and individual choice.

A unique nature and destiny is also demonstrated by the Quileute wolves—they are not the same as the Children of the Moon, whom Marcus hunted almost to extinction. Their alliance with the vampires of Forks is completely unprecedented. But Jacob Black and his pack, even in this fairy tale, operate outside the magical realm of the American Dream, much as Native Americans have sought their own sovereignty and been excluded from opportunities for educational and material success in colonial and postcolonial North America. The Founding Fathers' City on the Hill came into existence only because they conquered the indigenous populations.[12] Younger Native Americans continue to struggle with the poverty and social problems endemic on many reservations, which keeps them from the material, community, and individual successes promised by the American Dream. The alternative Native American dreams of their own nation and self-determination cannot coexist with the dominant and dominating hegemony of the United States.

The Quileutes in Meyer's story are bound *to* their roles as guardians—which are crucial—and *by* the boundaries of the reservation, their territory. While Jacob, who ditches school on "the Rez" and excels as a mechanic, is worthy, moral, and magical, he is never on equal footing with the wealthy, white, upper-class Edward.

While Bella may flirt with Jacob, and momentarily toy with the idea that she and he should have been together, Jacob was never going to be the prince in her story. He is not white, unnaturally beautiful, or wealthy. He cannot, by virtue of his race, species as shape-shifter/wolf, and socioeconomic position help her to rise, socially or economically, nor can he even help her to "evolve" into a being like himself, as Edward can. The American Dream may allow Beauty to befriend the wolf, but in order to live (or die?) the dream that says she *can* have it all, she must marry the Beast/Prince and herself become transformed.

CinderBella and Her Sisters

Much like Hansel scattering breadcrumbs through the dark forest, Meyer has peppered her books with fairy-tale references. The very cover of *Twilight* tempts the reader, Snow White–like, with its rosy red apple.[13] Isabella Swan's own name is itself a fairy-tale signifier, her first name meaning "beauty" in its abbreviated form, and the surname reminiscent of many tales, from the "Swan Maidens" to "Six Swans" to the "Ugly Duckling" (the latter's transformative aspect is one that Bella by inference applies to herself, since in her own mind she does not fulfill the beautiful potential of her name until her "undead" life). But what of the American Dream for our fairy-tale heroine?

J. Emmett Winn points to a number of Cinderella stories, such as *Working Girl* (1988) and *Pretty Woman* (1990), which incidentally is also a Disney film, as examples of ongoing mythologies of the American Dream.[14] Beautiful, hardworking, and moral (in spite of Vivian's occupation as a prostitute in *Pretty Woman*), the female characters Winn discusses rise above their circumstances and enrich the lives of those around them. However, Winn does little to discuss the fact that Cinderella stories are the specifically *feminine* form of the American Dream. From drudgery and strong expressions of morality to sartorial transformation, these stories bear striking similarities. Even when the woman in question attains a desired career as a part of her new life, it is always through her relationship to a man. While for men the ways to achieve their dreams, and even the dreams themselves, have changed over time, for women landing the prince remains a constant in the climax to their stories. Carlisle and Edward are shining examples of masculinity and progress, whereas Bella is depicted as old for her years and is by implication an old-fashioned heroine.

The Twilight Saga's female characters follow narrative arcs that color them as either worthy, and therefore accepting of their fates, or as shallow and selfish and therefore open to criticism and punishment of some sort. Bella's story and those of Esme and Rosalie echo the fairy-tale legacies of both pre- and post-Perrault stories. The clearest influences in these stories, however, largely seem to come from the twentieth-century productions of Disney studios. Meyer's grim tales are inflected by twenty-first-century sexual politics. With their focus on "morality" at the expense of education, or honesty about teenage sexuality, they are in some ways more conservative than their seventeenth-century predecessors.[15] While Bella may flirt with her wolf to gain information, and get into bed with him to get warm, she remains fully clothed at all times. She bears little resemblance to the pre-Perrault Little Red Riding Hood, who does a striptease for the wolf before escaping out the back door: her attempts to help in the battle against Victoria's minions in *Eclipse* consist of self-sacrifice and self-harm, not cunning.[16] And while Edward climbs to her room every night, all activity between him and Bella remains charged yet chaste. Unlike the story of Rapunzel, there is no punishment for promiscuity and giving birth to illegitimate twins for our twenty-first-century heroine—she does not let down her hair until she is properly married.[17]

When Bella first meets Esme, she is reminded of an ingénue of the silent-film era. Moments later, Bella observes that "[I]t was like meeting a fairy tale—Snow White in the flesh." (*Twilight*, 282.) The reference to silent films and Snow White hearken back to the original American celluloid Cinderella, Clara Bow in *It* (1927). This reference, despite the "waves of caramel colored hair," intersects neatly with Walt Disney's first feature-length animated film, *Snow White and the Seven Dwarfs*, released in 1937. Both Clara Bow's character, Betty Lou, and Snow White know "someday my prince will come," both have pale complexions, and both have heart-shaped faces framed by bobbed hair. But there are some differences worthy of examination. Clara Bow's It-girl is the classic flapper of the 1920s, a time of frivolity, flagrant displays of wealth, and unease about changes in the postwar sexual behavior and roles of women. The "It" factor refers to sexuality. As hemlines rose, women gained the vote, and more and more women entered the workplace, Clara Bow's portrayal of Betty Lou encompassed both the hedonism and the anxiety of the era.[18] Despite the monumental changes that were occurring, the ideal presented by Hollywood's dream factory was still marriage, even in a text such as *It*. However, the flighty, manipulative, and sexualized behavior of Betty Lou, in spite of the Cinderella ending that implies that she was a "good girl," suggests that ultimately Esme more nearly resembles Disney's *Snow White*.

Carlisle is Esme's prince, and his "kiss" saves her life following her suicide attempt after losing a child. Esme has hobbies in architecture and the restoration of furniture and buildings, but this is described as something in which she dabbles rather than the "calling" pursued by Carlisle. This interest in houses is an extension of Esme as "homemaker," much like Disney's Snow White, who whistles while she works and worries terribly that the dwarfs have no mother. And the cottage Esme constructs for Bella and Edward is also straight out of *Snow White* or 1959's *Sleeping Beauty*. Esme's mothering instincts and her capacity for love and devotion are what make her the ideal companion for Carlisle. She is devoted to her "children" in spite of the threat that having a human girl in their midst poses; she wouldn't care if Bella had "a third eye and webbed feet" if it made Edward happy. (*Twilight*, 286.) While Esme may be the (unbeating) heart of the Cullen family, however, it is Carlisle who is its head and the leader of their way of life.

At the end of the Great Depression, *Snow White*, whose princess Esme resembles so strikingly, marked the beginning of Walt Disney's dominance as the chief peddler of fairy tales and dreams—and not only to an American audience. Walt Disney is himself representative of the American Dream in the early twentieth century: having pulled himself up by his bootstraps, he built his success in the 1930s, when destitution and despair were the lot of so many, and ended up the chief controller and dictator of the "happiest place on earth."[19] For many people growing up in the twentieth and twenty-first centuries, Disney *is* the chief source for fairy tales. This all-American studio and corporation have taken tales that originated in Europe and retold and repackaged them to the entire world in a kind of reverse colonization of the imagination. Often known as the "great sanitizer," "Disney's trademarked innocence operates on a systematic sanitization of violence, sexuality, and political struggle," purging these where they had been present in earlier versions of these fairy tales.[20] But as Naomi Wood pointed out, the "squeaky clean" feel of Disney texts was a part of the "American prurience that was so appealing and acceptable to his audiences."[21]

Certainly the "classic" Disney princesses in *Snow White, Cinderella,* and *Sleeping Beauty* represent beautiful heroines whose excellence in the domestic arts and beautiful bell-like singing voices are what commend them—much like the "feminine ideals" of the mid-twentieth century. *Cinderella* makes wishes on soap bubbles and passively receives the gifts of her fairy godmother. It is not she who seeks to find her own way to the ball, but her furry companions who go to work, making a dress fit for royalty. She is beautiful and blond—and blank. Her identity is defined first by her subordinate position in her family there among the cinders, and then as the "wife" of Prince Charming. Her dreams go no further than being on the arm of someone who can elevate her from being a servant in one household to presiding over another—neither of which belongs to her. The 1950 Disney *Cinderella* does not need to be named to be present in *Twilight,* but a direct reference does tie the two texts together. The spells of Cinderella's fairy godmother shimmer when Carlisle engages Jacob in a discussion of his DNA:

> "Your family's divergence from humanity is much more interesting. Magical almost."
>
> "Bibbidi-Bobbidi-Boo," I mumbled. He was just like Bella with all the magic garbage. (*Breaking Dawn,* 237.)

Jacob introduces another princess, *Sleeping Beauty*, overtly into Meyer's text in his less than cordial relationship with Rosalie: "The look on Rosalie's face made it clear that I wasn't welcome to one of them. It made me wonder what Sleepless Beauty needed a bed for anyway. Was she that possessive of her props?" (*Breaking Dawn*, 253.)

Rosalie's long blond hair and breathtaking beauty, even among the Botticellian vampires, reinforce the connection to the 1959 animated feature. Rosalie herself has told her story as a fairy tale gone awry.

Renowned for her physical beauty, Rosalie was the daughter of an aspiring middle-class family in the 1930s, a family that never felt the effects of the Great Depression. While the Hales had wealth, their position in banking suggests that their material well-being was at the expense of others who lost everything during the hardships of the early 1930s. So while they fulfilled the upwardly mobile part of American mythology, they did not possess the other requirement of moral strength and a willingness to help others.[22] Dreams of wealth without the desire or the capacity to improve the lives of those around you are empty dreams. And in *Twilight* the princess of such dreams, Rosalie, was similarly without substance. Rosalie, in *Eclipse*, attempts to explain to Bella why she should hold on to being human. For Rosalie, being turned into a vampire was more a punishment than a reward: a punishment for a shallow existence premised on little more than her good looks and her sense of entitlement. The fairy tale that had been promised in life—"This was everything they'd dreamed of. And Royce seemed to be everything I'd dreamed of. The fairy tale prince, come to make me a princess. Everything I wanted, yet it was still no more than I expected. We were engaged before I'd known him for two months."—ended in gang rape. (*Eclipse*, 157.) Beauty is a potential trap in many fairy tales, and without the moral center of self-sacrificing devotion of a true fairy-tale heroine, Rosalie's unhappiness continues in her afterlife.

It would be wrong to imply that Disney heroines have not changed over time, even though, ultimately, the end result of fulfillment through marriage has been maintained. Ariel (*The Little Mermaid*, 1989) and Belle (*Beauty and the Beast*, 1991), the two princesses who essentially rebooted the appeal of Disney animated magic for a new generation, represented significant change from their sweet, mop-wielding, predecessors. Both heroines have been somewhat influenced by feminism in their intellectual curiosity and their possession of much more bravery and capacity for action than Cinderella. Ultimately they too marry to rise socially, above the sea and out of "this provincial life," and their dreams of new ideas and experiences fade with the closing kisses of these stories. The women in the Twilight novels also exhibit feminist traits, both historical and contemporary, or they would simply have no appeal to a twenty-first century audience. But they too have their eyes on the prize of marital bliss.

For example, Rosalie's whole existence seems to revolve around just being beautiful—but there are tongue-in-cheek references to her skills as a mechanic in both the books and the *Twilight* movie. This is more than a jibe at the incongruity of a beautiful blond emerging from underneath a car. It resonates with skills Rosalie may well have acquired during World War II, when in a time of national emergency women were being told (by a woman also called Rosie), "We can do it!" and encouraged to take on the jobs and skills of men, before being encouraged back to the kitchen and the bedroom at war's end.[23] But technical skill is not required of these radiant women and is indulged because they will never need to use it as a profession, unlike Jacob, whose class and ethnic background in these depictions seem to necessitate knowledge of a "trade" rather than aspiration to a profession.

Bella is introduced to the reader as sacrificing the life she loved in the sun so that her irresponsible mother can pursue her own happiness. Renée's happiness itself revolves around remarriage to a minor league ballplayer, her own entrée to the American Dream through "the American pastime." Bella then moves into the dark and gothic atmosphere of the town where her father is the chief of police, but like so many fairy-tale fathers, he is benign but largely absent. Bella may not sing while she does housework, but she takes on the role of housewife for her father much like her 1950 predecessor. Bella's blankness of mind for Edward poses a mystery, and it is one of the things that attract him. Along with devotion, beauty, and self-sacrifice, this feminine silence is often present in many fairy tales and has over many centuries acted both as a punishment of young women and a feature that attracts male fairy-tale heroes.[24] Her silence of mind and her silence with regard to keeping the secret of the Cullens' existence both become gifts in the end, since Bella's blankness becomes the means of saving her entire family from the games of the Volturi.

Bella toys with the idea of college but mainly as a device for the only ambition she ever clearly expresses—maintaining her hold on Edward. Before her relationship with Edward solidifies, we hear of Bella working to supplement her meager college fund, and we later learn she has applied to a university in Alaska (mainly because she could use this as a ruse to disguise her own transformation into a vampire). However, we never know what it is she might like to study or what she might like to pursue in terms of a career. Much like Belle in *Beauty and the Beast*, Bella does not really fit into "provincial" Forks. Like Belle, her longings for more are not clearly articulated, and this "more" seems to be fulfilled by both Beauties' choice of Beasts.

Beauty and the Beast was first published in French in the first half of the eighteenth century (translated into English in 1759), and includes clear evidence of class struggle and the aspirations of the merchant class for the trappings and privileges of the aristocracy.[25] It is a part of what folklorists call the "Cinderella cycle" of tales, and follows a familiar trajectory of feminine self-sacrifice and devotion being ultimately rewarded through marriage. The Disney text subtracts the element of class conflict, despite the obvious socioeconomic differences between Belle and the Beast. In this way, and in dressing Belle in a way reminiscent of the cinematic version of the original American fairy tale *The Wizard of Oz*, we have a truly American fairy tale that fits with the "classless" society of American Dream mythology.

Pre-vamp Bella makes a great deal of not accepting expensive gifts—a part of her "morality" is her rejection of the trappings that highlight the inequalities between herself and Edward. Along with Bella's father's profession, other indicators of Bella's class difference from the Cullens are constant throughout the Twilight novels. Like any Cinderella, her premarriage wardrobe is scanty and occasionally supplemented by the good fairy Alice. Bella's father's profession and income mean that the house they live in is small and shabby, and she has access only to antiquated communications technologies. Bella's car is an ancient Chevy truck that, while safe, has none of the style or speed of any of the vehicles in the Cullens' garage. CinderBella never complains about her circumstances, and that is a part of her charm. But where she protests extravagance extended in her direction before her nuptials, she has no such qualms in accepting the benefits of the Cullens' wealth after marriage, especially when this can assist her transition from human to vampire.

Conclusion: What Price the Glass Slipper?

The Twilight Saga is very much a twenty-first-century morality tale with a fairy-story ending. It is also a "survival story with hope" that invokes and enacts the premises, and promises, of the American Dream in all of its forms, both masculine and feminine. The Cullens represent morality, wealth, and the unique qualities of the New World vampires from the seventeenth century to the present. They work hard at staying secret, staying together, and maintaining their "vegetarian" diet. Bella makes sacrifices to keep her family happy and never complains about her limited lot in life. Her selflessness and character as a good girl mark her as exceptional in portrayals of young women in contemporary popular culture. She is also an exceptional "newborn" vampire—even for her New World family. But the things that make Bella's narrative an extraordinary vampire story make her a rather ordinary Cinderella. Beyond being a Cullen, she has no ambition, and unlike Carlisle and Edward, she seems unlikely to carve out her own separate path. And while the ultimate battle may take place after Edward and Bella's wedding, and while

Bella plays an active role in her family's defense, the curtains still close on a kiss to last forever after.

Edward laughs off what in Meyer's saga are merely myths about vampires. However, the "truths" communicated by the American fairy tale remain. Moral good little girls can marry princes and become more talented through that marriage, stay beautiful, and never need to worry about juggling work and child care—but only if they adhere to whatever society dictates as moral and good, and only if they accept marriage as the ultimate happy ending. Bella fulfills the self-sacrifice quotient required of a fairy-tale heroine in the numerous conflict scenarios where she offers herself up to fate in order to try to save those around her. She is often selfish and self-indulgent but always self-sacrificing when it comes to those she loves. Bella works hard, remains a virgin until marriage, and refuses an abortion even when her own life is at stake. And she is rewarded. In the ultimate wish fulfillment, Bella escapes the pains of aging in a society that purports to venerate knowledge but is really enamored of that most fleeting of shiny toys—youth. "Forget Princess, I want to be a Vampire" sums up an entire culture whose ideal of having it all conflicts with the realities of income differences and sexual inequality that still characterize American society. All happily-ever-afters come at a cost, and the price Bella pays is her life.

Notes

1. Fairy-tale theorists, such as Jack Zipes and Robert Darnton, argue that the roles for women in such tales were much more fluid in the oral storytelling cultures that predated Perrault. In fixing the tales in published literature (at a time when private and public spheres and a strict demarcation of gender roles were becoming more rigid for emerging middle classes) that had a strongly didactic function, the strictures on feminine behavior became much more apparent. Even in the literary traditions of the seventeenth, eighteenth, and nineteenth centuries, however, there is much variation according to changing behavioral norms and the socioeconomic, cultural, and religious backgrounds and genders of the authors. There have, of course, been many more producers of fairy-tale texts than the three cited in this section, but these are the three most well-known examples in the progression from oral to literary to cinematic texts. See, for example, Jack Zipes, "Breaking the Disney Spell," in Elizabeth Bell, Linda Haas, and Laura Sells, eds., *From Mouse to Mermaid: The Politics of Film, Gender, and Culture* (Bloomington and Indianapolis: Indiana Univ. Press, 1995), 21–42; Jack Zipes, *Why Fairy Tales Stick: The Evolution and Relevance of a Genre* (New York: Routledge, 2006); and Robert Darnton, *The Great Cat Massacre and Other Episodes in French Cultural Theory* (New York: Basic Books, 1984), 9–74. There remains, as Zipes

points out in a number of his works, great potential for subversion in the fairy tale even in the face of such monolithic dream factories as Disney studios.

2. Zipes, *Why Fairy Tales Stick*, 27.

3. See Cal Jillson, *Pursuing the American Dream: Opportunity and Exclusion over Four Centuries* (Lawrence: Univ. Press of Kansas, 2004). See also J. Emmett Winn, *The American Dream and Contemporary Hollywood Cinema* (New York: Continuum, 2007).

4. Peggy Orenstein, "What's Wrong with Cinderella?" *New York Times*, December 24, 2006, www.nytimes.com/2006/12/24/magazine/24princess.t.html.

5. I wish I could claim to have ownership of the "dying young, staying pretty" idea. I first heard it articulated in the season 2 episode of *Buffy the Vampire Slayer*, "Lie to Me," where a former friend of Buffy's, Billy Fordham, who has terminal brain cancer, articulates it as the ideal of every American teen. Fordham's quip may have origins in a famous quote supposedly attributable to 1950s teen idol James Dean: "Live fast, die young, and leave a beautiful corpse." There is also a 1979 song by punk band Blondie titled "Die Young, Stay Pretty."

6. Darnton, *The Great Cat Massacre*, 59.

7. In fact, Bella herself makes reference to some of these tales: "It seemed that most vampire myths centered around beautiful women as demons and children as victims; they also seemed like constructs created to explain away the high mortality rates for young children and to give men an excuse for infidelity." (*Twilight*, 116.) What she doesn't mention is the voluptuousness and inferred homosexuality of many male and female vampires in literary and cinematic texts, including Bram Stoker's *Dracula*, which was first published in 1897, and Joseph Sheridan Le Fanu's *Carmilla*, published in 1892, to all of their cinematic incarnations throughout the twentieth century. It is highly unlikely that any homosexual vampires exist in the Cullen-verse, and while the consumption of blood can incite a fury, its orgiastic quality seems to relate more to gluttony than to sex. For commentary on aspects of sexual transgression in *Dracula* see, for example, Christopher Craft, "Kiss Me with Those Red Lips: Gender and Inversion in Bram Stoker's *Dracula*," *Representations* 8 (Autumn 1984): 107–133.

8. Jim Cullen, *The American Dream: A Short History of an Idea That Shaped a Nation* (New York: Oxford Univ. Press, 2003), 10, 38.

9. "American exceptionalism" is a term originally coined by Alexis de Tocqueville, the famous French writer who was so enamored of the nascent democracy in the United States in the nineteenth century. Originally this was intended to convey a sense of difference through a nation made up of immigrants making a new life distinct from the old. A factor that encouraged this "difference" was life on the frontier. The term has come into much wider usage in the twentieth century, particularly after World War II, and has come to stand for the things that make America distinct and distinctly "virtuous" in contrast to the rest of the world. For an overview of the history of this idea, see Deborah Madsen, *American Exceptionalism* (Edinburgh: Edinburgh Univ. Press, 1998).

10. Jillson, *Pursuing the American Dream*, 29.

11. This is not to say that Carlisle's feelings are not those of love and loyalty, but he has a commitment to a bigger picture in his faith in God and God's will.

12. Jillson, *Pursuing the American Dream*, 58.

13. "What's with the Apple?" is an FAQ on Meyer's Web site, to which she responds with the following:

> The apple on the cover of *Twilight* represents "forbidden fruit." I used the scripture from Genesis (located just after the table of contents) because I loved

> the phrase "the fruit of the knowledge of good and evil." Isn't this exactly what Bella ends up with? A working knowledge of what good is, and what evil is. The nice thing about the apple is it has so many symbolic roots. You've got the apple in Snow White, one bite and you're frozen forever in a state of not-quite-death. Then you have Paris and the golden apple in Greek mythology—look how much trouble *that* started. Apples are quite the versatile fruit. In the end, I love the beautiful simplicity of the picture. To me it says: *choice*.

The Official Website of Stephenie Meyer, FAQ page, www.stepheniemeyer.com/twilight_faq.html.

14. J. Emmett Winn, *The American Dream in Contemporary Hollywood Cinema* (New York: Continuum Books, 2007).

15. Abstinence classes instead of sex education, in addition to abstinence pledges and leagues in high schools, have been a part of a growing politics of the religious right in the United States, which in spite of/because of these attempts to keep young people ignorant and/or chaste "leads the industrialized world in teen-pregnancy, abortion and sexually transmitted disease rates." Susan Rose, "Going Too Far? Sex, Sin and Social Policy," *Social Forces* 84, no. 2 (December 2005): 1207.

16. For an involved and fascinating examination of all the incarnations of Little Red Riding Hood, see Jack Zipes, ed., *The Trials and Tribulations of Little Red Riding Hood* (New York: Routledge, 1993).

17. In the first edition of *Die Kinder und Hausmärchen der Brüder Grimm*, published in 1812, Rapunzel falls very obviously pregnant and reveals herself to the witch in asking: "Tell me Godmother, why my clothes are so tight and don't fit me any longer?" "Wicked Child," cried the Fairy. In the second edition, published in 1819, Rapunzel betrays herself thus: "Tell me, Godmother, why is it you are so much harder to pull up than the young prince?" Friedrich Panzer, ed., *Die Kinder und Hausmärchen der Brüder Grimm*, cited by Maria Tatar in *The Hard Facts of the Grimms' Fairy Tales* (Princeton, NJ: Princeton Univ. Press, 1987), 18.

18. See Cynthia Felando, "Clara Bow Is *It*," in *Film Stars: Hollywood and Beyond*, ed. Andy Willis (Manchester, Eng.: Manchester Univ. Press, 2004), 8–24.

19. Elizabeth Bell, Lynda Haas, and Laura Sells, "Introduction: Walt's in the Movies," in Bell, Haas, and Sells, *From Mouse to Mermaid*, 2–3.

20. Ibid., 7.

21. Naomi Wood, "Domesticating Dreams in Walt Disney's *Cinderella*," *The Lion and the Unicorn* 20, no. 1 (1996), muse.jhu.edu/journals/lion_and_the_unicorn/v020/20.1wood .html.

22. See Jillson, *Pursuing the American Dream*, 71, where he uses *The Great Gatsby* (first published in 1925) as an example of the bankruptcy of the dream where only the pursuit of material wealth is present.

23. For an examination of the not-so-successful campaigns to mobilize American women during World War II, see D'Ann Campbell, *Women at War with America: Private Lives in a Patriotic Era* (Cambridge, MA: Harvard Univ. Press, 1984). "Rosie the Riveter" has become an icon for the mobilization of women and a recognition of women's skills. At the time, however, this was not enough to overcome much of the backlash against women who joined untraditional trades and professions in the war effort.

24. Successive chapters of Marina Warner's *From the Beast to the Blonde: Fairy Tales and Their Tellers* (London: Chatto and Windus, 1994) discuss the history and power of the myth of feminine silence.

25. Jerry Griswold, *The Meanings of Beauty and the Beast: A Handbook* (Toronto: Broadview Press, 2004), 27, 59.

Courting Edward Cullen

Courtship Rituals and Marital Expectations in Edward's Youth

Catherine Coker

Bella Swan's perceptions of Edward Cullen are colored by literary influences, particularly *Wuthering Heights* and the novels of Jane Austen, as well as what she believes to have been the cultural norm for young couples early in the twentieth century: visits on the porch and early marriages. If Edward and Bella had really known each other in the early twentieth century, however, they would have been caught up in changing patterns of social behavior and gender norms; their courtship would probably have been quite different from what she imagines. This chapter explores Bella's assumptions about history and how they are colored by her reading habits. In addition, I will discuss the true place of courtship in twentieth-century America and how this information adds to our knowledge of Edward and Bella.

The Influence of Romance

The courtship of Edward Cullen and Bella Swan is presented through a peculiarly literary lens. Throughout Meyer's novels,

Bella is often reading novels and plays, including the works of Jane Austen (such as *Mansfield Park* and *Pride and Prejudice*), Emily Brontë (*Wuthering Heights*), and Shakespeare (*Romeo and Juliet*). These novels generally serve as a contrast to the action in Bella's world. For example, the parallel plots of Romeo and Juliet's doomed romance and Edward and Bella's separation in *New Moon* color our expectations of what will happen to them. Likewise, the social romances of Austen, when compared with Bella and Edward's own interactions, provide us with a shorthand for understanding why they so often misunderstand or fail to communicate with each other, as well as why Bella treats her supernatural friends so differently from her human ones. By portraying Bella as a precocious bookworm who finds it easier to relate to fictional people than real ones, Meyer writes her as both a reader and a stand-in for the reader of Meyer's own works: girls with books reading about a girl with books. As such, Bella and Edward themselves join the classic canon of literary lovers, such as Elizabeth Bennet and Mr. Darcy, for many teenage readers.

Bella and Edward also become their own critics as they discuss these novels throughout the Twilight books, commenting on their own similarities to literary characters such as Catherine and Heathcliff:

> "The characters are ghastly people who ruin each other's lives. I don't know how Heathcliff and Cathy ended up being ranked with couples like Romeo and Juliet or Elizabeth Bennet and Mr. Darcy. It isn't a love story, it's a hate story."
>
> "You have some serious issues with the classics," I snapped.
>
> "Perhaps it's because I'm not impressed by antiquity." He smiled . . . "What is it that appeals to you?"
>
> [. . .] "I'm not sure," I said. . . . "I think it's something about the inevitability. How nothing can keep them apart—not her selfishness, or his evil, or even death, in the end. . . . Their love *is* their only redeeming quality."
>
> "I hope you have better sense than that—to fall in love with someone so . . . malignant."
>
> "It's a bit late for me to worry about who I fall in love with," I pointed out.

"But even with the warning, I seem to have managed fairly well." (*Eclipse*, 28–29.)

To many readers, this passage verges on becoming meta-commentary on the series. Many critics view Edward in an extremely negative light: for his almost pathologically controlling nature, for his obsession with Bella, and for his relationship with a girl some ninety years his junior. It is telling, however, that here he contrasts himself with Darcy, a literary ideal, as well as labeling an early-nineteenth-century book an "antiquity." He is implicitly stating that he considers himself antiquated as well, even though he was born in the early twentieth century. This action places "history" at a distance from the reader, as well as from Bella and Edward. "History" becomes something far away, events that transpire in a foreign land rather than referring only to the passage of time. This distancing functions for readers a lot like the common witticism "To Americans, a hundred years is a long time, and to Europeans, a hundred miles is a long way" functions for travelers: as a shorthand for understanding cultural differences. In the case of Bella and Edward, the cultural differences are the result of the passage of time, a generation gap from the time period when Edward was a young man to Bella's present day. Bella consistently reads Edward's human self (the "historical Edward" of 1918) as an exotic personage both removed from the man she knows but a man she would like to idealize. She also daydreams about an idealized, historical version of herself that she would like to pair with this human Edward and that gives their relationship the simpler, romantic history she craves.

Bella's literary choices and her conversations with Edward also influence her youthful belief in romance and courtship. Her inner thoughts about her relationship with Edward focus on an eternal unity and perfection. Her uncritical approach to the classics ignores the stories they tell: Romeo and Juliet have a perfect love because they die within a week of meeting; Cathy marries Edgar Linton instead of Heathcliff; Elizabeth and Darcy at least marry happily, but as with most romances, the story ends at the marriage.

Most twenty-first-century readers therefore find Bella's interpretations of these stories problematic: she does not think about a career or a source of income; she does not consider children until she is already married and pregnant. The future is reduced to a fear of growing old—specifically not death itself, but of no longer being seventeen. Her eighteenth birthday precipitates the crisis in which Edward temporarily leaves Bella, before he returns to her with the expectation of a marriage that she initially rejects for superficial reasons that will be further discussed later. Bella thus essentially views life as an extended adolescence, a view at odds with the woman who works, manages her family's finances and household, and is otherwise engaged in the business of "real life." Her life is suspended because of romance.

Bella's point of view is best expressed in her fantasy of being courted by Edward in the early twentieth century: "I saw myself in a long skirt and a high-necked lace blouse with my hair piled up on my head. I saw Edward looking dashing in a light suit with a bouquet of wildflowers in his hand, sitting beside me on a porch swing. I shook my head and swallowed. I was just having *Anne of Green Gables* flashbacks." (*Eclipse*, 277.)

This literary flashback evokes a specific response from readers who recognize the reference. L. M. Montgomery's novel *Anne of Green Gables* was published in 1908 and is now a part of the young adult literary canon. The story focuses on Anne Shirley, adopted at the age of eleven by a pair of middle-aged sibling farmers. The book and its sequels follow Anne through her adolescence, education, marriage, and community life. They conclude with the end of World War I, at which point she has had six children and raised them to adulthood. Since Edward became a vampire during this same time period (1918), Bella's association of these childhood novels with him again reveals her adolescent expectations of romance—the kind of romance where there is sex, but it is veiled; where there are a minimum of hardships, emotional, physical, or monetary; and where the ending is always happy. Unsurprisingly, Meyer's own novels follow this same trend, focusing more on Bella and Edward's courtship rituals than on the other plotlines, to the point that the final volume revolves primarily around their emotional and physical relationship.

In the final book, *Breaking Dawn*, Bella and Edward marry and consummate their love. Since the series is still classified as young adult, Meyer "fades to black" on the love scene itself, though the physical ramifications after their two lovemaking sessions—including Bella's bruised body—are discussed at length. Edward refuses to make love to Bella again until she has become a vampire herself, and their honeymoon quickly becomes tense with emotional and physical frustration. The tension escalates when Bella discovers she is pregnant with a half-vampire that grows at an alarming rate. Edward urges Bella to abort the unnatural fetus, and she refuses—a decision that sparked controversy among both readers and critics. Bella gives birth to a daughter, Renesmée, and Edward turns Bella into a vampire to save her life after a messy, fanged caesarian section. The rest of the novel focuses on Bella's adaptation to the vampiric lifestyle and the political machinations of other vampires. The story ends with peace restored and Bella and Edward and their family settling down to a cozy, eternal ever-after.

The Place of Twentieth-Century Courtship

At the very beginning of the twentieth century, middle- and upper-class courtship took place under the watchful eyes of family members, often at the woman's home. There, it was expected that the woman would entertain the man, providing tea and snacks, engaging in light talk, and perhaps showing off such accomplishments as singing or playing music. The invention and availability of the automobile changed this: it became the fashion to "go out," especially if one lived in an urban environment with easy access to cinemas, dance halls, and dining establishments. Since men were more likely to hold steady employment, it then became their responsibility to provide entertainment on these dates.

A popular joke from the 1920s involves a young man asking a city girl if he might "call on her." When he arrives, according to the punch line, "she had her hat on," which is to say that she was ready to go out on a date rather than stay at home with the young man. The humor plays on gender expectations: a boy arrives, expecting to be fed and amused, only to find a girl expecting the same thing! Thus the new world of dating is unexpectedly and improbably equalized through the location of the actual date.[1] In *New Moon* this shift in customs is brought to life when Bella and Jacob and their friends drive to a cinema outside of Forks to watch the latest horror film: they buy the film tickets and food (the boys paying for the girls) and travel to a different city in order to be entertained.

In contrast, the dating and relationship mores of the late twentieth and early twenty-first centuries are equally complex, if less straightforward. Women striving for economic and sexual equality with men often find themselves beset with questions their grandmothers never asked—or never asked publicly, at least. Who calls whom to arrange a date? When both parties work, who is expected to pick up the check for an evening's outing? And what about the issues of birth control and family planning, living together before marriage, and so on, ad nauseam? Many types of books (fiction, self-help/advice nonfiction, and scholarly studies) have attempted to dissect the most common practices, but the answers tend to remain up to the individual. Nonetheless there are some patterns that can be distinguished: early dates tend to take place outside of the home, at restaurants or movies. After a comfortable level of intimacy has been reached, the couple will meet and interact in the home. "I will cook dinner" is to many an offer of exceptional intimacy in a time when many busy people subsist on fast food, frozen meals, or delivery and take-out food. In addition, people having first dates through the new online dating sites, or simply meeting one another for first time after meeting electronically, are cautioned to always meet in a public space for safety or for a quick exit if the date isn't going well.

This evolution of dating is of particular note in Meyer's series. Bella and Edward's dates at first follow the modern-day script. In *Twilight*, Edward takes Bella to an Italian restaurant after he saves her from muggers; he buys her a meal of mushroom ravioli and sodas. Later they spend time outdoors together; his physical revelation of his vampiric powers takes place in a sunny meadow. After they have declared their love for each other, Edward and Bella then spend most of their time in their homes, often with family members around monitoring them, albeit for different reasons. Charlie Swan watches Edward with the same suspicion most men have when then their teenage daughters are romantically involved. In contrast, the Cullens' awareness of Bella derives from their supernatural abilities—they can't help but be aware of the only human on the premises. In addition, they too want to keep Bella physically safe—at first because they don't want to have to leave the area if Edward's interactions with Bella go disastrously wrong in some way, then later because they genuinely care for Bella as a member of their family.

In the latter books, however, Edward and Bella's courtship becomes more old-fashioned, with almost all of their interactions outside of school taking place in the home. Edward watches sports on television with Charlie when he is at the Swan household; he plays the piano for Bella when they are at the Cullens'. At night, Edward surreptitiously (and chastely) "sleeps" with Bella in her own room, unbeknownst to Charlie. This practice is similar to the eighteenth-century practice of bundling or tarrying as sometimes practiced in colonial America. One member of a courting couple would be sewn or tightly wrapped in bedding to sleep next to the other prior to marriage; sometimes a wooden board was physically placed between the two. It was assumed that the couple would also make physical contact (teenage hormones have not changed in the last two centuries, after all!) but be restrained enough not to go "all the way," since they would be placed mere rooms away from sleeping parents. The aim was for the couple to establish the intimacy of marriage and ensure that they were compatible without actually engaging in sexual intercourse. In the Twilight novels, of course, sexual intercourse is prevented only by Edward's ironclad will and early-twentieth-century morals.[2] Bella presents herself as a modern-day girl who would like to proceed to the next steps of a relationship on her terms. She gets her wish only by meeting Edward's own expectation: that of marriage.

Essentially we therefore have a couple whose courtship rituals go further back in time as their own relationship progresses. As Edward and Bella grow closer, they do more activities together inside their homes, rather than going out on dates. Instead of taking Bella out to films or meals in restaurants, Edward takes her to his family's home. The two come to the mutual conclusion that they are destined for eternal love very early on, though Edward (in his own words, a masochist) attempts to discourage Bella's interest at first. Their early marriage and childbearing reflect the norms of ages past rather than the current day—norms that Bella is less than eager to embrace herself, at first.

Gendered Expectations and Conflicted Desires

Because of the quite different cultural expectations Bella and Edward each have for their courtship, they face a conflict over how to proceed with their relationship. Edward wants marriage; Bella just wants to *be* with Edward. There are reasons for Bella's resistance to matrimony: her parents married young and quickly divorced. More important, however, Bella does not want to be *that girl*: "The one who gets married right out of high school like some small-town hick who got knocked up by her boyfriend! Do you know what people would think? Do you realize what century this is? People don't just get married at eighteen! Not smart people, not responsible, mature people! I wasn't going to be that girl. That's not who I am." (*Eclipse*. 275–276.)

Bella's venom and contempt for *that girl*, the girl she doesn't want to be, come from deeply embedded middle-class expectations. Her town of Forks is a stand-in for Everywhere Middle Class, America: the high school students all have cars instead of using public transportation; everyone's parents are apparently employed, and the students themselves are also employed; the local upper class consists predominantly of the Cullens themselves, who each have flashy cars and designer clothing despite the fact that only their patriarch, Carlisle, is gainfully employed.

Bella is herself middle-class bordering on working-class. Her father, Charlie, is a police chief who always drives his police cruiser and does not have a personal vehicle. Their closest social ties are with the Black family from the nearby Quileute reservation. The descriptions of Bella's possessions usually emphasize that they are old or hand-me-downs: the used truck rebuilt by Billy Black and the motorcycle that is restored by Jacob Black; the computer with a dial-up modem when most Internet users have high-speed cable connections; worn paperback books and comfy, tatty quilts. Bella has an after-school job and is used to maintaining careful accounts of everyday finances after a lifetime of taking care of an irresponsible mother. In contrast, the Cullens (with the exception of Carlisle, who is the town doctor) are all well dressed, unemployed, and seemingly spendthrift. Bella often notes to herself how expensive the items are that the Cullens surround themselves with—and they are expensive. Without hesitation they buy new, imported high-end cars for one another as presents; Carlisle gave a tropical South American island (with a furnished house to boot) to his wife, Esme, as a gift. Bella's unspoken anxiety about these class differences becomes clearer when she is about to officially meet the Cullen family.

> "Look, I'm trying really hard not to think about what I'm about to do, so can we go already?" I asked.
>
> "And you're worried, not because you're headed to meet a houseful of vampires, but because you think those vampires won't approve of you, correct?"
>
> "That's right," I answered immediately. (*Twilight*, 320.)

Though Meyer doesn't put it in so many words, Bella finds it easier to navigate the supernatural world of vampires and werewolves than the demands of being a lower-middle-class teenager in a wealthy household. Meyer spends pages and pages describing Bella's anxieties over social interactions with her classmates, her lack of real friends, and her preference for spending her time studying or reading instead of socializing. In the latter books Bella also frets about saving money for college, unwilling to allow the Cullens to pay for an education at an elite institution. Unspoken is the implication that if Bella were to accept their generosity, she would feel herself to be less in their eyes.

Bella is put in the position of having to prove that she is worthy of Edward, much like the heroines of the nineteenth-century romances she adores. She must overcome racial and social boundaries—the high school cafeteria, with its cliques; the supernatural stratification of human, werewolf, vampire; even the vampiric hierarchies of the "vegetarian" Cullens and the traditional vampiric nomads and the Volturi—in order to be with her love. In addition, Meyer assigns Bella what would have been traditionally male behaviors in the early twentieth century: her role as the sexual aggressor for instance, as well her resistance to marriage despite her intention to commit to a relationship with Edward; her working outside of the home and her focus on finances. She even takes the male role of resisting emotional involvement with Edward, primarily because she believes she cannot be worthy of him as she is. Much of this belief is in her own mind—both Edward and Jacob regularly compliment her on her intelligence, her bravery, and her beauty: to them, social class and money are of far less importance than these attributes, which Bella possesses in spades. Nonetheless, she feels herself to be an inferior. She gains confidence in herself only after she becomes a mother and is willing to fight any battle necessary for the life of her child.

Just as Bella displays attributes traditionally seen as male, Edward's actions in the domestic sphere—playing the piano, spending his leisure time reading and listening to music—feminize him. Bella's endless comments on his perfect physical beauty, as well as the descriptions of his body as being like stone or diamonds, literally objectify him. Edward becomes the object that Bella must win and be worthy of—Edward must be courted.

Other Lives in Other Universes

Since we know the story of how Edward and Bella's courtship played out in the twenty-first century, I think we should ask ourselves the same question Bella asks: what would their lives have been like if they had had the normal lives of teenagers during specific times in history? I would like to provide some possible answers, recreating the historical context of different periods—showing how their relationship would have been influenced by the social movements and events of each period. The specific time and place of the courtship, as well as how Bella imagines her courtship, highlights Meyer's own approach to history in the text: by placing history at a distance (an "antiquity" akin to Bella's historical romance novels), she implies that Bella and Edward's own courtship takes place "out of time." By returning real historical elements to the saga, we end up providing a resistant reading of the text. Media studies scholars Henry Jenkins and John Tulloch use the term "resistant reading" to describe a process of essentially reading a text against itself (something that many fans do in their own minds) in order to examine the "many important questions about the ideological power of the mass media and the relationship between 'the viewer and the viewed.'"[3]

We have already observed how the roles of class and gender have shaped Bella and Edward's interactions and their relationship. By providing a resistant reading of Bella and Edward's courtship and comparing their interactions with real historical details, we will be rewriting the series' presentation of Bella and Edward so that they reflect real historical details rather than the characteristics and clichés of most romance fiction. For instance, in Meyer's series, Bella's resistance to being *that girl* nonetheless foreshadows, and finally culminates in, Bella's becoming the very creature she does not want to be (married, pregnant), as well as who she does want to be (a beautiful vampire). This is the "correct ending" for the protagonists of Bella's beloved romances—who often end up married and happy—except of course for the vampire part.[4] In what follows, I would like to show how Meyer's world reflects the values of some truly alternate universes, as well as the probable outcomes of the situations that Bella and Edward face, if they had taken place during different historical periods.

The Year 1918 through the Roaring Twenties: A Brief Historical Digression

The early twentieth century was a tumultuous time in America. In the year 1918, when Edward died at the age of seventeen, the Spanish influenza ravaged much of the world. The United States had entered World War I the year before, and the conflict would not end until late in 1918. The Prohibition movement was at its apogee, and the sale, manufacture, and transportation of alcohol would become illegal the following year. The women's suffrage movement was at its height, and it would be two more years before the Nineteenth Amendment was ratified, allowing women to vote. Women had had limited access to higher education for half of a century, though many colleges and universities were still male-only. The sexes were often separated socially, although the gap was steadily closing.

In two more years, the Roaring Twenties would introduce real changes in women's appearance and their roles. Flappers—the iconic, liberated young women of the period—would dance and smoke in dark jazz clubs, the term transforming from slang for a spunky teenager to a word that was shorthand for a liberated and hedonistic lifestyle. Birth control and condoms were available, though obtaining information about them was often difficult. The first novels of Ernest Hemingway and F. Scott Fitzgerald were published in this decade, and they tackled topics such as premarital sex, the horrors of the Great War, and the ugly side of class and gender relations.

Sitting on the Porch Swing: The Anne of Green Gables *Remix*

If Bella and Edward had been born around the turn of the twentieth century, their lives could have been close to what Bella imagines: her fantasy was very similar to some couples' relationships in that generation. One historically realistic version of their story would have had Bella and Edward living in a small town outside of Chicago, if they had been middle-class.

It is 1918 and the Spanish influenza seems like a nightmare occurring in another world. It has not touched them, though Edward sees the images in the news reports in the cinema. He also sees what is happening overseas—and he yearns to be a soldier, but he can't bring himself to leave his family just yet. And then there is Bella to consider. Bella and her family do not go to the playhouses to see the movies, but he tells her about them as they sit together on the front porch swing. The next year, the two marry quietly and celebrate the war's end. Edward is in medical school when Bella becomes pregnant with her first baby. After Renesmée is born, Edward quietly obtains contraceptives, and Bella waits several years for another child, this time a boy. The years pass; their son is drafted in 1944, but he does not participate in the worst battles of World War II. Renesmée marries in the postwar celebrations—her own son will be drafted to fight in Vietnam. Edward and Bella both die quietly in the late seventies, having watched from afar two sexual revolutions and two world wars.

Edward Masen and the Flapper: A Not-That-Girl Remix

Another, equally realistic, scenario could have taken place if Edward and Bella had grown up in Chicago itself in the late teens. If they had led lives more typical of sophisticated city dwellers, their story would have played out quite differently.

Bella is still determined to never be *that girl*, and to her parents' horror she bobs her hair and leaves home at a young age. Edward meets her at a dance party his fellow students drag him to. To his bewilderment, he meets a spaghetti-strap vision in blue; amid the smoke and booze of Prohibition, he dances the night away. They marry hastily when it becomes clear that Renesmee is a reality and divorce just as hastily when Renesmee is lost to complications stemming from poor medical care. Edward and Bella do not see each other again.

That Girl, *Yes and No: A 1950s Remix*

Interestingly, Bella imagines her and Edward's courtship only in the early twentieth century and in the early twenty-first century. What would their dates have been like had they taken place halfway between these two time periods?

In the 1950s Bella *would* have wanted to be *that girl*—most young women of that time period did. She very much wanted to get married and have children because, as she was often told, that's the life that young women want. Bella vaguely wants a husband and child; it's only when she meets Edward that she knows exactly who she wants her husband to *be*. Like many other young adults, they marry after high school. Bella spends a year at college before dropping out to have Renesmée; Edward stays in school and obtains several degrees. Bella and her parents (Charlie and Renée are still married, although not exactly happily) are all thrilled when he becomes Doctor Masen.

Bella and Edward have several children. Bella takes care of them at home while Edward works long hours. Once the children are all in school, Bella isn't quite sure what to do with herself any longer. Finally, she decides to go back to school and finish her degree; she had always loved studying literature. Edward reluctantly agrees, though he sometimes wonders aloud what the children will do without their mother. He wonders even more loudly when Bella decides to go on to graduate work. Bella is one of a handful of women scholars in her program: some professors are openly dismissive of her. At home, Edward says he is supportive of "what she does to entertain herself," though Bella would hardly call writing a dissertation on Jane Austen entertaining exactly.

In the early 1970s, they divorce. Bella gets the children to school in the morning, works during the day, feeds the children supper in the evening, and writes at night. She goes to a consciousness-raising group on the weekends and, after many years, realizes that although she wanted to be *that girl*, the one who wanted to make her man happy and sacrifice everything for him and her children, she isn't. She is *that woman* instead—the one who managed to make herself happy and successful despite protests from all sides. Very few can say that, and she is proud.

The Static Age: A Twenty-First-Century Remix

If Bella and Edward had met when and where they did in the Twilight Saga, and their courtship had simply reflected the norms of gender and social class of that decade, it would have been different yet again.

It is the twenty-first century. Edward Masen is a normal teenager in Forks, Washington, though his parents have a two-income household that is a little more prosperous than Bella's and Charlie's home. The two students are remarkable for their above-average academic abilities and are often paired together in classes; they quickly become an item. Bella loses her virginity to Edward after the senior prom. Their relationship combusts when they go to separate colleges, she to study literature and he in an intensive premed program. They each date a series of lovers; Edward marries in graduate school and divorces a few years later. In their early thirties, Edward and Bella reconnect through Facebook and tentatively begin to date again. Where it will end this time remains unknown.

Conclusion: "She Had Her Hat On . . ."

If the scenarios presented here were rather more complicated and less happy than those most readers would expect from Meyer's novels—well, so it goes, and that is the nature of life rather than books. It should be noted, however, that while none of the stories focus on perfect unions, they do focus on human beings trying to make their way in the world, and perhaps succeeding—at least to themselves. After all, the works of Austen, the Brontës, and Shakespeare also offered resistant readings for their own centuries, times when the possibility of love overcoming class distinctions (like the social gulf between Jane Eyre and Mr. Rochester) was almost as remote as the likelihood of a young woman falling in love with a vampire.

One thing all of these courtships have in common is the idea of love overcoming all obstacles because of a young woman's determination. Bella's determination to court Edward, to ultimately be worthy of him (in her own eyes), and to *have* Edward fuels a passion that transcends what many would consider acceptable levels of behavior from a high school student/graduate, which is what fuels much of the controversy and criticism of the series. If we were to reverse the circumstances, however, and say that Bella could *never* be worthy of Edward because of her lack of (and here the reader can pick and choose among a variety of issues) beauty, class, education, gender, wealth, or other abilities natural or supernatural, would readers not object to such an ending, and again offer alternative versions of their own to soothe the savage readership? Bella is many things, but a passive bystander is not one of them.

Finally, we should return to the old joke about the young woman who "had her hat on" when her date came to the door. The trajectory of a particular courtship often rests on expectations, as does a reader's enjoyment of a book. Bella expects certain actions and behaviors from her romance novels; Edward has his own expectations of courtship formed through a mortal life in the early twentieth century and a supernatural life that spans into the early twenty-first. The readers of Stephenie Meyer's saga also have expectations as to how these characters should act, whether these expectations are based on romantic fiction or on the social norms of a particular historical era. For all of these reasons, our expectations are subverted by Meyer herself—which is perhaps a joke on us.

Notes

1. Beth L. Bailey, *From Front Porch to Back Seat: Courtship in Twentieth-Century America* (Baltimore: Johns Hopkins Univ. Press, 1989), 13.

2. Of course that doesn't explain why he's in bed with a teenage girl to begin with, but that's why it's fiction.

3. Henry Jenkins and John Tulloch, *Science Fiction Audiences: Doctor Who, Star Trek, and Their Fans* (New York: Routledge, 1995), 262.

4. Although given the popularity of recent works such as *Pride and Prejudice and Zombies* and *Sense and Sensibility and Sea Monsters,* presumably it is only a matter of time before *Mansfield Park and Vampires* is available.

PART TWO

Some Family History

The Cullen Coven

Jasper Hale, the Oldest Living Confederate Veteran

Elizabeth Baird Hardy

Years after the American Civil War ended in 1865, many Union and Confederate veterans of the nation's bloodiest conflict often gathered together, reconciling their long-ago differences, commemorating their shared struggles, and mourning their dwindling numbers, until, at last, they had all "crossed over the river" to join their comrades who had perished in combat or succumbed to disease in camp. Each of these men was shaped by a war that was, particularly for Confederates, a transformative experience of loss and suffering. For Major Jasper Whitlock of Texas, the War between the States was only one of two wars that altered his peculiar existence.

Despite the fact that Jasper, clearly the most enigmatic of Stephenie Meyer's Cullen family, is a fictional creation, his role as a Confederate veteran is deeply rooted in the actual historical experiences of men who fought, and quite often died, under the Stars and Bars. Jasper attends high school in the tiny town of Forks, Washington, pretending to be the eighteen-year-old foster son of

Dr. Carlisle Cullen; he is actually a battle-scarred vampire with a wife, a number of advanced degrees, and a history of successful forgery that has helped his adopted family retain its secrecy for over fifty years. In many ways, though, he is neither a twenty-first-century teenager nor a sophisticated modern adult. He is a veteran from the 1860s, exhibiting qualities common to the vast majority of Confederate soldiers, as well as suffering from some of their same sorrows. Only Jasper, forever frozen in his teens, cannot age and grow beyond his years of Confederate service, which merged into a very different war; so, for him, the war is an ever-present influence, despite being a fragile human memory.[1] Understanding the Civil War as Jasper may have experienced it can lend a greater depth of understanding to his character, including his emotional struggles, his interests, and his attitudes. It also helps to shed light on the ways in which his "other" war was very like the one he knew as a human soldier.

While there was no "generic" Confederate soldier, the average man in the Southern army was young, a farmer of little or modest economic means; he did not own slaves and was more likely to perish from disease than from enemy shot and shell. He seldom wore a smart gray uniform, wearing instead his own homespun wool, linen, or cotton shirt, vest, trousers, braces, jacket, and drawers. His hat was likely the same one he wore on the farm or into town. Needed items were often sent to him by his family, particularly as the Confederate army ran ever lower on supplies. If he did have a uniform, it might be very different from that of a fellow soldier. Each state, and even regiments from the same state, used different suppliers and designs, and officers had their uniforms tailor-made; thus even those men who dressed in issued clothing might not be "uniform." The regimental flags under which these men fought exhibited a similar diversity of design, few of them what twenty-first-century Americans would see as the "typical," controversial Confederate flag.

Each soldier was, of course, an individual. On average, men were shorter in the nineteenth century than they are today, but service records reveal that many Confederate soldiers were, like Jasper, over six feet tall. Though quite a few made their "mark" when they enlisted, using an X to sign their names because they could neither read nor write, others were literate. Social class and geographical background also had an impact on the particular experiences of individual soldiers. Most young enlistees were inspired by the war stories of their fathers and grandfathers, but the specific stories varied by region; in states like Georgia or the Carolinas, these might be tales of the American Revolution or the War of 1812. For Texans like Jasper, in a state that had been part of the Union for fewer than twenty years, those inspiring stories were likely of the recent Mexican War, in which so many Civil War commanders gained their combat experience. Despite the soldiers' individual natures, there were common experiences shared by hundreds of thousands of very real Confederate soldiers and one very intriguing fictional vampire.

Because the Girls Are Watching

The Confederate soldier has often been maligned because popular opinion has confused the reasons individual soldiers enlisted with the reasons the war occurred. While the causes of the American Civil War are complex, convoluted, and controversial, the average Confederate soldier thought little of slavery or tariffs as he signed his name or made his mark, received his enlistment bounty, and was mustered into the service of his state. He may have had some vague idea about states' rights or some sense of moral outrage against "Old Abe Lincoln" and his call for Southern troops to "put down" the rebellion in South Carolina, but for most young men who enlisted, the war was not a political opportunity, but a personal one.

Soldiers' motivations for enlistment changed at various points during the war. When Jasper—too young to serve—lies about his age in 1861 and becomes a soldier, he exhibits some of the most common motivations for the first enlistees before the Confederate army began to scramble to replace the men dead in the ground at once-obscure places like Antietam and Chancellorsville. He was not alone in his subterfuge: young men in both the North and the South employed clever means to surmount the obstacle of age.

As Civil War historian James R. Robertson relates, "Because eighteen was the minimum age for enlistment, many underaged boys were known to write '18' on a slip of paper, insert it into a shoe, and when asked by the recruiting officer how old they were, respond truthfully, 'I'm over eighteen.'"[2] The Confederacy began implementing Conscription Acts in 1862, compelling many soldiers to volunteer in order to spare themselves and their families the shame of being drafted into service. In fact, by 1863, the governor of Jasper's Texas promoted the idea of requiring all males sixteen and older to enlist.[3]

Enlistment later in the war also included more soldiers who were older, settled, and imbued with a sense that they were protecting their homes and families. The first wave of enlistees, some forming companies even before their individual states seceded from the Union, had adventure on their minds.[4] These starry-eyed young men, like Jasper, primarily joined the army for the thrill and excitement the war promised. "The dominant urge of many volunteers was the desire for adventure."[5] They expected the war to be brief, a single glorious battle in which they would trounce the Union forces and return as heroes. Like Jasper's adopted younger brother Edward a generation later, they were worried that the war might end before they had the opportunity to fight in it. Thus Jasper and thousands of boys and young men like him went off to war to have an adventure, to see some of the world, and of, course, because the girls were watching.

The use of women as recruitment tools was a shamelessly effective practice, especially early in the war. Later recruits might have been motivated by a desire to protect their wives and sweethearts, or even by the money that could be used in their support, but the first volunteers were often encouraged by pretty girls at community recruiting events. These young ladies dressed patriotically, presented flags made from their own silk dresses, and sometimes served large dinners for the men who agreed to join the army. These tactics clearly played to the use of beauty and sexuality as an advertising tool that has been employed to sell everything from alcohol to automobiles, but it also worked upon something deeper: the Confederate soldier's innate sentimentality, particularly with regard to the "fairer sex."

A very cursory overview of popular 1860s song titles quickly reveals the deeply sentimental attitude toward women presented by the popular culture of the era. Men of this period were often quite expressive with their emotions, even if they weren't gifted like Jasper, and soldiers North and South embraced these songs and their idealized portrayal of women. From plaintive parlor songs like "Aura Lee" and "Loreena" to rousing marches like "The Girl I Left Behind Me," the tunes beloved by the boys in blue and gray reflect the importance of feminine inspiration in their lives. In addition to the ladies' obvious charms, women frequently represented home, domestic safety, and all of the comforts of the family hearth, deeply appealing to a man who was away from familiar surroundings, perhaps for the first time in his life. Thus, the lady praised in the songs and poems loved by, and sometimes composed by, many a lonely soldier was not necessarily his sweetheart; his mother was the focal point of many tunes, from the Federal favorite "Just Before the Battle, Mother" (which Confederate troops merrily lampooned as a song about Union cowards) to "Do They Miss Me at Home?" Thus, any woman, from a dewy maid to a gentle matron, could be presented as an object of sympathy and nostalgia in the popular culture of this period, a view of women clearly accepted by many Civil War soldiers. They tended to be a highly sentimental lot, carrying locks of a sweetheart's hair, photographs, well-worn letters, and other mementos with them in camp and battle. They begged for letters from their mothers, wives, sisters, and sweethearts and were so protective of the contents of these missives that they often burned them before battle to prevent an enemy soldier from reading personal correspondence found in a dead man's pocket. Jasper, with his innate receptivity to emotion, would undoubtedly experience such sentiment acutely.

Young Major Whitlock is not immune to the feminine charms, to his ruin, and his protective nature toward the opposite sex is an attribute he carries forward into his new life as an immortal. When he stops on the road between Houston and Galveston to see if three pale lovely ladies need help, Jasper is operating from a deeply rooted cultural command to protect the "weaker" sex: "I assumed they were stragglers and dismounted at once to offer them my aid."

(*Eclipse*, 293.) Confederate soldiers were sometimes depicted in popular culture as knights of yore, and Jasper does not serve in the army long enough to see the war shudder to its decidedly unromantic close, disabusing the surviving veterans of any such notions. In late 1862, when Galveston's women and children were being evacuated to safety, many officers still felt they should behave as knights would. Their notions of knighthood were not grounded in actual historical reality, but rather in the idealized medieval world presented in the wildly popular early-nineteenth-century novels of Sir Walter Scott. Literate soldiers were more likely to have been exposed to these romanticized heroes and their deeds of derring-do; thus, officers were more likely to see themselves in the role of knight than were the less-educated men they commanded, but even a man who could not read might have been exposed to tales that contributed to his perception of the roles of knights and ladies. Even though Jasper has some inkling of the danger he is in, he is programmed by his culture and his training to regard women as objects of protection, not as dangers to himself and others. "I had not been taught to fear women, but to protect them." (*Eclipse*, 294.) Chivalrously, Jasper attempts to offer assistance to Maria, Nettie, and Lucy. It is his last act as a human being.

Despite the disastrous effects of his assumptions, Jasper continues to function as the chivalrous Southern soldier even in his immortal life. He remains loyally devoted to Maria, like a knight to his lady, even as he tires of the war in which she has embroiled him. His devotion to her, grown from his human nature, has a powerful hold on him, but his sentimentality eventually frees him from her clutches. At Peter's refusal to destroy the newborn Charlotte, Jasper should have killed them both, but he lets them escape, the act of a sentimental nineteenth-century man rather than of a vampire warrior. He later leaves with them, able to break Maria's hold on him primarily because his heightened emotional awareness reveals her plans to eliminate him and because he, like so many of his fellow soldiers, longs for peace and respite from war. He wants a home, the nineteenth-century realm dominated by women.

Jasper's sentimental attitude toward women is most obvious in his relationship with his beloved Alice. She is clearly able to defend herself, yet he constantly feels the need to protect his "frightening little monster" from harm. (*Eclipse*, 396.) He is extremely careful of his mate, leaning over her, "his posture protective" at the approach of James's coven. (*Twilight*, 372.) Alice lies to him about her chances of survival in Volterra because she knows he will chivalrously rush to her rescue and die in the process; she calls him an "overprotective fool" for getting himself hurt trying to prevent her from being in combat. He will do anything to protect his beloved, including terrifying J. Jenks into secrecy or disapproving of Carlisle's decision to accept an enemy's surrender. Though he is later protective of and kind to his new sister, in the pivotal family meeting in *Midnight Sun*, Jasper is willing to kill Bella if her life will threaten Alice's, ultimately backing down only at Alice's insistence.

The irony of his defending tough little Alice is also historically grounded. White women of this period, particularly in the South, where they were less likely to be factory workers or other independent wage earners, were depicted in Southern popular culture as creatures in need of protection. Certainly, such protection was welcomed by some women; but others, especially those in rural, frontier areas, were perfectly capable of taking care of themselves, their farms, and their children, tasks in which they participated fully long before the war began. Very few white Southern women were lounging on verandas drinking mint juleps. As the war dragged on, they increasingly took on the roles left vacant by their fathers, brothers, husbands, and sons, thus fulfilling the ironic double duty of taking a man's place and doing his work while still being viewed as the delicate creature he fought, and gladly died, to protect.

Tenting Tonight

The dreary everyday life of the common Confederate soldier undoubtedly contributed to the idealization of the opposite sex; camp life was far from glamorous and only sporadically exciting. A good description of Civil War army life would be long periods of boredom punctuated by brief moments of absolute terror, all on an empty stomach or meals of hard crackers and spoiled meat. After his enlistment, Jasper would have been placed in a company, likely with other enlistees he knew from his community, as most recruits served alongside their family members, friends, and neighbors. While this did make the men feel more at home in the army, it also had a number of disadvantages. Since the men from individual families and communities were serving together in the same unit, one disastrous charge could annihilate every male member of a family or community; battle trauma was increased for soldiers when the comrades they lost were also family members or childhood friends; and when some individuals decided that they had gotten their fill of the army and wanted to desert, they might take all of their associates with them. If they succeeded in deserting, they left their regiments understaffed, but if they were caught, they could be shot, affecting their communities even more dramatically than if they had died in combat.

Once the company was formed, the men were sent to a training camp to learn how to drill, march (or for cavalry, ride in specific formations), and fire their weapons. Camp Lubbock was near Jasper's hometown of Houston, but there were many camps of instruction throughout the state to which troops might be sent.[6] After completing training, the new company was officially mustered into Confederate service. Jasper appears to have served only in Texas, or to have been sent back there for the initially unsuccessful Confederate defense of Galveston. This may indicate that he was a member of a state militia, serving only in Texas and not officially part of the regular Confederate army, but since he identifies himself as a Confederate officer, that seems unlikely. Other troops might be sent further afield. One of the many frustrations of Confederate soldiers was the fact that they enlisted to protect their homes but were frequently forced to fight far from home in other states. While soldiers waited for combat or marching orders, they spent their time in camp.

Camp life was often a difficult adjustment for citizen soldiers who had previously worked long days on farms or in other gainful employment. The endless routine of drilling served partly to help raw recruits become soldiers, but also gave them something to do. Soldiers devised a variety of diversions, not all of them condoned by their superiors. Some men engaged in noble pursuits like religious meetings, music, reading, or even dancing, but others gambled, told tall tales, or fought among themselves. A few of the more popular pastimes perhaps were some of Jasper's favorites, following him into his life as an immortal. Bell Wiley's seminal text on Confederate life, *The Life of Johnny Reb*, details some of the entertainments practiced by soldiers: "Next to music, Johnny Reb probably found more frequent and satisfying diversion in sports than in anything else. When leisure and weather permitted, soldiers turned out in large numbers for baseball."[7] The "great American pastime" that Jasper plays with his adopted family in *Twilight* may have also been a favorite when he was still Jasper Whitlock. Like the Cullen family version, Civil War baseball often had its own peculiar set of rules depending on the number of players and their skill levels. The snowball battles and wrestling matches that Jasper enjoys with his brother Emmett also reflect Civil War interests. Though Jasper may have had little occasion to see snow while he was in Texas, soldiers in theaters farther north often fought epic snowball fights, creating missiles loaded with rocks or ice. Wrestling was also a frequent diversion that also supported the gambling addictions of the noncombatants. Jasper, too, is a gambler, betting with Emmett on how many humans Bella will kill after her transformation.

Two more edifying pastimes common to Civil War soldiers were chess and reading. Chess was one of the many games in which the more thoughtful soldiers competed, but they likely did not encounter the challenges Jasper later faces when playing his clairvoyant mate, Alice, or his mind-reading adopted brother, Edward.[8] Bella reports that when she played Jasper, "He buried me"; she is one of the few people who does not have an unfair advantage over him. (*Eclipse*, 57.) He is also a scholarly individual, pursuing the study of philosophy at Cornell, not his first degree, when the Cullens briefly leave Forks. Many Civil War regiments had their own traveling libraries, and reading materials were one of the items soldiers most often requested when writing home. Everything, from periodical materials to popular Dickens novels, was greedily read by soldiers, although the most popular text was definitely the Bible.

Of course, life in a nineteenth-century army was not all fun and games. Civil War battle was a horrifying experience, and men who had once considered themselves courageous sometimes sought any opportunity to escape. Since desertion was punishable by execution, more clever would-be deserters turned to forgery, creating for themselves furloughs, or passes to excuse their absences from the army. The less clever of these might try to test the limits of their forging ability. One soldier reportedly forged a furlough for one thousand days and even brazenly signed it "General Robert E. Lee."[9] As a member of the Cullen family, Jasper is in charge of handling all of their illegal documents, working with a Seattle forger to create birth certificates, driver's licenses, Social Security cards, and other necessary items for people who do not age and frequently require new identities. Perhaps this interest dates back to his Confederate service and has endured, along with his pursuit of certain hobbies. Although Jasper says he was never superstitious or believed in ghost stories, the popular camp entertainment of telling tall tales may also have prepared him for a life of lies and deception.

The Rattle of Musketry

Combat for the common Civil War soldier was an experience so life-altering that even those who endured it often struggled for the words they needed to capture the brutality and horrors they witnessed. Jasper's other war, as a lieutenant for the power-hungry Maria, was a savage one, but it may not have been so very different from the conflict experienced by mortal Confederates. In many ways, the Southern vampire war may have given him a lifetime of experience similar to what his fellow soldiers endured in the remaining years of the Civil War. When Jasper shows Bella his battle scars, she is horrified, despite being unable to clearly see his pattern of bite marks with her human vision. "[W]hat *happened* to you?" she asks. (*Eclipse*, 286.) War of any kind marks soldiers, and Jasper is no exception.

The first battle of Galveston, which Jasper refers to as a skirmish, was just one of many dramatic episodes in the Civil War history of the pivotal Texas seaport that, at war's end, was the only open port still in Confederate hands. Although Jasper never sees action on famous fields like Gettysburg or Shiloh, the first battle of Galveston was part of a complex series of events. On July 2, 1861, the Union steamer *South Carolina* arrived off the coast of Galveston to commence the blockade of Southern ports. A month later, the same ship fired into a crowd of onshore civilians gathered to watch the land-based Confederate batteries sink another Federal vessel. A man was killed, setting in motion a "general exodus among citizens and business owners. . . . Many . . . fled to Houston for the duration of the conflict."[10] Not everyone had left the island city, however, for when the Union bombardment began in earnest on October 4, 1862, a messenger underwent a harrowing journey to the Federal flotilla to beg a ceasefire for the evacuation of women, children, and noncombatants. He also dropped a few hints about yellow fever, making Galveston seem less inviting. Interestingly, the bulk of these negotiations were apparently conducted by a very persuasive but unnamed major.[11] The Confederates were granted four days to remove the women and children from the city. Since the truce was never formalized in writing, however, the Confederates did not see any reason they should not remove other items from the city: troops, food, supplies, weapons, and pretty much anything else of value. In this outflow of civilians, cattle, and matériel, it is not surprising that an officer like Jasper, with his naturally calming presence, would be of great service. By the time Galveston was reclaimed by the Confederates, in whose hands it would remain for the duration of the war, his human life had ended. His war, however, was just getting started.

Up through the Ranks

In large part due to his unique gifts, Jasper is quickly promoted to the rank of officer in the Confederate army. He knows that his meteoric rise to the rank of major is largely due to what his father called "charisma," but which he later recognizes as his latent gift for manipulating emotions. His promotion past older men with more experience may not merely be a result of this gift. Such impressive trajectories upward through the ranks were not unusual. In the early days of the war, as both armies sought to provide officers for hordes of new volunteers, men with regular army, state militia, or even Mexican War experience were called into service, but they were far too few, and officers' commissions were often handed out for a variety of reasons other than competence.

A military rank might be given as a reward for political favors; some potential officers had powerful financial influence that made them attractive candidates even if they could not march in a straight line or fire a weapon; and some men were promoted because, like Jasper, they were likeable. William C. Davis notes the lack of uniformity in methods of officer selection: "In the end, both governments utilized a host of means in choosing officers. The rule of the day was that there were no strict rules of procedure. What was policy was simply whatever means succeeded in getting a man a commission."[12] While high-ranking regimental officers had to have their commissions approved by the state's governor, a major like Jasper achieved his rank in a fashion well suited to putting popular people in positions of command: "In a nation that was fiercely democratic, that did not entirely trust the professional military, and that always vocally lauded the ability and judgment of the 'common man,' volunteer regiments . . . had the long-held tradition of electing their officers."[13] Usually, the men in ranks elected their captains, who then voted among themselves to select the regiment's major, as well as the colonel and lieutenant colonel; the latter two were then submitted for approval. Such a system undoubtedly worked in favor of the compelling Jasper, but it also led to problems in leadership structure. To ease the opprobrium of forcing companies to remain in the army beyond the deadline specified in their original terms of enlistment, the Confederate government often allowed for the restructuring of commands and the election of new officers. Unfortunately, this sometimes meant that competent but demanding officers were not reelected, and charming and ineffective men took their positions.

Jasper appears to have been a good officer, but many others who rose to rank through charm were not so competent. Cronyism and charisma put many an ill-qualified man in charge of troops whom he could not lead adequately. "The simple need for more officers in a hurry . . . always placed untried and untrained men in hundreds of vacancies every month."[14] Such officers were not only an embarrassment to the army, but they were also downright dangerous, putting the men in their command at more risk than those they were fighting against. Jasper, though his promotion rests on personality rather than on skill, is an effective military leader. By the time of *Eclipse*, he has not been in full-scale battle for half a century but naturally takes over as combat instructor, bringing to bear his skills and experiences to prepare the Cullens so well that they and the La Push wolf pack handily defeat Victoria's army. Each member of the Cullen family has particular skills and abilities that aid the group, and Jasper's soldiering expertise is one of his contributions, an expertise not so willingly given to the ambitious Maria in her quest for revenge and extended power.

Japser's military abilities are valuable to Maria, and although Jasper is at first pleased by the trust she places in him, his duties quickly take an emotional toll. In order to keep Jasper, the fastest and strongest of her newborn vampire army, from killing all the other young "recruits," Maria puts him in charge of them, "as if I were being promoted." (*Eclipse*, 296.) The vampire wars and the unique way in which Maria conducts her successful campaign actually mirror the historical American Civil War. Like the actual Civil War, the vampire wars are struggles for the control of territories, what Jasper calls "herd lands." They are also struggles in which effective "generals" like Maria use innovative and subtle techniques to ensure success. At the beginning of the American Civil War, troops still used Napoleonic tactics: two armies in straight lines shooting at each other across an open field. The changing firearm technologies of the period rendered such strategies suicidal; by the end of the war, trench warfare had evolved, and commanders who could use effective and fresh strategies were often those who claimed victory. In just such fashion does Maria use Jasper to implement her new plan:

instead of straightforward bloodbaths between covens and their out-of-control newborns, Maria, with Jasper's invaluable assistance, creates a trained, effective army of new vampires, much as a Civil War training camp shaped farm boys and shopkeepers into competent soldiers.

Of course, the ultimate irony in both the real army and the fictitious one is that these soldiers must be sacrificed to realize military goals. As General Lee states so memorably in Michael Shaara's landmark historical novel *The Killer Angels*: "To be a good soldier you must love the army. But to be a good officer you must be willing to order the death of the thing you love."[15] This is precisely the struggle faced by both actual Civil War commanders and by Jasper, for once he creates Maria's efficient fighting unit of newborns, he takes them into battles in which they are frequently destroyed: "[T]hey were pawns, they were disposable." (*Eclipse*, 298.) When the newborns are no longer strong enough to serve their purpose, Maria orders Jasper to kill them. True Civil War commanders did not slaughter their men so deliberately, but those leaders who were most effective, unfortunately, were those who could treat their men as tools to be used, and possibly destroyed, in the achievement of larger goals. The Union's Ulysses S. Grant, capable of relentlessly flinging his soldiers at impenetrable lines, is thus the commander who is lauded as the effective general, rather than George McClellan, so protective of his army that he hardly ever wanted to engage the enemy; McClellan's attitude reportedly prompted President Lincoln to quip that if General McClellan had no plans to use the army then Lincoln wanted to "borrow" it.[16] Men under McClellan's command certainly were safer, but those fighting and dying under Grant had a higher margin of victory.

The Lingering Shadow

Inevitably, many of the commanders who so effectively used their troops to achieve their ends suffered long-term emotional consequences as a result. Both officers and men in the ranks experienced emotional conditions ranging from mild depression to what would be diagnosed today as severe post-traumatic stress disorder (PTSD). Although "the diagnosis of PTSD was not formalized until 1980," it is likely that soldiers in every war in human history have suffered from some form of what has been variously called "combat fatigue," "shell shock," or just a bad case of melancholy.[17] In the Civil War, likely PTSD sufferers were often charged with malingering or desertion. Recent studies indicate that younger soldiers, like Jasper, were more likely to experience combat-induced psychological problems.[18] Long after the war, such men might react to their previous combat experience with anything from anxiety to full-scale hallucinations and flashbacks. PTSD was far less noticeable than the catastrophic wounds left on the bodies of many surviving soldiers. Firearms of the period made amputation a regular, necessary practice, and made common the sight of a veteran missing one or more limbs. Like Jasper and his layers of battle scars, Civil War veterans bore visible evidence of their time in combat, but the scars on their souls and minds were often even more painful than those on their bodies.

Civil War veterans also frequently exhibited symptoms of depression. Jasper, particularly before he meets Alice, suffers from several PTSD-related symptoms as well as acute depression. Part of his depression is undoubtedly a result of his unwilling conversion. Civil War conscripts frequently suffered from depression in which the obvious causes (seeing death, confrontation with one's own mortality, loss of friends and family members, and a feeling of helplessness) were compounded by the fact that they were forced to serve against their wills.

Conscripts also, as one might suspect, were far more likely to desert, as Jasper eventually does upon learning that he doesn't have to live in a combat zone as Maria's field marshal and executioner. Yet, even after he has escaped combat, Jasper is a victim of depression, craving happiness so much he actually annoys Bella with his hovering to enjoy the joy she exudes. Lifelong depression was not unusual among Civil War veterans. Confederates also had to contend with the fact that they had been defeated and frequently disenfranchised by the policies of Reconstruction. In Jasper's case, the depression is exacerbated by his natural sensitivity and by the fact that—unlike his human comrades in arms, whose period of military service would have been, at most, five years—he fights a nasty war for nearly eighty years. Even after leaving Maria and traveling with Peter and Charlotte, Jasper is depressed and eventually strikes out on his own. His relationship with Alice transforms him, but he is still a more serious, somber man than his brothers, clearly marked by both his human and immortal combat experiences.

Jasper is a warrior. Although it is only one facet of his complex character, it is, in many ways, what defines him and how he views himself. Like thousands of other Confederate veterans, he has struggled to build for himself a life beyond his military service, but its echoes follow him long after the guns were stilled at Appomattox. In fact, while his former foes and comrades from the Civil War live on only in memories, crumbling letters, and fading photographs, Jasper remains, his Confederate experience fixed in his memory and forever affecting his character and the way he responds to circumstances and individuals. Whether he is masquerading as the teenage Jasper Hale, the adult Jasper Cullen, or the vampire super-soldier Jasper, he is still, deep in his silent heart, Major Jasper Whitlock of the Confederate Army, a man whose strange journey has been transformed by the same experiences that changed the lives of his long-dead foes and friends of the 1860s.

Notes

1. There is a bit of a math problem with Jasper's age. He states in *Eclipse* (page 292) that he was not quite seventeen when he lied about his age to join the Confederate army. Though he could have enlisted a bit before the war officially began in April 1861, Jasper should have been only eighteen at the time of his transformation, around the First Battle of Galveston, October 4, 1862. He would not have been nineteen until sometime after April 1863. Meyer has listed his "permanent" age as twenty in her notes and supplemental texts for the books; see "Personal Correspondence #1," *Twilight Lexicon*, www.twilightlexicon.com/?p=34, but this seems to be the fake age he gave when he was enlisting.

2. James R. Robertson, *Soldiers Blue and Gray* (Columbia: Univ. of South Carolina Press, 1988), 25.

3. Sam Houston, *History of Texas, Together with a Biographical History of the Cities of Houston and Galveston: Containing a Concise History of the State, with Portraits and Biographies of Prominent Citizens of the Above Named Cities, and Personal Histories of Many of the Early Settlers and Leading Families* (Chicago: Lewis Pub, 1895), 92.

4. Texas's secession process was unusual in that it was put to a statewide referendum rather than being decided by representatives. Texas left the Union in March 1861.

5. Bell Irvin Wiley, *The Life of Johnny Reb: The Common Soldier of the Confederacy* (Baton Rouge: LSU Press, 1978), 17.

6. See James E. Williams, "Confederate Military Camps in Texas," *A Revised List of Texas Confederate Regiments, Battalions, Field Officers, and Local Designation*, http://members.tripod.com/jamesewilliams/texasconfederate.html.

7. Wiley, *The Life of Johnny Reb*, 159.

8. Robertson, *Soldiers Blue and Gray*, 89.

9. Thomas L. Norwood, ed., *Letters, 1863–1865*, Lenoir Family Papers, Southern Historical Collection, University of North Carolina, Chapel Hill, NC.

10. Edward T. Cotham, Jr., *Battle on the Bay: The Civil War Struggle for Galveston*. (Austin: Univ. of Texas Press, 1998), 35.

11. Tenna Perry, "Major Civil War Battles in Texas," *Pagewise*, www.essortment.com/all/civilwarbattle_rlev.htm.

12. William C. Davis, *Rebels and Yankees: Commanders of the Civil War* (New York: Gallery Books, 1990), 30.

13. Ibid., 35.

14. Ibid.

15. Michael Shaara, *The Killer Angels* (New York: Ballantine, 1992), 191.

16. Ward Hill Lamon, *Recollections of Abraham Lincoln 1847–1865* (Chicago: A. C. McClung and Co., 1895), 200.

17. Erica Weir, "Veterans and Post-Traumatic Stress Disorder," *Canadian Medical Association Journal* 163, no. 9 (October 31, 2000): 1187. Masterfile Premier, via EBSCOHost, www.nclive.org.

18. Bruce Bower, "Combat Trauma from the Past," *Science News*, February 11, 2006, 84. Masterfile Premier, via EBSCOHost, www.nclive.org. For more on PTSD during the Civil War, see John Talbot, "Combat Trauma in the American Civil War," *History Today* 46, no. 3 (March 1996): 47–54. Masterfile Premier, via EBSCOHost, www.nclive.org.

Smoky Mountain Twilight

The Appalachian Roots of Emmett McCarty Cullen and His Family

Elizabeth Baird Hardy

To some people, the Appalachian Mountains seem frightening, even dangerous, with their endless ridges and imposing peaks, their trackless, entangling forests, and their prolific wildlife. To others, the ancient mountain chain, which rises in northern Alabama and runs all the way to Nova Scotia before dropping off into the ocean, is seductively beautiful, its charms nearly irresistible, prompting poet James Still to proclaim, "I shall not leave these prisoning hills."[1] Such a paradox can also be seen in the Cullen family created by Stephenie Meyer for her Twilight Saga. They, too, are both extremely dangerous and extremely alluring, a connection with the mountains that they once inhabited and the place where one member spent his entire human existence. Although Emmett McCarty left behind his Appalachian life to join the Cullen family, he is still in many ways a product of that environment and its complex culture, both reflecting and contradicting many of the stereotypes that have been attributed, with varying degrees of accuracy, to

Southern Appalachia and its people for centuries. In fact, the entire Cullen family exhibits some aspects of Appalachian culture, which may be a product of the time they spent among the mountains' misty coves and hollows.

The Prisoning Hills

To understand the man Emmett was and the vampire he is, it is important to understand the landscape where he spent the first twenty years of his life and the culture that shaped him. Emmett was originally from Gatlinburg, Tennessee, a popular tourist town today, but once just one of many tiny towns scattered across the vast Appalachian region.[2] Emmett's mountains, the Smokies, are actually part of the Unaka chain of the Appalachian region, and they take the name "Smoky" from the mists that frequently drape the region, a name more appropriate than "Appalachia," a corruption of the name of a northern Florida tribe of Native Americans.[3] Over the years, folklore has attributed the mist that drapes the mountains to everything from animals stirring up dirt to Native American spirits to the smoke from moonshiners' stills. Regardless of the meteorological or supernatural reasons for the smokiness, it is easy to see why it might contribute to the region's appeal for the Cullens. With the mist, dampness, and cloud cover of the Eastern Appalachian Mountains, this region bears a strong resemblance to gloomy little Forks, Washington. Plant life is even similar, with the Appalachians boasting a surprisingly diverse array of flora, from alpine firs to tropical ferns.

European settlement came slowly to Appalachia, both due to the rugged terrain and the indigenous peoples who claimed the region as hunting territory. Although the British forbade colonial settlement past the crest of the Blue Ridge and later incited native peoples to fight against those who violated the edict, white settlers still came. Some even made their own treaties, such as the 1772 agreements reached between the Cherokee and the Watauga Association in what is today eastern Tennessee. In a similar fashion, Carlisle Cullen and his family, in 1936, engineered their own treaty with the Quileute tribe in the Pacific Northwest. They might have created just such a pact with the few remaining Appalachian native people if they had encountered any during their stay in the Smoky Mountains a few years earlier, but by the 1930s, nearly all of them had been gone for a hundred years; the Cherokee, the area's dominant tribe, had been forcibly relocated to Oklahoma by the United States government by way of the tragic Trail of Tears, but many elements of the Cherokee culture linger in the region. Small remnants of the tribe remain in and around the town of Cherokee, North Carolina, close to Emmett's home in Sevier County, Tennessee.

Like Emmett's human family, most of the early settlers were Scotch-Irish. A staggering variety of different groups participated in settling the mountains, but according to historian and author Tyler H. Blethlen, "even the lowest estimates of Scotch-Irish ancestry still acknowledge this as the largest single group in Appalachia, and as such it played a powerful role in shaping the region's culture."[4] Seeking religious and political freedom, as well as opportunities to own land and be left alone, the early settlers made their homes in coves and valleys where they could raise their families and their crops without interference from outside authorities or nosy neighbors, much as the Cullens themselves later sought privacy in the mountains. After both the American Revolution and the War of 1812, American soldiers were often paid with land grants to remote mountain property.

Gatlinburg, Emmett's hometown, was apparently settled in 1807 by a widow, Martha Jane Huskey Ogle, and her family. Descendants of the original settlers remain in the region, lending family names to streets and businesses. Emmett's McCarty fictional family also lingers in Sevier County, with several actual families of that name in both Gatlinburg and Sevierville. Ironically, one branch of the McCarty family today runs a local funeral home. Belying the crowded streets and sidewalks of today's Gatlinburg, the original settlement evolved through a process that spanned several generations, as families grew and spread further up the steep slopes and into the narrow valleys of the region, creating small pockets of settlement inhabited by farmers and their families in tightly woven kinship and community groups.[5] While somewhat secluded, Appalachian people have never been completely isolated. In fact, in Emmett's 1930s Appalachia, the mountains were already going through radical and permanent transformations.

The Ring of the Ax, the Whistle of the Train

The first few decades of the twentieth century brought pivotal changes to the region. The Appalachia Emmett would have known would have been very different from the one settled by his great-grandparents. For generations, mountain people had adapted to the area's climate and geography, but had little lasting effect on the mountains themselves. By 1935, however, the forests that carpeted the hills were already showing the effects of the great chestnut tree blight that, by midcentury, eliminated all of these mighty trees, once the dominant members of the Appalachian canopy. The forests were also being leveled by growing logging interests. In the late nineteenth century, railroads began to make possible the extraction of Appalachia's many valuable resources, from the coal of the Ridge and Valley and Cumberland Plateau sections to the timber that had blanketed the ancient mountains for centuries. As timber resources began to diminish elsewhere, the mountains became a focus of commercial interests, and logging changed from a seasonal occupation practiced by farmers harvesting particular trees for their own needs and supplemental income into a major commercial operation owned by outside investors. While mountain people sold or lost their land in questionable legal transactions, industrialism gained a greater foothold in the area, bringing in logging and mining operations and the railroads to support them. Emmett thus grew up in a world where outside economic forces were affecting both the culture of Appalachia and the mountains themselves, while bringing both positive and negative opportunities and influences with them.

As farmers were separated from their land, they frequently became employed by one of the industries reshaping the region.

Thus, mountain people became loggers and coal miners, occupations that were dangerous and often dehumanizing. Emmett's section of the mountains contains no coal, but he and his family might have been employed in one of the many timber operations in East Tennessee. Although this work could bring in "cash money," it severed the mountaineer from kinship groups and traditional practices and employed him in the wholesale environmental destruction of the wilderness he had once treasured. In addition, as folklorist Michael Williams observes, "the boom and bust cycle of the timber industry ultimately left those who had become dependent on cash wages poorer than ever."[6] Without jobs or land, mountain people sometimes sought their fortunes elsewhere, leaving their beloved mountains for "public work" in cities and towns, while others stayed and tried to retain their dignity and their traditional lifestyles.

The timber industry also devastated the forests themselves. Visitors to the Great Smoky Mountains National Park usually see the forests as pristine, almost primeval, but many trees are relatively young, having grown back after the devastation of logging left the hillsides bare and exposed to erosion. The changes to the forest, both from humans and from the losses inflicted by the chestnut blight, contributed significantly to the decline of one of the region's most iconic native animals, and one critical to the story of Emmett Cullen. Today, those who visit the park are frequently rewarded with the sight of one or more black bears shuffling along the highway or even, to the horror of park officials, raiding trash cans, but in the early twentieth century, according to *National Wildlife*, the bear population was in serious decline: "Scientists speculate that only a few bears were left in the high elevations of the [Great Smoky Mountains] park when Congress created it in 1934."[7] Relying primarily on chestnut mast for food, the black bear had been an important member of the diverse biological web in Southern Appalachia. Early settlers depended on the many species of game to supplement their farming, eliminating animals that were dangerous to them or their meager crops. Bears, which would eagerly raid orchards, topple bee stands, or empty gardens, were hunted even after their numbers were so reduced as to remove them as a threat.

Bear hunting evolved into a regional pastime as well as a means to acquire food and remove a problem. Bear hunters proudly bred dogs, such as the Plott Hound, specifically for bear hunting, and every mountain community has its tales of legendary bear hunters.

It is not entirely clear whether Emmett was bear hunting or just in the wrong place at the wrong time when he was attacked. He was alone, and although some bear hunters prefer to hunt alone, even today, bear hunting is usually a team sport.[8] In early-twentieth-century bear hunting, a hunter might track a bear for several days, placing him in a position like Emmett's, so isolated that only Rosalie, a hundred miles from where the Cullens lived, could hear his struggle. Long-term tracking was necessary after the bear populations became so diminished. While black bears can easily reach several hundred pounds, many of the bears hunted in the early twentieth century were small. Apparently Emmett was not so lucky, as his bear was more than a match for him. Emmett did seem to have been missing both the firearm and the bear dogs that were used by every Appalachian bear hunter. With Emmett's thrill-seeking personality, though, it is not hard to imagine that he might have taken the bear on "bare"-handed, just for the challenge.

A "Real" Mountain Man?

In many ways, Emmett seems to fit the stereotypical image of a mountain man: physically powerful, prone to violence, passionate, and fond of a good joke (especially at someone else's expense). The standard image of Appalachian people is a controversial and painful topic, particularly for mountain people themselves, who often shudder at the sight of cartoon hillbillies emblazoned on souvenir shops and restaurants throughout the region. Much excellent scholarship has been conducted over the past few decades, analyzing the complexities of this still-rampant stereotyping, but it has not eradicated the tendency of the media and mainstream culture to see mountain people as "other": sometimes comical, often dangerous, but always as "not us." As historian Jeff Biggers observes, "No other region has been so misrepresented by the mass media."[9]

The Cullens, too, struggle against myth and misperception. Much of what Bella Swan discovers on the Internet about vampires turns out to be untrue about the Cullens and their kind, and even the truth has been twisted, such as their aversion to sunlight being interpreted as an intolerance for ultraviolet rays. Appalachian people, too, continue to be saddled with untruths and exaggerations, as even accurate characterizations of their culture are often distorted. For example, most mountain families tended to be large, like Emmett's, but this trend, common among nearly all rural, agrarian people for whom many hands make light work, has been twisted to portray fecund mountain people as animalistic.

As early as the 1820s, tourists were already coming to the mountains to enjoy the fresh air and supposedly healing waters. As tourists came, so did "color" writers, seeking material for their work. It has been speculated that such writers may have actually "invented" Appalachia as a separate and distinct place. They certainly helped to create the public image of the people who inhabited the region. The Appalachian "type" tends to fall at one end of the spectrum or the other: on the positive end, there is the frugal, artistic keeper of the past who lives a simple but spiritually fulfilling life in touch with all nature, and who represents a wholesome, honest America that exists nowhere else. On the other end of the scale is the depraved, xenophobic, ignorant backwoodsman, the product of incest and disease, prone to drunkenness and violence and engaging in criminal behavior rather than doing anything that might require effort. Both of these images are demeaning and exaggerated, and yet both have been wholeheartedly embraced by American culture, appearing in our movies, cartoons, and novels.[10]

Writers and photographers sought the types who would reinforce their preconceived notions of the region and its people. Visiting "picture-men" often insisted that subjects take off their shoes before posing with the old washtub that no one had used since Grandma purchased her washing machine. When Bayard Wooten created the images for Muriel Earley Sheppard's haunting but controversial *Cabins in the Laurel* in 1935, the same year Emmett and Rosalie met, she sent "mountain people back into their houses to change into homespun or linsey, should they appear in store-bought clothes . . . to find their hand thrown pots, to replace the store-bought ones in use."[11] The reality did not fit the fixed image, and it was discarded. As Ted Olsen reports in *Blue Ridge Folklife*, "By the early twentieth century, the stereotyped negative image of the southern mountain people—by now generally tagged with the label 'hillbilly'—had become entrenched in the popular imagination."[12]

The image is so codified in mainstream media that even individuals from other parts of the United States are considered "hillbillies" if they display the characteristics associated with the type. For example, the original, iconic "hillbilly" couple," Ma and Pa Kettle, whose appearance in the 1947 film *The Egg and I* led to a series of spin-off films and influenced the better-known Clampetts of *The Beverly Hillbillies* fame, didn't hail from Appalachia or even the Clampetts' Ozarks. In an ironic coincidence, they in fact came from the Olympic Peninsula in Washington, where the Cullens moved in 1936, shortly after "adopting" Emmett.

Those seeking to preserve the mountains also embraced and promoted the image of "typical" Appalachian people. One of the most important voices for the establishment of the Great Smoky Mountains National Park was Horace Kephart. His seminal study *Our Southern Highlanders* both demonstrated the beauty and diversity of the Appalachian people he observed and helped to cement the skewed image of Appalachian people that continues to be widely accepted.[13] The Smoky Mountains were inhabited by a variety of families before their land was purchased or condemned for the creation of the park. Yet, the only dwellings that have been preserved or reconstructed are those that, for the most part, reinforce the perception of mountain people as log-cabin-dwelling farmers from another time. While this charming and nostalgic image is popular, it is not entirely accurate.[14] Emmett and his large human family would have been just as likely to have lived in a timber frame house as in a quaint log cabin, and they might have been business owners rather than subsistence farmers, especially as the park brought economic growth to Gatlinburg and other surrounding towns. While the McCartys may have still eaten cornbread and pork at most meals, they also would have been able to acquire food and other products commonly available throughout the country at the time.

The hillbilly image has several distinct, frequently cited components; in an examination of how Emmett and the other Cullens do and do not fulfill these expectations, it is useful to look at several elements separately, some of which are clearly actual cultural features, although exaggerated or misrepresented by the media. Like all people, Appalachian and otherwise, Emmett is an individual, and the ways in which he reinforces or disproves cultural stereotypes are expressions of his own unique personality. In addition, the other members of the Cullen family exhibit many Appalachian characteristics, regardless of where they came from.

Keeping Themselves to Themselves

Stories abound of mountain people who ran from, or shot at, the first car they saw. Although such accounts may be based in fact, they are retold not just for humor but also to emphasize the idea of mountaineers as completely cut off from the world. Such total isolation has frequently been exaggerated as a justification for both philanthropy and exploitation, but most Appalachian people have not been any more isolated than other rural Americans. In 1933, residents in what would soon become Shenandoah National Park were described as "almost completely cut off from the current of modern life . . . not of the twentieth century."[15]

Yet recent archaeological studies of the homes destroyed by the Park Service after the eviction or relocation of the residents reveal store-bought toys, imported tableware, and soda and medicine bottles. The stereotype of the isolated mountaineer was used to justify the seizure of their land for the park, but material evidence tells another story. In this case, and in many others, mountain people were viewed as isolated even if they ordered regularly from Sears and Roebuck, drove Model Ts, and lived only a few miles from the store and the post office. This fictionalized isolation also connects with the assumed xenophobia of mountain people. Like most people, Appalachians have historically been wary of the unfamiliar, and when one considers the impact that industrialization and logging had on their region, it isn't hard to see why.

Emmett was certainly not completely isolated in his human life. Gatlinburg was a boom town in the 1930s, and Emmett would have had access to most of the same conveniences and news sources as other Americans at the time. Although some contemporary community studies claimed mountain people had no organized religion, Emmett refers to Rosalie as his angel, and Carlisle as God the Father. He also mentions sermons he has heard about the forgiving nature of God.[16] In fact, despite the missionaries sent into Appalachia, many communities had long-established churches, like Gatlinburg's White Oaks Baptist Church, founded in 1835. Nor is Emmett afraid of the unknown. When he tells Bella his story, he notes that the others were surprised that he was never really bothered by his transformation into a mythical creature, easily embracing his strange new reality. Contrary to the stereotypes about Appalachians, Emmett is also not suspicious of "outsiders"; his beloved Rosalie is from New York, and despite her objections, he is very friendly toward Bella, welcoming her heartily into the family. He delights in new experiences, looking forward to a trip to the Amazon to try his abilities against an anaconda and taking Rosalie to Africa on one of their many honeymoons.

In their complex charade as humans, however, all of the Cullens mirror the delicate balance between isolation and cultural connection seen in the history of Appalachia. Although they are very comfortable with the human world, they still keep to themselves like many mountain families that enjoyed the same clothing, music, and other trappings of mainstream culture while still living in coves and "hollers" off the beaten path. The Cullens' separation from the larger world is self-imposed, to protect their secret, and those mountaineers who were pitied by the larger culture for their isolation were frequently secluded by choice. While the Cullens are also operating from a similar sense of self-preservation, they also want to protect humans from their presence.

Them's Fightin' Words

Despite their civility, the Cullens are dangerous, and Appalachian people, too, regardless of their sophistication, have had to struggle against the image of the violent mountaineer. No stereotypical "Mountain Man" is complete without a rifle, a fact that has created problems for colleges with "mountaineer" mascots. The tool once critical for self-protection and the provision of food has now become a symbol of mountain violence. Ironically, the very outside forces that encouraged the perception of mountaineers as violent brutes lurking in the bushes with Winchesters actually turned this image into a self-fulfilling prophecy. The American Civil War began outside Southern Appalachia, and few of its major battles were fought near the region, but mountain people were preyed upon by soldiers of both armies as well as by those using the war as an excuse for theft and "meanness."

Although the violence originated elsewhere, it festered in Appalachia, and mountain people who became more prone to violence in self-defense were viewed as inherently hostile.[17] When industrial forces began to vie for the region's resources, violence sometimes erupted as workers were imported, creating cultural tensions, exacerbated by economic and social pressures. Some of the region's infamous feuds were actually begun by families with competing visions for their communities' industrial futures.[18] The timber camps and coal towns created by industrialism also became hotbeds for violence. None of these subtleties is reflected in the blanket assumption that mountain people are by nature violent.

Emmett embodies some aspects of this Appalachian stereotype. He is constantly spoiling for a fight, expressing disappointment when it looks like he will lose his opportunity to fight Demetri, and he enjoys competition of any kind, from wrestling with Jasper to hunting the largest prey possible, to demonstrating combat techniques for the Cullens' Quileute allies. Taking down a bear, for him, is just as much a form of entertainment as it is survival; when Edward points out that Emmett doesn't have to fight with his food,

Emmett replies, "Yeah, but who else am I going to fight with? You and Alice cheat, Rose never wants to get her hair messed up, and Esme gets mad if Jasper and I *really* go at it." (*Midnight Sun*, 149.)

Violence, in its sterilized, "safe" modern manifestation, competitive sports, is also a critical part of Emmett's character. He enjoys all games and sports, both as observer and as participant. The Cullens' massive television and its vast array of channels provide him with a wide variety of professional sports. In addition to playing the Cullen favorite of baseball, Emmett begs Edward to join the family in what must be a particularly violent game of football, and he and Jasper play "chess utilizing eight joined boards . . . and their own complicated set of rules." (*Midnight Sun*, 142.) One of the most frustrating parts of Emmett's role as human high school student is downplaying his incredible physical ability in gym class: "Throwing games was an affront to his personal philosophy." (*Midnight Sun*, 242.) Any kind of contest, violent or not, is appealing to Emmett, perhaps allowing him to control his instincts and channel his aggressive tendencies.

Unlike some of his family members, Emmett has occasionally faltered in his commitment to the Cullen diet. While Carlisle and Rosalie have never tasted human blood, Emmett has sometimes "fallen off the wagon" and preyed on humans. Yet he is never depicted as truly malicious. Instead, he is prone to physical displays because he enjoys using his talent of prodigious strength, and although he is easily the most terrifying member of his family, his playful nature offsets his menace. Like the bear with whom he is so often associated, Emmett can be both a formidable predator and a playful comedian.

Taking a Joke

Although mountain people have frequently been the butt of jokes made by mainstream culture, they usually enjoy a good joke, particularly at the expense of those who view themselves as superior to others. This "leveling" is both entertaining and a reflection of the resentment mountain people have often expressed toward those who desire to patronize or exploit them; as Williams writes, "A vein of mischievousness seems to run through many who live in the region."[19] Appalachian people also sometimes use humor to take themselves down a notch, making what seem like self-deprecating, humorous comments when they are complimented. Humor is used on friends and family as mountain people seek to keep those they love from becoming self-important.

Just as Emmett relentlessly teases Bella, Appalachian people have often employed humor as a form of affection, leading to the common mountain statement, "If we didn't love you, we wouldn't pester you." Emmett's teasing is certainly one of his most prominent characteristics; and by joking, Emmett makes himself less terrifying. When he and the rest of the family consider confronting the vampires in Seattle, Emmett's enthusiastic "Let's go. I'm dead bored" is both a pun since he's "undead" and a device to take the menace out of his desire to destroy others. (*Eclipse*, 284.) His affection for Bella is almost always expressed as humor, particularly when she is still mortal and clumsy. In *New Moon* when Emmett leaves the room for a moment, he asks her, "Don't do anything funny while I'm gone" because he finds her entertaining. (*New Moon*, 26.) As Bella states, "[H]e thought my bizarre human reactions were hilarious . . . or maybe it was just the fact that I fell down a lot that he found so funny." (*Twilight*, 485.) In true Appalachian fashion, Emmett's teasing makes Bella feel accepted and loved rather than humiliated.

Come In and Sit a Spell

Ironically, the same Appalachian stereotype that paints mountain people as violent and xenophobic also portrays them as hospitable and generous, happy to feed a complete stranger and insist he stay the night. Horace Kephart claimed that the mountain people he knew during his early-twentieth-century sojourn in the Smokies welcomed him despite his outsider status; his belongings and person were always safe and unmolested, as he was under the protection of his mountain hosts and friends. "Outsiders," including teachers, missionaries, and doctors, were often surprised at the ways in which they were embraced by supposedly "backward" communities. Because such visitors brought skills and services mountain people respected and desired, they were usually treated with deference and hospitality.

Although Carlisle does not mention his experiences as an Appalachian doctor, it is likely that he was welcomed into the area, as the early twentieth century saw many communities in the region recruiting doctors who could supplement their limited medical resources with modern treatments and surgical techniques and aid the overworked doctors already practicing. While most Appalachian people resisted offers of charity and resented being patronized, they often enlisted doctors and educators in order to improve their communities. Settlement schools, such as the Pi Beta Phi School established in Emmett's Gatlinburg in 1912, provided public education to communities that had limited options, and residents worked hard to donate land and pay teachers to make it clear that they were employing these outside professionals rather than serving as recipients of others' kindness.

Mountain people, in their resistance to and resentment of charity, nonetheless have a history of happily giving to others. The Cullens exhibit this dichotomy, as they are all generous, from Edward's lavish gift-giving to Esme's desire to feed and clothe homeless werewolves. Yet, they are self-sufficient, uncomfortable asking for help, preferring instead to rely only on one another.

A Bear of Very Little Brain

The desire for improved access to education and health care also demonstrates that mountain people often sought improvement for both the mind and the body. There is no question that Emmett is a physical presence, so much so that Charlie, confusing him with Edward, is immediately concerned about Bella's new interest. When she later challenges her new brother-in-law to an arm-wrestling match, she hesitates: "He was just so *huge*." (*Breaking Dawn*, 518.)

Emmett's strength is the element of his human personality carried forward into his immortal life, allowing him to serve as a fearsome guard for his family and to assist Rosalie in her hobby of automobile maintenance—as her jack. The powerfully strong mountain man is a figure brought into the view of popular culture primarily by tall tales featuring real mountain men Daniel Boone and Davy Crockett, and often involving wrestling matches with bears or other superhuman feats. As mainstream culture became more distanced from the physical struggle for survival, the boisterous mountain man became an ever-more-appealing figure.

However, the mountain strong man is usually seen as having more brawn than brains. With limited access to education and plenty of hard work to build up his muscles, the mountain man is generally portrayed as all body and very little intellect. At first, Emmett seems to fit neatly into this type, with his prodigious strength and lack of obvious interest in intellectual pursuits. Bella thinks of him as "so brave and thoughtless that he was never the least bit cautious." (*Eclipse*, 312.) He clearly prefers wrestling to reading, yet Emmett is no fool. It is he who suggests that the Cullens' friends, who have joined them against the Volturi, may be able to talk to their opponents rather than resorting to violence. Despite his natural desire for competition, Emmett also understands the power of negotiation, which, in fact, becomes the salvation of the entire Cullen family and their allies. He also recognizes the value of Bella's plan to evade the tracker James.

Unlike Edward, Emmett can rationally see what should be done. His practical, often lighthearted, evaluation of situations reveals him as a savvy and deft thinker who is anything but a "dumb jock." One of his cleverest moments is the careful way he uses a televised University of Florida football game to defuse tension when Charlie sees Renesmee and the drastically changed Bella. By drawing Charlie into their mutual interest in sports, he subtly alleviates the tension of the moment and makes Charlie feel at home cheering on the Gators. Clearly, Emmett's mind is just as powerful as his muscles.

Gloom, Despair, and Agony

Appalachian people are generally portrayed as fatalistic, a quality perhaps related to the emphasis on predestination that was a feature of Calvinism, a form of early Protestantism common among the Scotch-Irish settlers who came to Appalachia. Emmett, however, is the eternal optimist, always focusing on the positive even in seemingly hopeless situations such as the confrontation with the Volturi in *Breaking Dawn*. He does not get discouraged or depressed: "Nothing ever bothered Emmett." (*Eclipse*, 283.) Edward attests that Emmett "doesn't hold grudges," and he never wallows by criticizing himself or others for their failings. (*Midnight Sun*, 77.) When Edward implies that Bella attacked humans on her first hunt, Emmett merely shrugs and lets it go.

Instead, it is little Alice—from the Deep South—who is a fatalist, believing wholeheartedly that what she sees will come to pass. Her Jasper, in his expectation that Bella will have trouble with the "rules," is also fatalistic, even frustrated at first, when she exhibits extraordinary control. Thus, interestingly enough, the two Cullens who are not from the mountains and who did not live with the family in Appalachia are those who most embody the "typical" mountain characteristic of "doom and gloom" fatalism.

In addition, the family's champion grudge-holder is Rosalie. While Emmett relishes the challenge of taking on James and later Demetri, he is not interested in revenge so much as he is anticipating a chance to do what he does best: protect his family and prove his superior strength. Rosalie, while she has never killed humans for food, tortured to death the men who had brutally gang-raped her and left her for dead, administering justice but also savoring her revenge. Even seventy years later, she still nurses a grudge against those who ruined her life. Emmett, although he hates losing a physical contest to anyone—bear, Jasper, Bella—and always wants rematches, does so not because he holds a grudge, but because he likes to prove that he is still the biggest and the strongest. Rosalie also takes a darker view, more in keeping with the fatalism ascribed to Appalachian people, claiming that "my story . . . doesn't have a happy ending—but which of ours does? If we had happy endings, we'd all be under gravestones now." (*Eclipse*, 154.)

By contrast, Emmett is unflappable, as happy in his vampire life as he would be in any other. Yet his positive outlook, while refuting the common perception of mountaineer as dour fatalist, confirms another aspect of the mountaineer type: childishness. Edward calls Emmett "such a child," and Appalachian people have been typically treated as children, incapable of managing their own affairs or resources and in need of "rescue" by the mainstream culture. (*Midnight Sun*, 149.) Although Emmett is certainly boyish, he is a fully capable individual with no need of rescue and little need for anyone other than his beloved Rosalie and his adopted family.[20]

Thicker Than Water

Appalachian family loyalty has been both praised as a virtue and lampooned as a cartoonish clannishness. The close settlement patterns and kinship ties of the region lent themselves to the creation of closely connected family groups, and as Berea College professor emeritus Loyal Jones states: "Family is the functional unit of the mountains. It is extended, far-flung, made up of individuals of diverse dispositions but held together by affection, obligation, and tradition."[21] Such a description easily fits the Cullens, only some of whom are "linked by blood and venom," but all of whom are fiercely loyal to one another.

While close family ties are certainly not a feature exclusive to Appalachian people, the ways in which these ties work in Appalachia and in the Cullen family are remarkably similar. It is in Appalachia that Carlisle turned Emmett, the last human he transformed; and as Emmett is wrenched from his large human clan, he becomes part of an equally closely bound group whose members repeatedly sacrifice and struggle for one another. Despite their very different personalities and opinions, the Cullens live together most of the time, with occasional breaks from one another. Historically, in Appalachian culture, newly married couples often established their homes near family members, allowing for some independence and privacy, but with proximity to family for mutual emotional and material support. The Cullens also follow this practice, with Rosalie and Emmett living in their own "weaning house" to avoid making the rest of the family uncomfortable with their youthful passion. Bella and Edward's cottage also follows this pattern. In addition, the Cullens have a network of "extended family" to whom they exhibit loyalty, from the Denali clan to the Quileute wolves to Bella's human family. Despite disagreements and misunderstandings, the Cullens seek to preserve these ties, to protect, like Bella's shield, those they love, much as any traditional family would.

The Way We've Always Done Things

The tension between the two opposing and connected forces of traditional thought and modernity has pulled at the culture of Appalachia for centuries. All residents of the region, whether consciously or unconsciously, are influenced by this struggle, and the Cullens, including Emmett, are no exception. Traditionalism is focused on the past, concerned with keeping everything as it once was, or at least the way it was perceived to have been in the often-idealized notions we cherish about the past. It also is focused not on the self, but on the family or community; thus a mountain person might sacrifice his or her personal ambitions for the family's good. Time, in the traditional worldview, is cyclical, with each year following the same basic patterns and rhythms and one's work being woven into the everyday fabric of one's life. In contrast, modernity has a linear view of time: one works until the end of the day, the end of the week, the time of retirement, and then one plays, with work sharply defined as separate from the rest of one's life. A worldview that endorses modernity also celebrates change for change's sake, and there is a distinct focus on the individual instead of the group or family.

Most Appalachian people, both historically and in the present, have had to decide how they will embrace or resist these two forces, and despite the common assumption that mountain people are all traditionalists, for the most part, a balance is achieved; for example, individuals may choose to treasure their family's past while still seeking career opportunities that are personally rewarding but not meaningful to the group. For the Cullens, there is a struggle for balance as well. Each member of the family has lost most of his or her human memories, and Alice has none whatsoever. Rosalie's determination to hold on to her human recollections, particularly of the gruesome crime against her, is evidence of a traditional worldview. She refuses to release those memories, and they add to her bitterness. Carlisle has balanced his grasp on the past much better, by collecting mementos that commemorate his human life but moving on without clinging to the past. Each Cullen is frozen as he or she was in life, the very essence of traditionalism, but they have all acquired attributes from the many time periods they have experienced. Thus, although Edward retains many of the manners and morals from his early-twentieth-century era of origin, he also enjoys modern sports cars and progressive music.

The Cullens' views on time also reflect a blend of traditionalism and modernity. There is some sense of time as linear as they follow modern routines of school and work in their pretense as humans, but Meyer's vampires do not view time as humans do: members of the ancient Volturi "count years the way [humans] count days." (*New Moon*, 517.) For the Cullens, time is mostly circular, with their patterns of relocation and infiltration in one community after the next that allow them to live unobtrusively. While they compartmentalize the less interesting elements of their human charade, such as the high school work of the younger Cullens, their views on work as a vocation are far more traditional. Carlisle's medical practice is not necessary for his family's survival, but as part of who he is, it often dictates their movements. With so much time on their hands and no need to sleep, each Cullen explores his or her own interests, pursuing knowledge and seeking degrees for personal growth rather than for a linear goal or professional gain.

The Cullens' family-oriented worldview is distinctly traditional, as the individuals sacrifice and struggle for one another. The entire family pulls up roots to accommodate Edward's misguided desire to protect Bella by leaving her, and they prepare to leave again after Bella's transformation as they have done frequently over the years when an individual has "slipped up" or a new member is added to the family. They are willing to die for one another, because protecting the family is, to them, far more important than individual survival.

Although the Cullens have all traveled widely and experienced most of what the world can offer, they are all still products of the places where their lives began. Emmett is a distinct, unique individual, yet he is also a man whose character and attitudes reflect the practices, history, and misconceptions of his human culture, a culture he has shared with those he loves. Strangely enough, the Cullens apparently have not returned to Appalachia, although they have come back to the Olympic Peninsula and other locations after an appropriate amount of time has passed. Perhaps Emmett dislikes the rampant tourism that has made his hometown indistinguishable from any other overcrowded, overcommercialized vacation spot. Perhaps, after all of those grizzlies, black bears don't seem like much fun anymore. Perhaps Emmett, always so comfortable with moving forward, has moved on. Although only Emmett is truly "Appalachian" in origin, all of the Cullens frequently function as mountain people, regardless of where they are living. They no longer reside among James Still's prisoning hills, but the mountains and their human culture linger within the Cullens themselves.

Notes

1. James Still, "Heritage," in *The Wolfpen Poems* (Berea, KY: Berea College Press 1986).

2. "Personal Correspondence 1," Twilight Lexicon, www.twilightlexicon.com/?p=34.

3. Chris Bolgiano, *The Appalachian Forest: A Search for Roots and Renewal* (Mechanicsburg, PA: Stackpole Books, 1998), 11.

4. Tyler H. Blethlen, "The Scotch-Irish Heritage of Southern Appalachia," in *Appalachia Inside Out*, vol. 1,: *Conflict and Change*, ed. Robert J. Higgs, Ambrose N. Manning, and Jim Wayne Miller (Knoxville: Univ. of Tennessee Press, 2002), 3. The Scotch-Irish should not be confused with people who are a combination of Scottish and Irish heritage, as the term actually refers to Scots who lived in Ireland for some time before later immigrating elsewhere, in this case, Appalachia.

5. For a wide variety of historical photographs of Gatlinburg, Sevier County, and the Smokies, see Steve Cotham's *Images of America: The Great Smoky Mountains National Park* (Charleston, SC: Arcadia Publishing, 2006).

6. Michael Ann Williams, *Great Smoky Mountains Folklife,* Folklife in the South Series (Jackson: Univ. Press of Mississippi, 1995), 8.

7. Rene Ebersole, "Black Bears on the Mend," *National Wildlife* 43, no. 5 (August/September 2005): 38–45, *Masterfile Premier,* via EBSCOHost, www.nclive.org. Despite the fact that Emmett is almost universally thought to have been mauled by a grizzly, a black bear, Appalachia's only indigenous bear, must have attacked him. Grizzlies, found in abundance in the Pacific Northwest, are much larger and fiercer, so it is not surprising that Emmett enjoys hunting them.

8. Greg Culpeper, telephone interview, July 13, 2009; Eliot Wigginton et al., *Foxfire 5* (New York: Doubleday, 1979).

9. Jeff Biggers, *The United States of Appalachia: How Southern Mountaineers Brought Independence, Culture, and Enlightenment to America* (Emeryville, CA: Shoemaker Hoard, 2006), xii.

10. For a thorough treatment of the film industry and Appalachia, see J. W. Williamson's *Hillbillyland: What the Movies Did to the Mountains and What the Mountains Did to the Movies* (Chapel Hill: Univ. of North Carolina Press, 1995).

11. John Ehle, "Foreword," to *Cabins in the Laurel* by Muriel Early Sheppard (Chapel Hill: Univ. of North Carolina Press, 1935, 1991), x. A few regional photographers actually allowed subjects to dictate how they were portrayed. See Ralph Lentz II, *W. R. Trivett, Appalachian Pictureman: Photographs of a Bygone Time* (Jefferson, NC: McFarland, 2001).

12. Ted Olsen, *Blue Ridge Folklife* (Jackson: Univ. Press of Mississippi, 1998), 64.

13. Horace Kephart, *Our Southern Highlanders: A Narrative of Adventure in the Southern Appalachians and a Study of Life among the Mountaineers* (Knoxville: Univ. of Tennessee Press, 1922, 1990).

14. See Durwood Dunn, *Cades Cove: The Life and Death of a Southern Appalachian Community 1818–1937* (Knoxville: Univ. of Tennessee Press, 1988.)

15. Audrey J. Horning, "Appalachia's Secret History," *Archaeology* 53 no. 1(Jan/Feb 2000): 44–52, *Masterfile Premiere,* via EBSCOHost, www.nclive.org.

16. "Emmett and the Bear," Stephenie Meyer.com, www.stepheniemeyer.com/pdf/twi_outtakes_emmett.pdf (accessed June 20, 2009).

17. For insight on the effects of the war on mountain people, see James Inscoe and Gordon McKinney, *The Heart of Confederate Appalachia: Western North Carolina and the Civil War* (Chapel Hill: Univ. of North Carolina Press, 2000).

18. Altina Waller's *Feud: Hatfields, McCoys, and Social Change in Appalachia 1860–1900* (Raleigh: Univ. of North Carolina Press, 1988) covers the economic and social pressures that shaped the Hatfield-McCoy Feud.

19. Williams, *Great Smoky Mountains Folklife,* 121.

20. For an excellent, if somewhat dated, analysis of media typing that infantilizes Appalachian people, see Horace Newcomb's "Appalachia on Television: Region as Symbol in American Popular Culture," in *Appalachian Images in Popular Culture,* 2nd ed., W. K. McNeil (Knoxville: Univ. of Tennessee Press, 1995), 315–329.

21. Loyal Jones with Billy Edd Wheeler, ed., *Laughter in Appalachia: A Festival of Southern Mountain Humor* (Little Rock, AR: August House, 1987), 24.

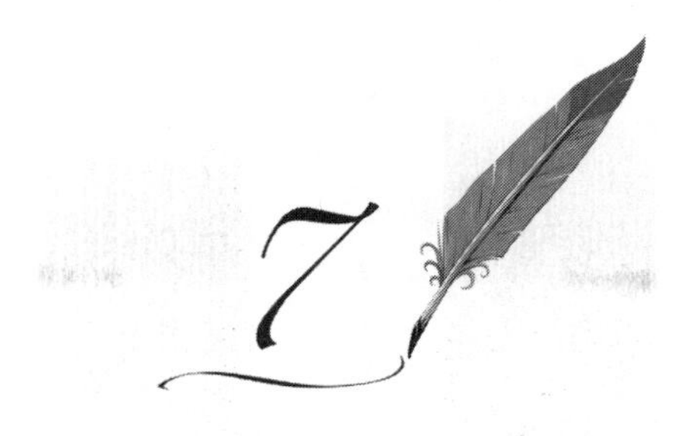

Better Turned Than "Cured"?

Alice and the Asylum

Grace Loiacono and Laura Loiacono

Throughout the Twilight Saga, Alice Cullen is a consistently bright, friendly, and welcoming presence in the Cullen household. She is a tiny pixie with an energetic and bubbly personality. Edward Cullen explains that Alice has "her own way of looking at things," sharing with Bella Swan an insight about the sources of Alice's constant enthusiasm and openness. (*Twilight*, 327.) Alice is able to accept Bella and offers immediate friendship in spite of the wariness coming from other members of the Cullen family. Alice's ability to see even imperfect visions of the future keeps her family, including Bella, alive or at the very least, safe. Her gift also has the added bonus of having allowed Alice to maintain a conscience as a newborn vampire, even when most others descended into uncontrollable bloodlust. It is safe to say that Alice is an invaluable member of the Cullen clan. They would be lost without her, and Bella would have been dead more than once.

Considering the asset Alice is to the Cullens, it is shocking that Alice, born Mary Alice Brandon, was such a burden to her human family that they chose to hide her away in a mental asylum. But it's true: Mary Alice Brandon's life ended alone and isolated in a room in a Mississippi asylum, in a death so traumatic that she remembers nothing of her human life. Alice's father chose to commit her to an asylum in 1920, a time when the treatment of the mentally ill was less about compassion and more about hiding away and "curing" society's undesirables. Alice's narrative reflects the history of the abuse of some of society's most vulnerable members.

Madhouses and Asylums

The asylums of Alice's youth were dreary and dark, much like the madhouses of the eighteenth and early nineteenth centuries. The founders of the first asylums had had good intentions, but it became obvious very quickly that the facilities built for treating mental illnesses were merely warehousing society's undesirables so that polite society and normal people would not be burdened by their troubling presence. The treatment of people in such asylums was brutal and humiliating. Patients were restrained with chains in filthy cells while the eighteenth-century public visited them as a rather macabre way to pass a leisurely afternoon. Widely held views of that era encouraged such harsh treatment. Charlotte Brontë's *Jane Eyre* offers an instructive insight into how "madwomen" were seen during this period: in the novel, Mrs. Rochester was kept hidden away in her husband's attic because she was "mad," with only a harsh and hard-drinking woman as a keeper and companion. But from Jane Eyre's standpoint, it was not strange that a woman who was deemed insane was imprisoned and kept away from society by her husband. This was also the type of treatment that Alice suffered at the hands of her family, when she was put in an asylum.

Physicians were not there to help. They were there to intimidate the patient so that he or she could be easily controlled. The insane were supposed to be "broken" and tamed like wild animals. The medical establishment in the late eighteenth and early nineteenth centuries generally agreed that "taming" was the goal of treatment, whether this was done through painful therapies, intimidation, or humiliation. Understanding and compassion were seen as mollycoddling and pampering people who could understand only a firm hand or even terror.[1]

Attitudes toward the mentally ill changed temporarily during the nineteenth century, although the improvement wasn't a permanent one. The mid-nineteenth-century approach toward the mentally ill, first proposed by Phillipe Pinel during the French Revolution and the Quaker physician Thomas Kirkbride in the United States, is encapsulated in the phrase "moral treatment." This idea of treating the mentally ill with caring and dignity was first introduced by the Quakers in the early part of the nineteenth century. By the middle of the nineteenth century, the idea caught on, and the United States had several institutions, both private and public, that claimed to provide patients with moral treatments.[2]

Moral treatment facilities were selective in how many and what type of patients they would admit. Occupancy topped out at 250 patients at a time in order to provide optimal care. The facilities used gardens to give the patients fresh air, tranquility, and exercise. Caregivers were said to be caring paternal figures. Intellectual stimulation was also a necessary part of the treatment, often in the form of talks and activities. A merit system provided rewards for the well-behaved and nonviolent reprimands for the disruptive. Every effort was made to convince patients that they were not broken beyond repair; they were treated as brethren and rational beings who could recover and become productive members of society. These asylums were more humane and apparently effective, but they didn't last.[3]

Moral treatment came up against resistance from the medical community, and lost. By the late nineteenth century, madness was once more seen as a physical disease that needed medical treatment, not kindness. The death knell for moral treatment truly sounded when neurologists returned from the Civil War, arguing that patients suffered from "mental disorders" that needed treatments based on "hard science." These enthusiastic doctors laid waste to the moral treatment movement. Mental illness was reimagined as a mental disease that could be cured only through harsh medical intervention.[4]

The number of people incarcerated in mental hospitals exploded during the last decades of the nineteenth century. A superintendent's or staff member's well-intentioned attempts to use kindness and empathetic rehabilitation could not prevail in the overcrowded and dreary environment of these new mental hospitals. These institutions used medical therapies as the primary method of treatment and made psychiatry more dependent on general medicine. Services and amenities were quickly cut from asylum budgets, as the demand for basic necessities to treat the hordes of new patients undercut the importance of moral treatment. The staff and administration of late-nineteenth-century asylums usually refused to "pander" to patients' needs, and instead were chosen for their willingness to accept low wages for hard work. Mental hospitals once again became harsh places, as new medical "treatments" were ushered in and compassion disappeared.[5]

The quality of life for patients in asylums declined while their numbers increased. Institutions that had been comfortably providing care for fifty patients had to stretch their services to accommodate four hundred inmates years later. This dramatic increase in the asylum population was caused by changes in the way families governed themselves in the early twentieth century. In earlier periods, members of upper- and middle-class families like Mrs. Rochester who were deemed to be mentally ill were usually kept at home with their families. The care offered by family members was usually more intimate and personal. But by the early twentieth century, ill relatives were seen as a drain on family resources. They were inconvenient, intolerable, and a strain on the family's emotional well-being.[6] Asylums were also being taxed with an influx of new patients from prisons and workhouses. This caused overcrowding of huge proportions and an even greater strain on already fragile and overworked asylum staff. By the time Alice was committed to an institution by her parents, asylums were as crowded as eighteenth-century madhouses had been.[7]

Public discussions regarding the mentally ill changed as well: before, these patients were seen as an inconvenience to their families, but now they were labeled as a true public danger. The new science of eugenics that emerged during the late nineteenth century argued that the insane were carriers of a "defective germ plasm"; if these people were allowed to reproduce, they would allegedly destroy the health of future generations of Americans. This "science" effectively separated people into two categories; the eugenic (well born) and cacogenic (poorly born, who allegedly had defective "germ plasm"). Anyone in the latter category was a drain on time, space, and resources. They were essentially walking time bombs that needed to be "disarmed" by being isolated from others.[8]

Eugenics also ensured that madness was shrouded in shame. Madness in one member of the family implied a possible madness in all of them, or in their descendants, because mental illness was seen as a result of generations of genetic decay in the family's germ plasm, which might be carried by other relatives as well. Alice's family likely used this to justify her incarceration in an asylum. Her family probably saw her as an embarrassment: a defective child rendered useless by generations of genetic deterioration, whose existence implied something unflattering about the "genetic health" of the rest of them. Her father likely felt that it was necessary to hide his daughter away to prevent her sickness, and the embarrassment caused by it, from spreading.[9]

Eugenicists promoted two strategies to keep the allegedly "genetically defective" patients isolated. First, the insane were to be sterilized or otherwise prevented from reproducing. By 1933, all U.S. states had outlawed marriages between those people deemed insane, since it was assumed that they would hand down their diseases to their children. The belief that insanity came from a defect in the family's genetic history brought about the fear that the flaw would continue to manifest itself from one generation to the next. The mentally ill, therefore, presented what was perceived as a real danger. The laws, however, did little good, since they were difficult to enforce. Carting the mentally ill off to insane asylums (the second strategy) was a more effective way of controlling their behavior and removing their freedom to make decisions and choices for themselves. It also prevented them from reproducing and thus spreading the "defective germ plasm." Eugenicists and the people who agreed with them argued that the insane should remain in asylums until they were past reproductive age. Others even supported compulsory sterilization of the mentally ill, which was practiced in several American states.[10] In asylums, patients were treated like animals to keep the cost to the "genetically healthy" majority to a minimum, and this was likely the environment that Alice encountered when she was placed in the asylum by her father.

Make a Commitment

Asylums in the early twentieth century were unforgiving places. The facilities were overcrowded, and the staff was overworked. The patients were isolated from their families and subjected to treatments and what passed for asylum discipline. Adriana P. Brinckle was an inmate in an asylum at the end of the nineteenth century. She recalls: "I saw a harmless patient who was sitting listlessly on a heat register attacked and beaten because she would not work. One nurse knocked her down and then called another with homicidal mania to join and they pounded the unfortunate creature until she was black and blue."[11]

Given the realities of living in an asylum, it stands to reason that the act of committing someone to an asylum would be a difficult decision, and not one that would be easy to carry out. At the very least, today we would expect that it should include bureaucratic checks and a large quantity of paperwork. But during Alice's youth many people, especially women, found that this was not the case.

The understanding of mental illness was then a sketchy thing, and illnesses were frequently confused with one another. There were also sexual biases built into the way people have been (and still are) diagnosed with mental illness. When Alice was young, women as a group were more likely to be diagnosed with psychiatric illness and were therefore more likely to be committed to an asylum.[12]

Women were supposed to complement men perfectly, supplying the qualities that men lacked. At first glance, Alice seems to have the qualities that made for a perfect, functional woman as her period defined the concept. The expectations of her culture were that women were always supposed to be happy and lively. Their temperaments were thought to include more patience and compassion than men's, as well. Any deviation from this template of femininity was seen by Alice's culture as a mental breakdown. Women or girls who attempted to become independent or be something other than a perfect wife, mother, or daughter were condemned as going against nature. That was just madness.[13]

The grounds for committing a daughter to an asylum could be as simple as a boyfriend that her family disliked, or a taste for books that her family felt made the girl willful and too intellectual. This is what happened to Jonika Upton, who was committed to Nazareth Sanatorium. She carried Proust with her at all times and had an artist for a boyfriend; in response, her family put her into an asylum for intensive shock treatment. She was quite different from the daughter her family wanted and expected, and so they sent her to an asylum to be "fixed." By the time she was released, she had no memory of the "inappropriate" boyfriend and had lost interest in her former intellectual pursuits.[14]

From her parents' point of view, Alice might have been the "perfect" daughter and sister during her human life, if only she hadn't been clairvoyant. Her vivacious, effervescent personality would have ensured that she fit her culture's expectations for what a woman was supposed to be. But her gift of premonition earned her a ticket to the asylum. When Alice has a premonition in the Twilight Saga, her behavior is far from what most would consider "normal": her eyes become unfocused and she stares into space at something only she can see. As Bella describes Alice's gift in *Eclipse*, "The vacant look in her eye told me that she was seeing something very different from the mundane lunchroom scene that surrounded us, but something that was every bit as real in its own way. Something that was coming, something that would happen soon." (*Eclipse*, 39.) Scenes like this would have been enough to make any parent worry, especially if they had been raised to believe that talents like the one Alice possessed did not exist, or should not exist. The visions understandably put stress on Alice. When she concentrates on seeing the future, Alice curls into herself and rocks back and forth, a sight that most early-twentieth-century parents would have found quite disturbing.

To Alice's family, it must have seemed as if Alice constantly got lost inside her mind. When she finally returned to the here and now, Alice would have warnings and a knowledge of the future that would have seemed odd and indeed crazy to her family. Even the most sophisticated parents would not understand her behavior, and Alice's family was apparently quite conventional. Her description of them implies that they were probably middle class or upper-middle class, but not "part of the social circle that made the papers." (*New Moon*, 401.) Alice would never be able to be the nice, sweet, average (nonclairvoyant) daughter her rather respectable family wanted. Alice's family took her visions as evidence of mental illness and as a rejection of her proper role as a dutiful daughter.

Alice could not stop her visions and she could not ignore them. It would have seemed like willful rebellion to her family when she did not stop seeing things she should have no way of seeing, at least in their view. This rebellion had to be dealt with harshly before it could spread and (in a culture where eugenics was very influential) destroy the entire family's social standing and reputation for being genetically "sound." The madness of one family member implied a defect in all of them, and a flaw in the family history. Having a mentally ill family member tarnished the lineage of the entire family and was a source of embarrassment and ridicule.

During the late nineteenth and early twentieth centuries, the definition of "madness" was definitely influenced by the sex of the patient. Before World War I, hysteria was the illness of choice when doctors in asylums diagnosed women. Adolescent girls were far more likely than adolescent boys or grown women to be seen as hysterical.[15] Girls who were judged to be hysterical were typically strong-willed, passionate, and bold. Their parents tended to expect a high degree of feminine decorum and tried to control every aspect of their daughters' lives. In such a family, the daughter's quest for freedom might lead to hysterical breakdowns, since these gave her some degree of control over her own life, and also her family. The quality of life for the entire family would be dependent on the fits and tantrums of their sick relative, which meant that they might often give in to the desires of the sick girl, while hiding her problems from the outside world.[16]

Alice's refusal to stop having her "fits" challenged her father's control over the family. The Brandons' family life had probably come to revolve around the fear that Alice might have a fit, or a desire to conceal her fits from others. The only way for them to put the world to rights would be to put their daughter in a place where she could be cured, or at least kept hidden.

During the 1920s, schizophrenia increasingly became the mental illness most associated with women. Schizophrenics were characterized by their blank faces and auditory hallucinations and delusions. Even though the disease couldn't have been a strictly female ailment (we know today that men and women suffer equally from it), schizophrenia became associated with feminine traits and roles during this period.[17] Unfortunately for Alice, her behavior made her a dead ringer for a sufferer of the disease. Her visions, and the blankness they cause in her eyes and facial expression while she has them, would have made her diagnosis and commitment to an asylum a simple matter for doctors of that period.

We might expect that putting a woman in an asylum should have required some kind of proof that the woman was in fact insane, or at least unable to take care of herself. But this was not always the case. Throughout the eighteenth and nineteenth centuries, women were usually classified as being similar to children in their legal status: they were under the guardianship (and legal control) of their fathers or husbands. This was only slowly changing during Alice's youth. A girl could thus be put into an asylum with no proof that she belonged there. A woman needed only to be considered "difficult," and her husband or father or family in general could have her declared insane. Asylums were used as a way to keep a lid on a daughter's (or even a wife's) rebellion, which families or doctors might declare to be symptoms of a psychiatric breakdown when no more convenient symptoms presented themselves. If the very act of rebellion was a sign of disease, then Alice stood no chance.[18] She could not conceal the fact that she displayed very obvious, accepted symptoms of psychiatric distress.

A daughter's assertion of independence could thus be grounds for putting her into an asylum and keeping her there without her consent. Even a girl with an "acceptable" personality and no social difficulties could be put into an asylum for the crime of not fitting in with her family, if her relatives so chose. Edith Lancaster was committed to the Priory, a private asylum in England, in the late nineteenth century because she decided to live with her lover instead of marrying him. Her physician's diagnosis was that Edith suffered from "over education," and her unwillingness to be a traditional wife made her "unfit to take care of herself."[19] Elizabeth T. Stone was committed to Charlestown's McLean Asylum in 1840 by her family because her religion was different from theirs. Although she showed no symptoms of insanity other than her religious conversion to a different denomination of Christianity, they tricked her into entering an asylum and kept her there without her consent and without cause. According to Stone, even the doctor of the asylum did not diagnose her as being mentally ill. She noted bitterly that "neither does he dare to say there was any disease, only my religion was different from my family, and for that he was hired to give a line [certify her mental illness] to deprive me of my liberty, and to be experimented on in a prison.[20]

Other women had complaints brought against them by their spouses. Alice Bingham Russell's husband had her committed as a way to gain unquestioned control over her property. He brought her to trial for insanity several times before she was found guilty and committed against her will.[21] If a woman was off guard or out of sorts for a moment, that could be enough to soil a lifetime of rationality, and once she was committed, she quickly became a nonentity. Russell observed sadly that "at your commitment you are without lawful rights, for you are legally dead and without influential interference if maliciously committed it can be lifelong."[22] Committing someone was in essence a way of silencing him or her and invalidating that person's existence. And if patients continued to insist that they were sane, this could even be taken as proof of belligerence in those whom others saw as crazy. At times, forcible commitment was even used as a method of divorce, when a husband would have his wife committed so that he could marry someone else.[23]

Being imprisoned behind the walls of an asylum against one's will was not as difficult as it should have been. It was even simpler in the case of a girl like Alice, gifted with an ability that no one understood. To her family Alice would have seemed willfully independent to the point of disobedient madness when she asserted that things were true that couldn't be; or perhaps they simply decided that she was sick and in need of the care that an asylum could provide. Her freedom was the price Alice paid for being different.

Crowd Control and Early Therapies

As the number of people housed in asylums grew rapidly during the late nineteenth century, control over the masses of mentally ill people became a bigger problem. Asylum authorities were outnumbered by patients, and maintaining control was a tenuous process. The main job of staff in an asylum was to ride herd over the patients and discipline them when necessary. Superintendents and asylum workers had tried and true ways of keeping patients under their thumbs that were quick and inexpensive, but it was an ugly business, keeping control over people who could not control themselves. The asylum employed a variety of horrifying methods to keep their patients quiet and compliant.

The first strategy the asylum used to control the patients it warehoused was rather obvious. Indeed, it seems almost harmless, at first glance: each patient in the asylum was given a strict schedule. Every minute of the day from waking in the morning until sleep at night was planned out. Patients knew when they would be awakened, when medication would be doled out, when treatments would be administered, and when they would sleep. The timetables controlled the flow of people and put the patients on the attendants' schedule. The same method was used to control people in workshops and inmates in prison. Jane Hillyer, a patient in an asylum, describes the effect of a schedule: "The few habits of ordinary living that remained with me were broken down by a new and rigidly enforced routine, having no connection with any phase of life I had ever known."[24] With one eye watching the clock, patients grew almost indifferent to their own time. They did not have to think about managing daily routines and activities, because it was done for them.[25]

If controlling the inmates' time was not enough to make them compliant and easy to control, then methods like restraint and beatings were deployed by asylum staff. Patients were often physically restrained in asylums. Kate Lee, an asylum patient in 1900, remembered seeing women being choked by two attendants as a method of restraining them.[26] She saw another tied to a chair with a sheet.[27] Inmates were also restrained in their beds. As Jane Hillyer recalled, "My hands were bound; my feet were tied to the foot of the bed with a cleverly made noose."[28] In *Twilight*, Alice is said to have been liberated from a dark isolated cell, where she had been kept for a long time by the vampire who turned her. She was "in that black hole" for such a long time that she did not even register the agonizing pain of transformation into a vampire. (*Twilight*, 447.)

Alice was kept in isolation, but there were more violent punishments for actively disobedient inmates. Beating patients was forbidden, but as long as no visible bruises appeared on patients, the rule was generally ignored. Sometimes a patient would be choked from behind with a wet towel or a pillow slip until he or she was under control. In other instances, the patient was hit with a hard bar of soap placed inside a sock, knocking the patient unconscious.[29] The mentally ill were thought to be lower than criminals and unworthy of humane treatment. Windows were barred and doors locked, and in overcrowded asylums, patients slept anyplace where even a sliver of space could be found.[30]

If rigid scheduling could not lure patients into complacency and beating could not control them, then other means were used to maintain order. Sedatives were administered to patients. These soothing, yet dangerous drugs were used on patients as a way to immediately calm them down and make them sleep in their small cells. Drugging could also be accompanied by restraining patients on their beds and putting them in a padded cell.[31] In the years before World War I, sedatives were part of the first wave of drug therapies. They had the dual effect of immediately calming patients down while also putting them into periods of prolonged deep sleep. Medications like morphine, before it was found to be highly addictive, were administered to uncontrollable patients to give them and their caregivers a moment of artificial peace.

Chloral hydrate, known more popularly at the time as Mickey Finns, was often used on asylum patients because it had reliable dosages and could be taken by mouth. Other medications, like apomorphine, caused a manic patient to vomit for up to an hour until he or she fell asleep, exhausted.[32] Barbiturates came into heavy usage in the 1920s, because they allowed a patient to sleep deeply after taking them and wake up feeling refreshed the next morning. Doctors researching ways to cure madness began to experiment with putting patients into deep sleep using these medications, and the results at first were reported as being promising. Barbituates eventually fell out of favor, however, since they presented a high risk of death to the patient.[33]

Asylum doctors also assumed that warm baths would have healing and calming effects, and they filled asylum rooms with bathtubs for "hydrotherapy," which they claimed had impressive success in treating patients. These therapies were actually adapted from older methods of punishing and tiring out disruptive patients.[34] The most blatantly brutal of the hydrotherapies was "drowning therapy." The patient was put into a coffinlike box with holes in the lid and was then submerged in a tank of water until there were no more visible air bubbles. Sometimes the person was submerged headfirst until his lungs were emptied of all air. Physicians theorized that once a patient was revived from a very near death, he or she could "start fresh."[35]

Variants on a warm bath were used in addition to the traditional version. The "needle shower" hit a patient with a highly pressurized jet of water. Asylum doctors felt this therapy stimulated the patient's heart. One form of hydrotherapy dubbed "the wet pack" (or "cold pack") prescribed wrapping the patient in a wet sheet, covering him or her in a wool blanket and then tying the patient to a bed for hours. The wet sheets would fuse to the patients as they dried and the insulation of body heat would cause the patient to feel unbearably hot.[36] This therapy was described as a punishment by Margaret Isobel Wilson in the 1930s: "The cold pack was considered one of the hardest ordeals for some. They dreaded it. Even a threat would pacify them and keep them quiet."[37] After treatment with the cold pack, the patient felt drained enough to go to sleep.

Early treatments for insanity were extremely diverse simply because no one truly understood the cause of insanity. A superintendent, Henry Cotton, even attempted to cure insanity by extracting patients' teeth! John Talbout and Kenneth Tillotson experimented with putting people into a state of hibernation for days by allowing their body temperatures to drop ten to twenty degrees.[38] From a modern point of view, the risks of these early therapies usually outweighed the reported benefits they offered; indeed, they often looked more like torture than treatment. And yet a patient in Alice's youth could have been subjected to any of them.

Shock Therapies

In *Twilight*, James reveals to Bella a past that Alice herself does not remember. In doing so, James discusses the reality of early-twentieth-century asylums and the treatment of mental illness during the time Alice was a patient. He says, "In the nineteen-twenties it was the asylum and the shock treatments. When she opened her eyes, strong with her fresh youth, it was like she'd never seen the sun before." (*Twilight*, 448.) Asylums were not discharging patients as quickly as they were receiving them, and severe mental illness increasingly seemed like a hopeless cause. People who were hospitalized rarely recovered, and warehousing them in asylums seemed to be the best anyone could do. It was against this backdrop of increasingly crowded asylums and poor "cure" rates that shock therapies emerged.[39] After years of no improvements and low expectations, these therapies provided some glimmer of hope that mental illness could be cured. The medical logic behind the treatment was that seizures or induced comas would destroy diseased brain tissue and therefore cure mental illness. The risks to the patient, however, were high, and the treatment itself was agony.[40]

The first of the shock therapies was insulin shock therapy, initially proposed by Viennese psychiatrist Manfred Sakel during the 1920s. He noted that putting addicts into deep, hypoglycemic comas resulted in a lucid, reasonable patient who awakened after being administered an emergency dose of glucose. Such comas are very dangerous, and if not monitored extremely closely, can prove fatal. Sakel experimented with deliberately putting psychotic patients into insulin comas, hoping that they might awaken recovered enough to be released. One insulin coma treatment was not a sufficient shock to produce any noticeable results, however. Patients had to be shocked twenty to sixty times over a period of a couple of months to produce the results Sakel sought. No matter how dangerous Sakel's studies seemed, they apparently worked, as he claimed that most of his study's participants were cured or improved by the end of the study.[41]

The reality of the treatment, however, was terrifyingly risky. In diabetic patients, hypoglycemic comas are a warning of impending hypoglycemic death, and patients in artificially induced comas could easily slip over into death.[42] The patient was kept under for twenty minutes to an hour and then revived by a shot of glucose.[43] Lenore McCall described the experience: "I don't want to come back. I stare at the wall beside me and nausea grips me. They make me come back every day, day after day, back from the nothingness. The sickness, the taste of blood in my mouth, my tongue is raw. The gag must have slipped today."[44]

Waking up from the coma was equally undignified and humiliating. The patients awakened from an insulin coma would experience what was almost a second infancy, losing the ability to speak and feed themselves.[45] They would often forget their adulthood and believe they were still children who needed to go to school. Nurses then served as surrogate mothers to insulin-shock patients. The injections of insulin made the patient feel miserable and willing to accept comfort from any quarter, like ailing children in need of a comforting mother. One treatment, however, was not enough to create a lasting change in the patient's behavior. The person would pass through the infantile stage of recovery and revert once again to her "mad" behavior. After multiple treatments, however, the diseased portions of the brain became damaged. "Cured" patients became detached and less emotionally invested in whatever their passions were before their treatment, while outwardly appearing more companionable. These changes—the so-called benefits of insulin treatment—were brought about because the insulin coma deprived the brain of oxygen, thereby killing cells in the brain. Insulin treatment also kept the asylum wards quieter, as beds were filled with comatose patients. Insulin treatments were used to treat schizophrenia until the 1950s, but a large majority of patients treated with insulin shock ultimately relapsed.[46]

Conclusion: Better Turned Than "Cured"?

Early-twentieth-century "treatments" forced on the mentally ill seem more like torture than therapy. Patients described electroshock, introduced into mental hospitals during the 1940s, as feeling as if they were burning alive or in the middle of an explosion. The treatments were also damaging, which was precisely why they were thought to have worked: because they damaged the patient's brain.

During the nineteenth and early twentieth centuries, a patient could be dragged, beaten, or tricked into submitting to commitment in an asylum and the regimen of treatments that might follow. It did not matter how he or she got to the hospital bed. It also became a common practice to use treatments, electroshock in particular by the mid-twentieth century, as a disciplinary method. Patients who misbehaved got more volts. Although it was not the only form of shock therapy, electroshock therapy is the form of convulsive therapy best known today. Jolts of electricity were passed through the temporal lobes of the brain, causing the body to seize and the patient to sink into unconsciousness. After each treatment it would take weeks for the patient's brain to return to normal functioning. The patients would become helpless and disoriented. Perhaps more frightening is the fact that the patient's intellectual and critical capabilities were diminished, as well.[47] This is a not very surprising continuation of what had happened with hydrotherapy in the earlier years. During the years that hydrotherapy was the dominant regime, patients who misbehaved were put in the baths and showers more often and for longer periods of time. Throughout this period all treatments were used to control and punish patients as much as they were used to "cure" them.

Alice, too, could have been tricked or forced into an asylum. Her special gift would have been easily misread as schizophrenia by those around her, and her parents might have hastened to commit her to conceal the "shame" of such poor "germ plasm" in their family. Once in the asylum, Alice could have been subjected to many of these treatments, since most were in use in American asylums during the period she spent imprisoned in one. Little wonder then that as James explains in *Twilight*, the agony and extreme heat of becoming a vampire hardly registered for Alice, because she had been in pain and darkness for so long. When Alice was turned, it must have felt similar to Bella's own transformation: "I didn't resemble the charcoal briquette I felt like . . . Every cell in my body had been razed to ash." (*Breaking Dawn*, 383.) But Alice, already in such pain, hardly noticed the horrific experience of transformation. What her human keepers had already done to her was, in the end, far worse than even a vampire's venom.

Notes

1. Robert Whitaker, *Mad in America: Bad Science, Bad Medicine, and the Enduring Mistreatment of the Mentally Ill* (New York: Basic Books, 2002), 3–15.
2. Ibid., 30–34.
3. Whitaker, *Mad in America*, 19–40.
4. Ibid., 36–38.
5. Ibid., 34–38.

6. Edward Shorter, *A History of Psychiatry: From the Era of the Asylum to the Age of Prozac* (New York: John Wiley & Sons, 1997), 46–52.

7. Ibid., 54.

8. Whitaker, *Mad in America*, 41–45.

9. Ibid., 41–45.

10. Ibid., 56–60.

11. Adriana P. Brinckle, in *Women of the Asylum: Voices from Behind the Walls 1840–1945*, ed. Jeffery L. Geller and Maxine Harris (New York: Bantam, 1994), 112.

12. Jane M. Ussher and Paula Nicolson, eds., *Gender Issues in Clinical Psychology* (New York: Routledge, 1992), 111.

13. Elaine Showalter, *The Female Malady: Women Madness, and English Culture, 1830–1980* (New York: Pantheon Books, 1985), 123.

14. Whitaker, *Mad in America*, 101.

15. Showalter, *The Female Malady*, 130.

16. Ibid., 132–133.

17. Ibid., 202–204.

18. Ibid., 158.

19. Ibid., 146.

20. Elizabeth T. Stone, in *Women of the Asylum*, 35.

21. Alice Bingham Russell, in *Women of the Asylum*, 193.

22. Ibid., 194.

23. Ibid., 197.

24. Jane Hillyer, in *Women of the Asylum*, 238.

25. Showalter, *The Female Malady*, 102.

26. Kate Lee, in *Women of the Asylum*, 210.

27. Ibid., 211.

28. Hillyer, in *Women of the Asylum*, 238.

29. Whitaker, *Mad in America*, 69.

30. Ibid., 70.

31. Showalter, *The Female Malady*, 203.

32. Shorter, *A History of Psychiatry*, 196–199.

33. Ibid., 200–207.

34. Whitaker, *Mad in America*, 75.

35. Ibid., 17.

36. Ibid., 76–77.

37. Margaret Isabel Wilson, in *Women of the Asylum*, 279.

38. Whitaker, *Mad in America*, 82–83.

39. Ibid., 84.

40. Showalter, *The Female Malady*, 205.

41. Whitaker, *Mad in America*, 85.

42. Shorter, *A History of Psychiatry*, 212.

43. Whitaker, *Mad in America*, 87.

44. Lenore McCall, in *Women of the Asylum*, 291.

45. Showalter, *The Female Malady*, 206.

46. Whitaker, *Mad in America*, 88–91.

47. Ibid., 96–101.

Carlisle Cullen and the Witch Hunts of Puritan London

Janice Liedl

In seventeenth-century England, a preacher's son pursued a short-lived career as a witch-hunter, seeking out the unnatural creatures hidden among the godly people of town and countryside. This man's name wasn't Carlisle Cullen but Matthew Hopkins. Unlike the Cullen clan's patriarch, Hopkins had no reservations about his career path. Matthew Hopkins rode to fame on his reputation as England's "Witch finder general" in the last great English outbreak of witch-hunting during the height of the English Civil War, sending hundreds of people, mostly women, to their deaths.

Carlisle Cullen was quite a different creature from Hopkins's driven witch-hunter, even before a vampire's bite transformed him. Raised by a dour widower who put the pursuit of his puritanical faith and witches ahead of the interests of his son, Carlisle put reason and compassion first. The son rejected his father's puritanical religion and extremist worldview, ideas that were already on the wane by the time Carlisle became an adult. Instead, Carlisle followed a code of ethics more in line with the intellectual trends of his own generation. Born in the midst of the Scientific Revolution and the early years of the Enlightenment, Carlisle rejected his father's religious hysteria in favor of rationality and the belief in divine benevolence more in line with his own generation. Understanding how he was raised in seventeenth-century London explains much about the man and the vampire he would become.

"The London of My Youth"

Carlisle Cullen was born about 1642 or 1643 to a London churchman and his wife. As with about one in twenty births before the advent of modern antiseptics and antibiotics, his mother died in childbirth. That Carlisle survived his childhood was fortunate: infant mortality was high at the time, and one in five children died before reaching the age of five. London's air was considered dangerous to the young and fragile, and the city was a vector for an amazing number of infectious diseases, thanks to poor sanitation and overcrowding. For the first years of his life Carlisle would have been in the care of a wet nurse, a woman who had recently weaned her own child and could thus breastfeed and nurture the orphaned boy. She might have stayed with the young Carlisle in his father's London home or in the countryside with a foster family. This wet nurse was the closest to a mother figure the little boy would have known. It must have been hard for Carlisle to see her go when his father decided the boy was too old for the nursery. Yet this very city was also what Carlisle characterized as "the London of my youth," so it seems likely that Carlisle spent his infancy and his youth in the heart of the metropolis.

At first glance, a seventeenth-century city bore little resemblance to a modern urban center. We feel as if we're looking into a strange fantasyland when Edward Cullen shows Bella Swan the small oil painting of "a miniature city full of steeply slanted roofs, with thin spires atop a few scattered towers. A wide river filled the foreground, crossed by a bridge covered with structures that looked like tiny cathedrals."(*Twilight*, 335.) Despite the fanciful words, Bella has convincingly described Civil War London as it was seen by contemporaries. Several famous panoramas record the city of this time, and they conform closely to what Bella saw. The Thames River was prominently featured in the foreground of virtually every picture of London, as it functioned like a highway for seventeenth-century commuters and traders. Ships sailed into the East End docks from Europe, the Americas, and the Far East loaded down with tennis balls, licorice, fine silks, and spices. Ferries and merchant ships wove their way up and down the wide river that, not far from the Tower of London, was spanned by the old London Bridge. Bella's description of the bridge seemingly covered in tiny cathedrals is surprisingly apt, for among the many buildings nearly filling the bridge's massive structures were residences, businesses, and chapels.

What was it like to come of age in seventeenth-century London, especially as the son of a minister? The Cullens, father and son, lived in the church residence known as a vicarage. Every Sunday, Carlisle's father would have preached a sermon in his parish church to the local residents, his parishioners. Carlisle would have attended his father's services, probably at first under the watchful eye of a household servant. As he matured, the pastor's son would have been expected to serve as an example of good behavior to all of the neighborhood residents. Strict churchmen like Carlisle's father also would forbid any sports or leisure activities on Sunday, except for pious activities like Bible-reading. But on the other days of the week, Carlisle might have played with other children of the parish.

The parish would have included anywhere from about fifty to over two hundred households. As part of the pastor's family, Carlisle would have been raised in relative comfort compared to many other Londoners. Like other churchmen, Carlisle's father was supported by a tithe: a tax of 10 percent on every parishioner's income. Depending on the size and wealth of the parish community, that tithe, as an annual income, would have ranged from £21 to over £100 (in today's currency that would roughly be the equivalent of $50,000 to $200,000).[1] This was at a time when a construction laborer might earn 10 pence a day and a household servant would take in £2 a year (room and board provided), but a gentleman's income rarely dropped below £1,000. However well-to-do their parish and their household, Carlisle wouldn't have been part of London's elite: a minister's son might be as well educated as a gentleman's, but he would neither dress nor live so well as the rich in such palaces as Somerset House or Arundel House.

Edward never tells us which part of London the seventeenth-century Cullens called home. Carlisle would likely have grown up in one of the 109 parishes sprawling northward from the north bank of the Thames (the south side, known as Southwark, was not officially incorporated into the City of London until 1551 and remained an afterthought in London politics for many years following). London was a boom town in the seventeenth century. The city was sustained on a growing wave of migration: country men and women coming to London in search of employment or opportunities. With a population estimated at 350,000 in 1650, London was growing faster than the rest of England and it was the third-largest city in all of Europe. London was also a breeding ground for disease and violence such that in the seventeenth century, many more people were buried in London's parishes each year than were baptized. Regardless, the city's population swelled throughout the century with newcomers from England's countryside and small towns. With constant migration to a city notorious for risk and disease, a coven of vampires could easily have preyed on unwary newcomers with no one the wiser.

Many people still crowded within the traditional boundaries of the city that stretched from the Tower in the east to Newgate in the west. To the south, London Bridge provided convenient passage to Southwark, where prisons, prostitutes, actors, and theaters abounded. Northward, the old city walls ended at Moorgate, but by Carlisle's day, London had far outgrown these old boundaries, sprawling outward in all directions as well as building upward in the city's center. Wooden houses, built up against one another and overhanging the narrow street, crowded the light out. There were many alleys in which to hide, and newer buildings rested on a warren of medieval or even Roman foundations. London might be thought of as a network of nearly continuous, connected buildings running from the Shadwell in the east end to Whitehall near Westminster Abbey and Palace, outside the city's boundaries.[2]

Whatever neighborhood he called home, Carlisle would have grown up under the watchful eyes of his father's parishioners, a child of the parish. The men and women whose homes and businesses filled the streets around the church and its vicarage would have known both of the Cullens. Perhaps they greeted Carlisle as he, like most London children, played in the crowded, narrow streets of their community. Possibly they sadly clucked over his lonely existence, with only his father and a few servants to care for him. Certainly, they kept a close eye on the widower's son. Londoners were notoriously protective of the children from their own parishes. We have accounts where humble men shielded children from being ridden down in the roadway or abused by strangers. One fourteenth-century case shows Londoners at their best: a crowd stopped a cook and a clerk who were beating a boy they came upon and themselves gave the bullies a sound thrashing. The courts later denied the men's claims, supporting the neighbors' assertion that the two "had no cause to complain."[3] Carlisle's willingness to defend Edward and Bella's daughter, Renesmee, against the Volturi in *Breaking Dawn* could have been inspired by his memories of the fiercely protective communities of old London.

Once Carlisle was six or seven, he would have begun his schoolwork, either under his own father's watchful eye or at one of the many London schools that catered to the sons of the city's well-to-do and educated citizens. Perhaps he attended St. Paul's School, the famous institution housed in the great cathedral's churchyard, close to the many booksellers who catered to the students and scholars. Or he might have studied at Christ's Hospital, which educated both poor boys and gentlemen's sons. Perhaps Carlisle's father ran his own parish school, as some London clergymen did, or simply chose to educate his son personally. In any case, Carlisle would have studied Latin and English, and possibly Greek and French as well. Given the senior Cullen's puritanical leanings, it's unlikely that Carlisle would have been allowed to indulge in many of the games and pastimes other London schoolboys enjoyed, whether playing ball on a

London field or wandering about the city singing ballads that critics such as Henry Chettle, a usually tolerant Elizabethan playwright and songwriter, characterized as immoral and obscene.[4] With such a puritanical and obsessive father, Carlisle would have likely had more books than friends.

"Just before Cromwell's Rule"

Even if Carlisle's father had been a more easygoing type, Carlisle's childhood couldn't have been comfortable. In the early 1640s, when Carlisle was born, all of Britain, especially London, was convulsed with the opening of the English Civil War, which lasted until 1649 (in Ireland and Scotland, fighting continued into the next decade). King Charles I was opposed by a Parliamentarian army that formed an early alliance with the Scots, whose Presbyterian leaders were fiercely opposed to the king's proposal that Scotland adopt the prayer book and the organizational structure of the English church. England and Scotland had actually been at war over this since 1637, a war that was mightily unpopular with many English subjects. Some preferred the Scottish-style church to the formal structure of the Anglican faith. Others suspected that the king's religious policy sought to bring the Church of England closer to the Catholic Church, which Henry VIII had broken with a hundred years earlier.

In the mid-seventeenth century, Catholicism was officially and unofficially condemned in England. Many saw this variety of Christianity as intensely anti-English, associated more with Guy "Guido" Fawkes, who had plotted to blow up king and Parliament in 1605. Some went so far as to equate the pope with the anti-Christ and accused Catholic priests of practicing witchcraft in the rites of the Mass.[5] Few English subjects rallied to the king's cause in what became known as the Bishop's War. Many of those who did deserted the royal army, leaving Scottish forces occupying some of England's northern counties and the king forced to summon a Parliament more interested in challenging the king than in assisting him. Supported by principled parliamentarians and religious extremists, Parliament went to war against the king's forces in 1643.

The king's troubles only increased during the years of Carlisle's childhood. The Parliamentarians retained control of London once civil war began, while Charles and his supporters fled to Oxford. Parliament made common cause with the Scots in their early battles against the king, not just because of politics, but also because many supporters of Parliament shared a religious proclivity for more austere forms of Protestantism, including Puritanism. When Parliament emerged victorious, Charles was executed outside of Whitehall Palace while Londoners watched. For the next two decades, their city was the center of a radical religious reform that sought to "purify" English culture and behavior according to Puritan standards. Even before the king's death, Puritans dominated London's religious scene. London churches were staffed by men who condemned theaters as useless frivolity, and celebrations of Christmas as anti-Christian. A few such Puritans went so far as to deny couples the chance to celebrate their marriage in the church under Oliver Cromwell's government in the 1650s, feeling that weddings were for civil authorities, not church ministers.

"His Father Was an Intolerant Man"

Carlisle's father seems to have fit in well with these religious extremists. Although Edward described the senior Cullen as an Anglican, that term better fits someone who remained obedient to King Charles and his archbishop, William Laud. Pastor Cullen couldn't have done that and still remained in London with Parliament in power. Carlisle's father was not a royalist but a reformer who sought to "purify" the English church of Catholic-style rituals and English society of decadent behavior, hunting witches as part of his godly duties. He would have prospered after the king's execution in 1649, as power centralized in the hands of the Parliamentary leader Oliver Cromwell. Carlisle's father was, in Edward's words, "enthusiastic in his persecutions of Roman Catholics and other religions," an attitude that sat well with Cromwell, who himself was strongly anti-Catholic. (*Twilight*, 331.)

The senior Cullen could have retained his London parish only if he adhered to the very strict idea of proper doctrine and behavior popular with Parliament's puritanical faction and many Londoners. Soon after war broke out, Parliament instituted a "Committee for Scandalous Ministers," which reviewed clergymen for bad behavior and "Popish" (that is, Catholic) leanings. In the first few months of its existence, the committee received around eight hundred petitions against established churchmen. The committee focused much of its energy on the London rectors and pastors who operated almost literally under Parliament's nose, weeding out ministers such as William Fairfax of St. Peter Cornhill, who was found guilty of innovation, scandal, and delinquency and was imprisoned in 1643.[6] Carlisle's father must not have raised the suspicion of the committee with his own religious practices in order to retain his position throughout the war and its aftermath.

In the same year that Fairfax was imprisoned for failure to adhere to the committee's ideal of a minister's conduct, Parliament established another religious institution, the Westminster Assembly. The new body was intended to create new models of church government and worship to be established across the country, as Parliamentary forces put the king's army on the defensive. The Assembly achieved little in the way of national church reform, however, instead concentrating on micromanaging London's religious staff and administration. Assembly members promoted Puritan ministers and undermined the traditional authority of bishops, but only in a piecemeal fashion. As long as the church leadership was so preoccupied with theological details, conforming Puritan ministers such as Carlisle's father could turn witch-hunting into a rather bloodthirsty hobby without raising any alarm.

Carlisle's early life was undoubtedly shaped by his father's religion and witch-hunting mission. Motherless and raised under Pastor Cullen's stern eye, Carlisle might easily have become as fanatical a witch-hunter as his father. But as his father searched through London's streets and alleys in search of ungodly creatures to destroy, witch-hunting was already in a steep decline. It's important to remember that such fervor was the exception, not the rule, even in the strongly religious culture of the 1600s. While no one advocated any sort of toleration for witchcraft or other demonic activities, many at the time were disturbed by the mind-set of overzealous witch hunters like Pastor Cullen, who fixated on "the reality of evil." What was this evil? As Eveline Brugger notes in her chapter in this book, in which she discusses vampires in European folklore, "vampire" was an unknown concept in Puritan England. So those Londoners who believed in ungodly creatures would have worried only about witches. For the senior Cullen, witches were as fearsome a threat as drug dealers in modern times, but even more urgent, as witchcraft threatened the soul, while drugs only harmed the body.

Another insight into the psychology of witch-hunters like Carlisle's father is offered by historian Wolfgang Behringer. Behringer believes that a shared mentality united witch-hunters in Europe and America. These men were all mentally hardened, prepared for the endtimes prophesied in the Gospels and immersed in a mind-set of extreme austerity. Behringer argues that "the character profile of the *authoritarian personality* not only applies to Fascist or Nazi voters, but also to those jurists, theologians, councillors or princes who embarked on the business of witch-hunting around 1600."[7] That personality type might have made for a great witch-hunter but probably not a loving and nurturing parent. Carlisle would have grown up to be emotionally self-sufficient with a fanatical father who saw his son more as a tool to carry on his own crusade than as an individual who should be encouraged to explore his own interests.

"When Monsters Were Not Just Myths and Legends"

It might be helpful at this point to return to the case of Matthew Hopkins, England's most successful witch-hunter, if only because of his own tireless self-promotion. Hopkins was born in the English countryside in the 1620s (as with Carlisle's birth, no records survive to pinpoint the date or location). He was a vicar's son who finally hit upon a witch-hunting career, which resulted in the execution of more than 250 people in eastern England for the crime of witchcraft. Hopkins carried out his hunts with an eye toward publicity: his exploits were written up in several contemporary books, one authored by Hopkins himself: *The Discovery of Witches*. Hopkins reportedly died of tuberculosis in August 1647, although folk legend has it that he was executed as a witch.[8] With Hopkins's early death, the enthusiasm for his witch hunts died, and the practice vanished in England over the next generation.

The most basic definition of witchcraft was laid out by George Gifford in 1587. He defined a witch as one that "works by the Devil . . . hurting or healing, revealing things secret or foretelling things to come."[9] Due to their presumed intellectual and moral weakness that made them jealous of men, women were considered especially susceptible to the devil's wiles. Older women, poor women, widows, or unwed mothers were thought to be especially vulnerable. John Stearne, who collaborated with Hopkins in his witch hunts, wrote two books documenting how they uncovered witches. For instance, his *Confirmation and Discovery of Witchcraft* (1587) explained how the Bible and certain signs could provide investigators with sure proof of a witch's demonic interaction.

Stearne and Hopkins found evidence by searching the accused witch's body or through painfully elicited confessions. Physical signs were known as witch marks and could be as innocuous as a mole or a wart. Stearne's guide told investigators to look for familiars in the forms of cats, dogs, ferrets, and rabbits that would suck at the witch mark to aid the witch in her dark magic. To preserve modesty, Hopkins employed a woman, Mary Phillips, to discover witch marks. Phillips assisted the investigators in many cases.[10] To gain a confession from a witch, the hunters used sleep deprivation and physical torture that could end with dislocated shoulders. The witchfinders also used "swimming" or ducking to determine whether the accused was innocent or guilty. In ducking, the accused was bound, hand to foot, and cast into a body of water; if she floated, she was presumed guilty, while if her body sank, she was not guilty. Hopkins and Stearne insisted that they used ducking only when the local community demanded it and also only when the weather was warm enough that the accused would take no harm.[11]

As opposed to the rather impromptu witch hunts run by Pastor Cullen and his reluctant son, Hopkins carried out his searches on the up-and-up. Stearne and Hopkins also complied with the laws about witchcraft and didn't act as vigilantes. When the hunters won a confession, they handed the witch over to the assize courts, where justices would review the evidence, convict the witch, and then arrange for her execution. Not all witch-hunters were so open and law-abiding. Many English men and women of the seventeenth century feared the supernatural powers wielded by witches and warlocks. Witches were supposed to be able to induce illness in humans and animals, cause crop failure, and even bring about miscarriages via their demonic pact. Suspected witches therefore posed a threat not only to the well-being of their neighbors but also to the spiritual survival of the community in which they resided.

If a witch was afflicting your family or your community, you didn't always want to wait for justice. Some, like Hopkins, found suspected witches and handed them over to the authorities. Others were inspired to take matters into their own hands: hunting the witches with the help of a mob. It is into this second category that Carlisle's father falls, for he taught his son to hunt out the demonic creatures at the head of a mob and not wait to have judges hear evidence. This was not unheard of at the time: in 1643 two different women were lynched by Parliamentary soldiers who feared that the women were using their devilish powers to aid the king's cause.[12] Fear of witchcraft led communities to mete out justice without resorting to the law, a kind of panic historians saw happening time and again during this era of the witch craze.

The witch crazes lasted from the late 1400s until the end of the seventeenth century. During the European witch crazes, tens of thousands of people died, executed either after official trials or as a result of mob justice like that practiced by Carlisle's father with his impromptu witch hunts through the London night. Churchmen were especially concerned with the threat posed by witchcraft as both a demonic opposition to Christianity as well as a sign of an unruly or ignorant populace. Governments, for much the same reason, passed new laws targeting witchcraft crimes, although their too-eager application was discouraged as destabilizing the political and religious order.[13] Legally sanctioned witch hunts took off in England after 1563, when the House of Lords passed "An Act against Conjurations Enchantments and Witchcrafts." The Witchcraft Act mandated punishments for various types of witchcraft crimes ranging from imprisonment and public pillorying to death. However, the level of proof required by this sixteenth-century legislation made prosecuting such a case a difficult task.

In 1604, a new statute eased the standards of evidence required for a conviction and no longer required proof of supernaturally caused harm for the witch to be found guilty. This legal change was made to please the new Stuart king of England, James I. While still king of Scotland, James had written a book on witchcraft called *Demonology*. The king believed that witches were full of malevolence toward himself and other good people. James blamed witches for plotting against him while he was king of Scotland, including an attack on his Danish bride, Anne, while she was sailing to Scotland. But even King James found that his credulity stretched only so far. When the false testimony of one twelve-year-old boy was enough to hang nine witches in 1615, the king rebuked his justices for condemning with so little evidence. Not only the king but other thinkers of the day began to openly doubt that witchcraft existed, at least as understood by the common people and the fanatical witch-hunters.[14] That sense of caution ebbed over the next decades and was utterly lost by the 1640s, when civil war and disorder left many grasping at the explanation that witchcraft offered for the many calamities in their lives.

"Carlisle Was a Disappointment; He Was Not Quick to Accuse"

Carlisle seems more in line with the skeptics of his era than with those like his father, who believed witchcraft was a constant danger. When Carlisle's father was organizing his searches for witches, werewolves, and vampires, the time was particularly ripe for this hysteria. Not just in England, but all across Europe, people were struggling and eager to blame someone else. As Wolfgang Behringer noted in his history of the witch hunts:

> The early 1640s, when large parts of Western and Central Europe were in turmoil, ravaged by rebellions, civil war and international conflict, were particularly fertile times for witch panics. The general feeling of uncertainty was presumably supported by another cluster of unfavourable years, and crop failure combined with man-made disruptions of commerce and trade. Not only England, but also France suffered from severe witch panics.[15]

Times change, and the problems of the 1640s were eventually forgotten. The Thirty Years' War in Central Europe was finally settled by the Peace of Westphalia in 1648. Britain's own peace was reestablished in 1660, when Charles I's son returned from exile and claimed the throne as Charles II. This "Merry Monarch" ushered in an age associated more with frivolity and leisure than Puritanism. The theaters reopened, and women began to appear on the stage as actresses, something scandalous and illegal when Carlisle was born.

It was in this new world of the English Restoration, when Carlisle was just twenty-three, that it became his job to take over his father's witch hunts. Very likely, the senior Cullen had not done much with his witch hunts over the past few years, because of both his age and the attitudes of the time. Across the country, too, few were now enthusiastic about the religious extremism of the past generation or the witch-hunts. As James Sharpe has noted, Hopkins's witch-hunting actions were the very excesses that English society in the 1660s now condemned as it looked back on the not-so-distant past.[16] But Carlisle was probably accustomed to obeying his father and took on the duty.

Ironically, what stands out in Edward's account of his adoptive father's time as a witch hunter is that Carlisle worked at witch-hunting enough to succeed in tracking down a fabled creature, an achievement far beyond his father's own experience. Edward tells Bella, "At first, Carlisle was a disappointment; he was not quick to accuse, to see demons where they did not exist. But he was persistent, and more clever than his father. He actually discovered a coven of true vampires that lived in the sewers of the city, only coming out by night to hunt." (*Twilight*, 331.) In contrast to Hopkins and Stearne, who worked closely with local authorities (and who also ran up enormous bills for their expert services that could amount to a quarter of a city's annual budget), Carlisle hunted his unnatural prey on the cheap and with far less official support.

Edward's description of a London mob armed with pitchforks and torches sounds a little melodramatic, especially given the senior Cullen's long and dismal record as a witch hunter. How many faithful would have remained to follow the witch hunters into the new era after decades of disappointment? Perhaps the following came out of admiration for Carlisle's clever idea to look to the sewers, the oldest part of the ancient city in which an ancient foe might hide. His intelligence, his speed, and his obedience to duty all spelled disaster for Carlisle, leaving him out front and vulnerable to the aged vampire who infected his blood and cut him off from the only family he had left. Now Carlisle had become one of the unnatural creatures that his father had devoted his whole career to eradicating.

The Soul of the Family

Being transformed into a vampire was, as Edward explained to Bella, a devastating blow to the gentle and ethical Carlisle. The dutiful son found himself in the grip of an irrational and presumably demonic power. Edward described to Bella his adoptive father's initial reaction: "When he knew what he had become . . . he rebelled against it. He tried to destroy himself." (*Twilight*, 336.) But Carlisle's efforts were in vain, even as he tried to starve himself to death. It was his fortunate discovery that the blood of animals could be as sustaining as that of people that gave Carlisle a new lease on life, as well as a new philosophy very much in keeping with the spirit of the age in which he was changed.

After Puritan excesses had gone out of fashion, European intellectuals popularized a worldview that built upon the scientific advances of the last several generations. Although Galileo had famously been persecuted a generation earlier when his astronomical arguments challenged church authority, in the latter part of the seventeenth century, more scientists and philosophers were challenging the status quo. This time period marked the early stages of the Enlightenment, and it's possible that Carlisle, as a young man in London, might have rubbed shoulders with such esteemed thinkers as John Locke, who we know visited London when he was admitted to Gray's Inn in 1658. At the same time that Carlisle was struggling to take up his father's mantle as witch hunter, Locke wrestled with concepts of natural law that eventually led him to argue in his famous *Essay Concerning Toleration* of 1667 that governments must tolerate varied opinions on religion as long as civil order wasn't threatened. This idea ran counter to the previous generations' assumptions that society had to be uniform in practice and belief: it laid the groundwork for a light-avoiding, free-thinking vampire to carve out his own unique identity. Like Carlisle, Locke would later travel to the continent to study in that exciting environment (although we have no record that any of his tutors at Montpellier were actually vampires).[17]

Carlisle also formulated a philosophy similar to the Enlightenment idea of Deism, an approach to spirituality that held that ethics and eternal truth were not exclusive to any one religious tradition but were knowable by reason. A generation before Carlisle was born, Edward Herbert argued that God could be known and worshiped through repentance and an ethical life: a philosophy far removed from the demanding doctrines popular with the battling religious sects of his day. In the last decade of the seventeenth century, another English philosopher, John Toland, published *Christianity Not Mysterious* in which he argued that only those religious principles knowable by reason should be followed.[18] Carlisle's generic, tolerant philosophy of life fits in more with the ideas of these and other Deists than with his father's Puritan doctrines. In becoming a vampire, Carlisle seemed finally to have found the freedom to turn away from the strident Puritanism of his father's day and embrace a new philosophy, a new faith, and a new life that wasn't far removed from the ideas put forward by his contemporaries. In doing so, he laid the groundwork for all of the other Cullen family vampires to follow.

Like Father, Like Son

Carlisle Cullen is critical to the Twilight Saga not only because he founded the Cullen family and its particular ways. Carlisle is especially important because he is Edward's role model. Time and again, Edward focuses on how his adoptive father embodies his own ideals. When Edward struggles with a desire to rip out Bella's throat and drink her intoxicating blood, in *Midnight Sun* he claims that it is not his own ethics, but his desire to be worthy of his father, that stops Edward from attacking:

> In my head, Carlisle's kind eyes did not judge me. I knew that he would forgive me for this horrible act that I would do. Because he loved me. Because he thought I was better than I was.—I would prove my father wrong about me. The misery of this fact hurt almost as much as the fire in my throat. I leaned away from her in revulsion—revolted by the monster aching to take her. (*Midnight Sun*, 13.)

Edward's desire to be worthy of his adoptive father's love and good opinion helps him to overcome his overwhelming urge to kill Bella and savor her blood. So, without Carlisle, not only would we not have had a chance for Edward and Bella to meet, but we can say without a doubt that Bella would not have survived such a meeting if another vampire had turned Edward.

Carlisle is the soul of the Cullen vampire clan: a position he attained precisely because of his experiences growing up in London during the 1600s. Both his father's religious fervor and his own rational intellectualism contributed to making Carlisle the man, or vampire, he would become. Carlisle may have rejected the extremes of his father's faith and mission, but spirituality remained important to him as he struggled with his transformation. Carlisle grew up with a vibrant community of Londoners that gave him a strong sense of community and a desire to serve that ultimately led him to pursue a medical career very much in the human world. Finally, his exposure to the scientific and Enlightenment influences of the time were critical elements in his devising a way to live ethically as a vampire that made it possible for Edward and others to join his clan. Spirituality, community, and rationality: all were components of Carlisle's upbringing that he adopted and retained as core elements of the Cullen family ethos.

Notes

1. Tai Liu, *Puritan London: A Study of Religion and Society in the City Parishes* (Newark: Univ. of Delaware Press, 1986), 23–33.

2. See Stephen Inwood, *A History of London* (New York: Basic Books, 1998), or Peter Ackroyd, *London: The Biography* (New York: Nan A. Talese, 2000). For 1640s London, see A. J. S. Nusbacher, *London's Civil War* (Stroud, Eng.: Tempus, 2006).

3. Barbara A. Hanawalt, *Growing Up in Medieval London: The Experience of Childhood in History* (Oxford: Oxford Univ. Press, 1993), 62–66.

4. Rosemary O'Day, *Education and Society, 1500–1800: The Social Foundations of Education in Early Modern Britain* (London: Longman, 1982), 33. Henry, Chettle, *Chettle's Complaint of England's Irreligious Youth Is from Kind-Hart's Dreame* (London: William Wright, 1593), Ci[r].

5. Sean Armstrong, "Superstition and the Idols of the Mind: How the Witch-Hunt Helped Shape the Scientific Revolution in England" (PhD diss., York Univ., Canada, 2004), 162–164.

6. Alice E. McCampbell, "Incumbents and Patronage in London, 1640–1660," *Journal of Church and State* 25, no. 2 (1983): 303–304.

7. Wolfgang Behringer, *Witches and Witch-Hunts: A Global History* (Cambridge, Eng.: Polity Press, 2004), 120, 163.

8. James Sharpe, "Hopkins, Matthew (d. 1647)," in *Oxford Dictionary of National Biography* (Oxford: Oxford Univ. Press, 2004), www.oxforddnb.com/view/article/13751.

9. George Gifford, *A Discourse of the Subtill Practises of Devilles by Witches and Sorcerers* (London: Toby Cooke, 1587), Bii[r].

10. John Stearne, *A Confirmation and Discovery of Witchcraft* (London: William Wilson, 1648).

11. Behringer, *Witches and Witch-Hunts*, 132.

12. Malcolm Gaskill, "Witchcraft and Evidence in Early Modern England," *Past and Present* 198 (February 2008): 39–46.

13. Brian P. Levack, "State-Building and Witch Hunting in Early Modern Europe," in Jonathan Barry, Marianne Hester, and Gareth Roberts, eds., *Witchcraft in Early Modern Europe: Studies in Culture and Belief* (Cambridge, Eng.: Cambridge Univ. Press, 1996), 112.

14. Gaskill, "Witchcraft and Evidence in Early Modern England," 43.

15. Behringer, *Witches and Witch-Hunts*, 131.

16. Sharpe, "Hopkins, Matthew (d. 1647)."

17. J. R. Milton, "Locke, John (1632–1704)," in *Oxford Dictionary of National Biography* (Oxford: Oxford Univ. Press, 2004), www.oxforddnb.com/view/article/16885.

18. Earle E. Cairns, *Christianity Through the Centuries: A History of the Christian Church*, 3rd ed. (Grand Rapids, MI: Zondervan, 1996), 377–380.

A Subtle and Dangerous Gift

Jasper Hale and the Specter of the American Civil War

Andrea Robertson Cremer

Images of the hero and the universe are devices that enable us to identify with (and thus enter) the world of the myth.

—*Richard Slotkin,* Regeneration through Violence

"Jasper is very interesting. He was quite charismatic in his first life, able to influence those around him to see things his way. Now he is able to manipulate the emotions of those around him—calm down a room of angry people, for example, or excite a lethargic crowd, conversely. It's a very subtle gift."

—*Edward Cullen (*Twilight, *308)*

Fans of the Twilight series can find mountains of merchandise to sate their appetites. One such item, a poster featuring Jackson Rathbone, the actor who portrays Jasper Hale in the Twilight films, sports the tagline: "Jasper—because he's so empathetic."[1] Jasper's very own motto refers to the supernatural ability he acquired after being transformed from human to vampire. He can control and shape the emotions of those around him, humans and immortals alike.

This trait makes Jasper one of the most appealing characters in the Twilight series. He appears in moments of crisis, the steady force of calm in the face of approaching storms. Deeply charismatic and terribly sensitive, Jasper offers the perfect portrait of genteel masculinity. Yet at the same time, Jasper's ability to read and control the emotions of those around him renders him the most unpredictable and dangerous of the Cullens. From his first appearance, Jasper's place within the family is ambivalent: "No one else seemed to know quite what to say, and then Jasper was there—tall and leonine. A feeling of ease spread through me, and I was suddenly comfortable despite where I was. Edward stared at Jasper, raising one eyebrow, and I remembered what Jasper could do." (*Twilight*, 324.)

Although Jasper's intentions appear to be out of kindness, Edward views this attempt to quell Bella Swan's fears with suspicion. The Cullen family culture is marked by deep love and loyalty among its members, but Jasper is treated as a possible threat to that stability, his level of commitment to its "vegetarian" lifestyle still unreliable. As Bella observes, "Jasper had more trouble sticking to the Cullens' diet than the rest of them; the scent of human blood was much harder for him to resist than the others—he hadn't been trying as long." (*New Moon*, 27.)

Of all the Cullens, Jasper emerges as the vampire whose hunger presents the greatest threat to Bella herself. At a Cullen family gathering to celebrate her eighteenth birthday, Bella slits her finger on a piece of wrapping paper:

> A single drop of blood oozed from the tiny cut. It all happened very quickly then. "No!" Edward roared. He threw himself at me, flinging me back across the table. It fell, as I did, scattering the cake and the presents, the flowers and the plates. I landed in the mess of shattered crystal. Jasper slammed into Edward, and the sound was like the crash of boulders in a rock slide. There was another noise, a grisly snarling that seemed to be

coming from deep in Jasper's chest. Jasper tried to shove past Edward, snapping his teeth just inches from Edward's face. (*New Moon*, 28–29.)

It is Jasper's inability to suppress his bloodlust that provokes Edward to temporarily abandon Bella in the hopes of protecting her from danger—a choice that plunges her into a severe depression that includes thoughts of self-destruction. This single event is the first step in a dangerous downward spiral that nearly ends both Bella's and Edward's lives. It took only a single drop of blood to transform empathetic Jasper into a raging beast who set off a chain of catastrophic decisions.

Jasper's role in the Twilight Saga mirrors a compelling historical archetype in American culture: the Southern gentleman-soldier. As Jasper's personal history is slowly revealed over the course of the Twilight series, we are introduced to several historical stereotypes regarding American masculinity and its relationship to violence. Jasper Hale embodies the ideal American man, balancing fierce independence, strong sensibilities, and brute force. But his character simultaneously exposes the dangers of a mythological Southern manhood: emotional volatility; a penchant, even lust, for violence; and an inherent selfishness that carries with it the threat of desertion.

By interweaving Jasper's past with the history of the American Civil War, Stephenie Meyer offers a glimpse into an ongoing debate about the role of violence and manhood in American society and history. This debate is not only about the individual man, but also about the character of the nation itself. As the Civil War remains one of the most defining events of modern American culture, Jasper's struggle with his violent nature, and the perpetual reminders that his role in the idealized Cullen family is the most unstable, all suggest that the United States itself remains a nation divided. Contemporary American society is tied to a regional past stained in blood, fearful that internal violence simply waits, latent but present, ready to break forth again and pit brother against brother once more.

A Time of Making Men

> The young men who have not ambition and moral courage to fight for the preservation of that rich legacy bequeathed them—and purchased for them by the blood of their ancestors will be scoffed at and looked upon as base cowards unworthy [of] the name of southern man.
>
> —*Sergeant R. A. Pierson, Ninth Louisiana Infantry*[2]

> "I didn't have quite the same . . . upbringing as my adopted siblings here. My beginning was something else entirely."
>
> —*Jasper Hale (Eclipse, 287)*

Like all vampires, Jasper Hale was born twice. First, to his human family in the nineteenth-century South, second to his vampire family in Texas amid the American Civil War. The era of Jasper's birth marked a turning point in the history of American manhood. The nineteenth century was a period marked by competing ideologies of masculinity, family, and government. A generation of men who did not identify with their Revolutionary forefathers sought ways to define their own place in society. No longer "Sons of Liberty," men in the youthful, rapidly expanding United States created new versions of manliness tied to conflicting economic, political, and social goals.[3]

This struggle to develop new versions of manliness occurred alongside other cataclysmic shifts in American culture, including the Industrial Revolution, the rise of chattel slavery, and the transportation revolution.[4] Rapid expansion of Euro-American settlers into the western parts of the continent increased the rivalries between North and South, while intensifying struggles over slavery and racial politics solidified social hierarchies. Amid such volatile changes, American men created new ideals by which to define their manhood. As historian Richard Slotkin notes, "Cultural anxieties and the competition of regional interest groups fostered a sectional divergence in the interpretation of this historical mission and hence of American character."[5]

Jasper's story echoes this conflict. Describing the antithetical practices of the Northern and Southern vampires, he says:

> "The North is, by comparison, very civilized. Mostly we are nomads here who enjoy the day as well as the night, who allow humans to interact with us unsuspectingly—anonymity is important to us all.
>
> It's a different world in the South. The immortals there come out only at night. They spend the day plotting their next move, or anticipating their enemy's. Because it has been war in the South, constant war for centuries, with never one moment of truth. The covens there barely note the existence of humans, except as soldiers notice a herd of cows by the wayside—food for the taking." (*Eclipse*, 289.)

Similar to the dichotomy Jasper describes, competing models of manhood that emerged in nineteenth century popular culture were of the industrious, self-made Northern man—whose interests were tied to the emerging free market and middle class—and the Southern gentleman who embodied the romantic figure of aristocratic nobility, high culture, and leisurely pursuits. The Southern man was not only master of himself, but of the women he claimed and the slaves he was likely to own.[6] Not only were such stereotypes steeped in mythologies of ideal manhood, they also remained accessible only to the upper classes. Both constructions of manliness excluded the majority of American men whose lives were tied to menial labor.

Archetypal Southern manhood emerged both in social practice and literature—dual forces working together to create a model that young Southern men seeking an identity could mold themselves on. The hero of this new Southern masculinity required "an innate nobleness of spirit, expressed not as some vague, natural moral sense but as a genuine gentility of spirit, of blood."[7] Slotkin describes this idealized Southern masculine archetype as that of the hunter—an appellation that describes Jasper to a tee.

He contrasts this archetype with the Northern ideal, who closely resembles Edward, the male who "resists change as he resists temptations to sin; he protects the feminine avatar of social virtues instead of seeking the woman of his dark wilderness dreams."[8] The hunter represents the other side of the coin to this more sexually conservative hero. While the entire Twilight Saga revolves around Edward and Bella's romantic struggle, rife with sexual tension, over the boundaries of their physical relationships, Jasper enjoys a fully developed relationship with Alice, the other member of the Cullen family whose extraordinary ability—glimpsing the future—guides their every action.

Although Jasper's devotion to Alice remains one of his most attractive traits, it throws his loyalty to the Cullen family at large into question. The conflict between individual passion and commitment to a higher moral code reveals yet another flaw in the mythical Southern male archetype as embodied by Jasper: the possibility of desertion. The theme of desertion will be revisited at the close of this chapter, but Jasper's relationship to Alice reflects yet another dimension of Jasper's embodiment of Southern masculinity. His first priority is to protect what he claims as his own—his home, his love (Alice), and his life. Manliness in the nineteenth century was founded upon the concept of mastery—financial, social, political.[9] The greatest test of that mastery, and the Southern male's manhood, took place during the years from 1861 to 1865, the American Civil War.

The Bloody Civil War: A Family Affair

> From noon until dark we endured the slow torture of seeing our comrades killed, mangled and torn around us.
>
> —*Captain Thomas L. Livermore, New Hampshire Infantry*[10]

> "Jasper belonged to another family . . . a very different kind of family."
>
> —*Edward (*Twilight*, 289)*

Competing versions of American culture at all levels—economic, political, and social—exploded into violence when the Confederacy fired on Fort Sumter outside Charleston, South Carolina, on April 12–13, 1861. For the next four years, the United States was plunged into a chaotic war that pitted "brother against brother" and soaked American soil from the Atlantic coast to the western territories with the blood of thousands.

America's violent past is also Jasper's violent past. Gradual revelations about Jasper's personal history in the saga reflect our own uneasiness about the internal violence that shaped modern American society. We're told at first that he's an expert in warfare and fighting, but not why. As a pitched battle of vampire against vampire becomes inevitable, it is finally revealed that Jasper's coming of age, as both a human and a vampire, was tied to his personal involvement in the Civil War:

> "When I was human, I lived in Houston, Texas. I was almost seventeen years old when I joined the Confederate Army in 1861 . . . My military career was short-lived, but very promising. People always . . . like me, listened to what I had to say. My father said it was charisma. Of course, now I know it was probably something more. But, whatever the reason, I was promoted quickly through the ranks, over older, more experienced men. The Confederate Army was new and scrambling to organize itself, so that provided opportunities as well. By the first battle of Galveston—well, it was more of a skirmish really—I was the youngest major in Texas, not even acknowledging my real age." (*Eclipse*, 292.)

But Jasper's aptitude as soldier and officer—based on two desirable masculine traits, strength and leadership—mask a darker story, one that the Cullens, and particularly Edward, are reticent to share with Bella.

> I wondered again what he'd [Edward] meant about Jasper's expertise. I really didn't know much about Jasper's history, just that he had come somewhere from the South before Alice found him. For some reason, Edward had always shied away

> from questions about his newest brother. And I'd always been too intimidated by the tall, blonde vampire who looked like a brooding movie star to ask him outright. (*Eclipse*, 283.)

Edward's secrecy functions on two levels: the first is his desire to shield Bella from the violence inherent in the vampire world—he continues to play the prescribed role of Victorian Northern gentleman—focused almost exclusively on protecting Bella's virtue. The second, however, raises the possibility of shame and fear with regard to violence in one's past. Not only are Jasper's choices derided, but we're led to believe that his former life might not have been completely left behind. Only when it is absolutely necessary is Bella allowed to see the "true" Jasper.

> Jasper's face was unreadable as he pushed the sleeve of his thin sweater higher up on his arm. At first my eyes could not make sense of the texture that was layered thickly across the skin. Curved half-moons crisscrossed in a feathery pattern that was only visible, white on white as it was, because the bright glow of the lamp beside him threw the slightly raised design into relief, with shallow shadows outlining the shapes. (*Eclipse*, 286.)

Jasper himself seems haunted by his past. The world he invokes when he finally tells his story is one filled with pain and regret, the musings of a battle-worn soldier still aching from the atrocities he has participated in and the horrors he has witnessed. The state of war is a state of exceptions to peacetime rules, rife with violence and the absence of the humane.[11] "'Before I tell you my story,' Jasper said, 'you must understand that there are places in our world, Bella, where the life span of the never-aging is measured in weeks, and not centuries.'" (*Eclipse*, 287–288.)

Jasper can't reconcile the man he wants to be, genteel and compassionate, with the man he believes he was and may still be, violent and irrational: "You've experienced the way I can manipulate the emotions around myself, Bella, but I wonder if you realize how the feelings in a room affect me. I live every day in a climate of emotion. For the first century of my life, I lived in a world of bloodthirsty vengeance. Hate was my constant companion." (*Eclipse*, 300.)

This violent past is written on Jasper's body in the form of scars that speak volumes about his involvement in mayhem and the destruction of other beings. This reality becomes even more jarring when Bella's vision grows sharper after her transformation into a vampire:

> Now that I could see, the scars were Jasper's most dominant feature. It was hard to take my eyes off his ravaged neck and jaw—hard to believe that even a vampire could have survived so many sets of teeth ripping into his throat. Instinctively, I tensed to defend myself. Any vampire who saw Jasper would have had the same reaction. The scars were like a lighted billboard. Dangerous, they screamed. How many vampires had tried to kill Jasper? Hundreds? Thousands? The same number that had died in the attempt. (*Breaking Dawn*, 402.)

Jasper's reserve in describing his experiences reflects another nineteenth-century masculine trait, bearing the burden of war without complaint—"honorable scars were necessary sacrifices."[12]

The possibility that violence from the past can rise up in the present becomes a reality in the Cullens' lives. Threatened by the vengeful plot of the vampire Victoria, the family relies on Jasper's previous war experience to defend themselves. Throughout this process, however, the family remains reluctant to embrace the necessity of war: "'We'll need you to teach us, Jasper,' Carlisle finally said. 'How to destroy them.' Carlisle's jaw was hard, but I could see the pain in his eyes as he said the words. No one hated violence more than Carlisle." (*Eclipse*, 306.)

Most of the Cullens go to war dragging their feet, with the exception of Emmett—the other hypermasculine character of the family, and Jasper, who appears to take pleasure in revisiting his role of officer and key strategist. This enthusiasm sheds light on the darker side of

Jasper's manhood. While surrounded by a family that abhors violence, Jasper is the most willing to take risks and cut ethical corners, even considering feeding on human blood to gain a slight advantage.

> "We want to be as strong as possible," he [Edward] explained, still reluctant. "We'll probably hunt again on the way, looking for big game."
>
> "That makes you stronger?"
>
> He searched my face for something, but there was nothing to find but curiosity.
>
> "Yes," he finally said. "Human blood makes us the strongest, though only fractionally." Jasper's been thinking about cheating—adverse as he is to the idea, he's nothing if not practical—but he won't suggest it. He knows what Carlisle will say. (*Eclipse*, 316–317.)

Or using Bella as bait for the enemy:

> "If Bella was actually there in the clearing," Jasper explained to her, "it would drive them insane. They wouldn't be able to concentrate on anything but her. It would make picking them off truly easy."
>
> Edward's glare had Jasper backtracking.
>
> "Of course it's too dangerous for her. It was just an errant thought," he said quickly. But he looked at me from the corner of his eyes, and the look was wistful. (*Eclipse*, 407.)

The other Cullens try to keep such violent tendencies at a distance. While they seek aid from like-minded vampires, they are reluctant to risk involving the "family" that created Jasper; a decision that again compares the "civilized" manner of the Northern vampires with the warmongering of Southern vampires: "Edward answered in a low voice. "Jasper thinks we could use some help. Tanya's family isn't the only choice we have. Carlisle's trying to track down a few old friends, and Jasper is looking up Peter and Charlotte.

He's considering talking to Maria . . . but no one really wants to involve the southerners." (*Eclipse*, 311.)

This description mirrors that of Northern critiques of Southern masculinity. Setting up a stereotypical comparison of civilized Northern men versus irrational Southern rebels, General Sherman remarked that he would not burn the college library while the rest of Columbia, South Carolina, was razed. "Far from destroying books, I will send them here. If there had been a few more books in this part of the world there would not have been this difficulty."[13] Where the North remains characterized by reason (in its own eyes, at least), the South suffers because of its alleged unrestrained passion.

This penchant for irrational destruction repels Carlisle and his family, but parallels between their experience and nineteenth-century warfare go even further. The battles depicted in the Twilight Saga revisit a central theme of the Civil War—the fight of brother against brother. Although the Cullens' "vegetarian" lifestyle sets them apart from most other vampires, they still recoil from the idea of killing others. The impending fight not only threatens the tranquility of their world, but it could also rip the very fabric of their tightly woven family to shreds.

> "This isn't good," Jasper said. "It's too even a fight. We'd have the upper hand in skill, but not numbers. We'd win, but at what price?" His tense eyes flashed to Alice's face and away.
>
> I wanted to scream out loud as I grasped what Jasper meant. We would win, but we would lose. Some wouldn't survive. I looked around the room at their faces—Jasper, Alice, Emmett, Rose, Esme, Carlisle . . . Edward—the faces of my family. (*Eclipse*, 309.)

The Cullens' preparations for, and debates over, their imminent battle with Victoria's army of newborn vampires mirror the problems faced by Union officers in the Civil War.

> What General Sherman described as the "awful fact" of the war was that victory would mean devastating loss of life through the

> Union ranks. As Charles Royster noted, "The South contained a certain number of men—he twice mentioned the figure 300,000—who would not stop fighting. If the North wanted to reunite the nation under the federal government, these men would have to be killed. Killing them would unavoidably entail the deaths of many Northerners."[14]

The peace-loving Cullens are unwillingly thrown into a war against their own kind in which casualties among their small family appear unavoidable. They fight only to protect their values and those they love; they have no other choice. Before that battle is even reached, however, the Cullens face another crisis: the possibility that their close-knit coven will break up because of "the weakest link" in their chain of kinship.[15]

Desertion

> "There is already a heap of men gone home," wrote a Mississippi private to his wife in November 1862, "and a heap says if their familys get to suffering that they will go [too]. A month later a distressed officer in Bragg's Army of Tennessee declared that "desertions are multiplying so fast in this army that almost one-third of it is gone."
>
> —*James McPherson,* Battle Cry of Freedom[16]

> "When you live for the fight, for the blood, the relationships you form are tenuous and easily broken. I walked away without a backward glance."
>
> —*Jasper* (Eclipse, *299*)

Jasper and Alice's relationship seems almost perfect throughout the Twilight Saga. Deeply in love and devoted to each other, their closeness represents an underlying threat that explodes onto the scene in the final book of the series, *Breaking Dawn*. While Jasper's idealized manhood paints him as a desirable partner, his connection to Alice provokes the question of whether he has any other loyalties.

> Jasper, again. It was strange. In the Cullen family, Jasper was always a little on the fringe, part of things but never the center of them. It was my unspoken assumption that he was only there for Alice. I had the sense that he would follow Alice anywhere, but that this lifestyle was not his first choice. The fact that he was less committed to it than the others was probably why he had more difficulty keeping it up. (*Eclipse*, 283.)

From the beginning of the series we learn that Jasper and Alice react to each other first and think of others later.

> "Where's Alice?" I asked Edward anxiously. He looked at the granola bar he was slowly pulverizing between his fingertips while he answered. "She's with Jasper."
>
> "Is he okay?"
>
> "He's gone away for a while."
>
> "What? Where?"
>
> Edward shrugged. "Nowhere in particular."
>
> "And Alice, too," I said with quiet desperation. Of course, if Jasper needed her, she would go. (*New Moon*, 54–55.)

In the second volume of the Twilight Saga, *New Moon*, Bella is deserted by Edward and his family primarily because of Jasper's inability to control his violent nature. This loss of control engenders ambivalence about Jasper's manhood. His strength has a cost.

> "How's Jasper?"
>
> She [Alice] sighed. "He's very unhappy with himself. It's all so much more of a challenge for him, and he hates feeling weak." (*New Moon*, 43.)

Beyond simple weakness, Jasper's loss of control suggests that his manhood remains tied to an animalistic penchant for unrestrained brutality. Inflamed by the sight and scent of Bella's blood, Jasper lashes out at his own family in the attempt to reach his prey: "Jasper struggled against Emmett's unbreakable grasp, twisting around, reaching toward his brother with his bared teeth, his eyes still past reason." (*New Moon*, 30.)

This lack of rational thought again invites the comparison of constructed male stereotypes—a sober Northern man pitted against the unrestrained, and terribly dangerous, Southern man. Edward—the "civilized" Northern vampire, is able to control his bloodlust even though Bella's blood tempts him more than anything ever has. Jasper cannot claim a similar connection to Bella, or a personal struggle with her blood in particular, yet even the minimal presence of blood sends him into a feeding frenzy—an outburst of crazed violence that can be remedied only by his physical removal first from the scene that then leads to the entire family's moving away from Forks to the more isolated vampire refuge in Denali, Alaska, a decision that leaves Bella alone and bereft.

This potential for abandonment reappears in the series' concluding book, *Breaking Dawn*. In the face of the crisis posed by the impending arrival of the deadly Volturi, Alice and Jasper vanish: "Carlisle turned the page around so that we all could read it. 'Don't look for us. There isn't time to waste . . . We're so sorry that we have to leave you this way, with no goodbyes or explanations. It's the only way for us. We love you.'" (*Breaking Dawn*, 558.)

The sudden absence of two key members of the Cullen family grieves both the Cullens and readers of the saga—such is the effect of desertion in literature and in history. Desertion evokes betrayal and loss, and it was often a harsh reality during the Civil War. Trauma from battle, untenable living conditions, and simple fear all fed into the steady stream of desertion by soldiers, which General Lee described in 1865 as an "epidemic," as fighting dragged on, battles became more bloody, and supplies dwindled.[17]

When Alice and Jasper leave amid the family's crisis, it calls into question whether true bonds of love and loyalty ever existed between the couple and the other Cullens.

> I'd always thought of the Cullens as a whole and indivisible unit. Suddenly, I remembered that it had not always been so. Carlisle had created Edward, Esme, Rosalie, and Emmett;

> Edward had created me. We were physically linked by blood and venom. I never thought of Alice and Jasper as separate—as adopted into the family. But in truth, Alice had adopted the Cullens. She had shown up with her unconnected past, bringing Jasper with her, and fit herself into the family that was already there. Both she and Jasper had known another life outside the Cullen family. (*Breaking Dawn*, 560.)

Even more than the strength of family ties, Jasper's individual character comes into question. Do his masculine traits include selfishness and self-preservation? Prior to his departure, Jasper has grappled with his place in the Cullen family. Bella's transformation into a vampire pits Jasper's version of who he is against Bella's experience as a new vampire. According to Jasper:

> Newborns [vampires] are dangerous, they are still possible to defeat if you know what you're doing. They're incredibly powerful physically, for the first year or so, and if they're allowed to bring strength to bear they can crush an older vampire with ease. But they are slaves to their instincts, and thus predictable. Usually they have no skill in fighting, only muscle and ferocity. (*Eclipse*, 290.)

Jasper's description of a newborn vampire parallels that of the uncivilized, hunter stereotype that he himself embodied while in the South. He anticipates that Bella will emerge as a newborn vampire full of bloodlust and brutality, but instead of treating this possibility with sobriety it becomes a form of entertainment.

> "Jasper's going to win the bet," she [Rosalie] said smugly.
>
> Emmett's laughter stopped immediately, and he studied me with appraising eyes.
>
> "What bet?" I demanded, pausing.
>
> He sighed. "They're betting on how many times you . . . slip up in the first year."
>
> "Oh." I grimaced, trying to hide my sudden horror as I realized what he meant.

> "They have a bet about how many people I'll kill?"
>
> "Yes," he admitted unwillingly. "Rosalie thinks your temper will turn the odds in Jasper's favor."
>
> I felt a little high. "Jasper's betting high."
>
> "It will just make him feel better if you have a hard time adjusting. He's tired of being the weakest link." (*Eclipse*, 343.)

When Bella's first days as a vampire counter Jasper's experience, he cannot accept that his vision of the vampire world might not have been accurate—an indictment of his personal choices rather than an innate characteristic he could not control.

> "I can't understand, I can't bear this." I watched in surprise as Jasper strode out the back door . . .
>
> [Edward to Bella] "He's wondering if the newborn madness is really as difficult as we've always thought, or if, with the right focus and attitude, anyone could do as well as Bella. Even now—perhaps he only has such difficulty because he believes it's natural and unavoidable. Maybe if he expected more of himself, he would rise to those expectations. You're making him question a lot of deep rooted assumptions, Bella." (*Breaking Dawn*, 465–466.)

Plagued by self-doubt and continuing to struggle against the violence within, Jasper seems to have reached a tipping point that necessitates his abandoning the family. He's one of the few Cullens who is not repelled by violence. His companions' inability to assess the strength of their enemies frustrates him: "'We fight,' he [Emmett] said calmly. 'We can't win,' Jasper growled." (*Breaking Dawn*, 549.)

Faced with insurmountable odds, Jasper and Alice flee without explanation. Their disappearance devastates the Cullen family, who can only assume that the young couple valued their own lives and love over the well-being of the family. Until the concluding chapters of *Breaking Dawn*, Jasper thus appears to play the role of deserter—the man who chooses himself over the greater good, whose true manliness is ultimately called into question because it is self-serving.

The Best and Worst We Could Be

> How true it is that, for a nation to be great, it must aim at something above its animal nature! We are in the act of transition from the animal to the intellectual. War, civil war, with its dread punishments, is not without its uses. In no other school than that of war can society learn subordination, in no other can it be made to appreciate order.
>
> —*John William Draper,* Thoughts on Civil Policy, *1867*[18]

> "In so many years of slaughter and carnage, I'd lost nearly all of my humanity. I was undeniably a nightmare, a monster of the grisliest kind. Yet each time I found another human victim, I would feel a faint prick of remembrance for that other life."
>
> —*Jasper* (Eclipse, *300*)

The tale of the Cullen family, and Jasper's individual journey, end on a hopeful note. Not the deserter he could have been, we presume Jasper will go on to an eternal life of contentment with Alice at his side. Despite the tidy conclusion of the Twilight Saga, Jasper's ongoing struggle with his destructive side points to a similar conflict in the American psyche. Like the conclusion of *Breaking Dawn,* the Civil War concluded with the restoration of the Union and the Reconstruction of the South, but it left many explosive cultural conflicts unresolved.

The competing masculinities of North and South were temporarily united; "the sores of war were closed by a culture of 'character.' . . . Soldiers on both sides had sacrificed equally and embodied the virtues of manliness and honor."[19] The violence of the past cannot be erased, however, and regional divisions still mar our society. Romanticized depictions of the war blind us to its terrible realities, just as Jasper's powers can make world seem better, but at the cost of distorting reality. When conflicted about her place within the Cullen family, Bella questions her own ability to gauge her safety, and even her free will of judgment, because of his presence: "I knew I couldn't trust my feelings with Jasper there." (*Twilight*, 411.)

The American Civil War remains a bloody beacon in the waters of the past, calling our attention, both fascinating and repelling us, forcing us to question our values and our very nature.[20] As Charles Royster pointed out, during the Civil War "Americans surprised themselves with the extent of violence they could attain."[21] Jasper Whitlock Hale raises the specter of the Civil War and with it the potential for violence within America's boundaries.

Just as Jasper was haunted by his past, our collective national character glances back over its shoulder, catching glimpses of smoke rising from razed cities and hearing cries of dying soldiers, ever wary about our haunted past rising from the grave to imperil our present. When we confess these fears, we doubt their truth, focusing instead on soldiers who embodied idealized masculine archetypes without considering the darker side of the violence embodied within them. After all, Jasper can "make you feel all warm and fuzzy about spilling your guts, don't forget that." (*Twilight*, 316.)

Notes

1. "Twilight Series," www.fanpop.com/spots/Twilight-series/images/1815435/title/jasper-hale.

2. "Reuben Allen Pierson to William H. Pierson," January 31, 1862, in *Brothers in Gray*, ed. Thomas Cutrer and T. Michael Parrish (Baton Rouge: Louisiana State Univ. Press, 1997), 77.

3. E. Anthony Rotundo, *American Manhood: Transformations in Masculinity from the Revolution to the Modern Era* (New York: Basic Books, 1993), 10–30.

4. James McPherson, "The United States at Midcentury," in *Battle Cry of Freedom* (Oxford: Oxford Univ. Press, 1988), 6–46.

5. Richard Slotkin, *Regeneration through Violence* (Norman: Univ. of Oklahoma, 1973), 397.

6. Lorri Glover, "Slaveholding and the Destiny of the Republic's Southern Sons," in *Southern Sons* (Baltimore: Johns Hopkins Univ. Press, 2007), 165–179.

7. Slotkin, *Regeneration Through Violence*, 462.

8. Ibid., 465.

9. On mastery and racial politics as the catalyst for new constructions of masculinity and manhood, see Gail Bederman, *Manliness and Civilization: A Cultural History of Gender and Race in the United States, 1880–1917* (Chicago: Univ. of Chicago Press, 1995).

10. From "Days and Events, 1860–1866," in *Voices from the Civil War*, ed. Milton Meltzer (New York: Thomas Crowell, 1989), 65.

11. Giorgio Agamben, *State of Exception* (Chicago: Univ. of Chicago Press, 2005).

12. Dora Costa and Matthew Kahn, *Heroes and Cowards: The Social Face of War* (Princeton, NJ: Princeton Univ. Press, 2008), 160.

13. Charles Royster, *The Destructive War: William Tecumseh Sherman, Stonewall Jackson, and the Americans* (New York: Vintage, 1991), 30.

14. Royster, *The Destructive War*, 338.

15. As Jasper struggles with his desire to hunt humans again, he is frequently described as "weak" or as the "weakest link" in the family—a label that he struggles with as it calls into question his ability to restrain himself as befits the ideal man of Northern "civilization." According to Gail Bederman, "The logic of 'civilization' gave coherence to potentially confusing blends of manliness and masculinity, self-mastery and unrestrainable passion, refinement and savagery, by rooting them all in "civilization's" larger narrative of millennial advancement towards a higher race and perfect manhood." *Manliness and Civilization*, 218.

16. McPherson, *Battle Cry of Freedom*, 613.

17. Ibid, 820–821. See also Charles Ramsdell, "Failure and Disintegration," in *Behind the Lines in the Southern Confederacy* (Baton Rouge: Louisiana State Univ. Press, 1944, 1972), 83–122.

18. Royster, *The Destructive War*, 381.

19. Costa and Kahn, *Heroes and Cowards*, 161.

20. On the legacy of the Confederacy in American culture, see Tony Horwitz, *Confederates in the Attic* (New York: Pantheon, 1998). For the influence of the Civil War on American popular culture, see Jim Cullen, *The Civil War in Popular Culture* (Washington, DC: Smithsonian Institution, 1995).

21. Royster, *The Destructive War*, xi.

Like Other American Families, Only Not

The Cullens and the "Ideal" Family in American History

Kyra Glass von der Osten

Do you realize what century this is?" Bella Swan demands when Edward insists that she marry him before he turns her into a vampire to spend eternity with him. (*Eclipse*, 276.) For her, young marriage (along with abstinence until marriage) could make sense only in another time, another world. To some extent she is right: Edward, or rather the Twilight Saga, does not know what century it is, or even which decade it is, since social changes can easily occur in only a decade. The Cullen family's behavior and sense of morality and norms have not developed according to the norms of a single time and place, but rather through a process that has changed the nature of the family throughout history. In some respects, such as Edward's rejection of premarital sex, the Cullens are very traditional; in others, like their apparent belief in equality between the sexes, they are not.

Commentators often attempt to describe texts as either conservative or liberal, feminist or antifeminist. These easy categorizations not only oversimplify texts but they also overlook how even seemingly conservative elements of a text can challenge social norms. Stephenie Meyer's Twilight Saga defies easy categorization. Often justifiably considered conservative because of their use of an "erotics of abstinence," the Twilight novels are also sometimes seen as both antifeminist and a celebration of the nuclear family.[1] At the same time these stories have some oddly subversive elements that go well beyond the obvious presence of vampires, werewolves, and the occult. What makes these novels so interesting is that these subversive aspects are often intertwined with the text's most conservative elements.

From early on in the Twilight series, Bella and Edward Cullen's relationship is characterized by a series of tensions: between tradition and modernity, between conservative and liberal definitions of family, and between nuclear and extended families. These tensions are reflected in the influences on Bella, both from romance as depicted in the classics—novels by Jane Austen, *Wuthering Heights,* and *Romeo and Juliet*—and her mother's own aversion to young marriage. They're also present in the saga's depiction of relationships and family structures. The lives of the Cullen family members have spanned several centuries, and their family structure reflects the diverse social norms encountered at various points in history. The Twilight novels place families at the center of its action, families that have sometimes been seen as aligned with "traditional family values" because of the series' focus on abstinence. Yet a closer reading of the text reveals that the families that function successfully in the saga often don't match the "traditional" concept of a family, because they don't adhere to the nuclear family structure of a biological father and mother and their unmarried biological children. At the same time, biological families with "normal" members in the saga are depicted as either broken or, more often, given only cursory mention. This chapter will examine the families in the Twilight series, focusing on their dual function as both keepers of some traditional values (like premarital abstinence) and as kinship units based on unusual and nonbiological structures that function to protect their members and provide them with love and support.

In his book *Past, Present, and Personal,* historian John Demos notes that in modern America "there is a diffuse sense of 'crisis' about our domestic arrangements generally—a feeling that the family as we have traditionally known it is under siege and may even give way entirely."[2] The Twilight series responds to this sense of crisis, but not by returning to the kind of 1950s nuclear family and purposeful domesticity that once characterized the "norm" for American households, if only briefly.[3] This "norm" is the sort of family that is usually thought of in contemporary discussions of "family values," an aspect of a conservative political movement that continues to be important today. In her book *Public Vows,* historian Nancy Cott refers to this movement as a "vocal minority, effective beyond its numbers in electoral politics in the 1980s and 1990s," who addressed "the degradation of family life" and gave voice to "the desire to reinstate a patriarchal model of marriage with the husband/father as the provider and the primary authority figure."[4] The Twilight Saga reflects this concern: it depicts modern American families as unstable but does not resort to the conventional nuclear family as a solution. Edward makes requests that Bella sees as old-fashioned, but at the same time other aspects of their family, such as the equality between Jasper and Alice, have clearly changed with the times and do not reflect the model of a "traditional family."[5] In this chapter I will analyze the nontraditional aspects of the Cullens and their extended family to show how the Twilight Saga incorporates family structures from a broad spectrum of historical moments, sometimes defying historical norms entirely.

The Failure of Twilight's Traditional Family

It is no accident that Bella's move to Forks at the start of the saga is tied to the fact that she comes from a broken home. Bella moves to Forks because she feels that her presence puts a strain on her mother and her mother's new husband, who must travel for his job. The novel makes it clear that Bella's mother's marriage cannot provide Bella with an intact and stable family unit, nor did Bella have a conventional relationship with her mother. Bella's mother is portrayed as scatterbrained, and Bella constantly feels that she must take care of her. This pattern is repeated with Bella's father; after moving in, Bella quickly assumes responsibility for cooking and worries about her father's ability to fend for himself if she isn't home in time to make dinner for him. One of the few other human families we get to know intimately is that of her friend Jacob Black, who is in a similar situation. Jacob's mother has died, his sisters rarely come home, and his disabled father, Billy, needs Jacob to serve as his caregiver.

Where the traditional biological family fails, the nontraditional, nonnuclear Cullen family—whose members are not biologically related—thrives: its members are able protect one another and take care of one another. The Twilight saga makes it clear that the Cullens are stronger than most vampires *because* they are part of a family, and Alice tells Bella that even James's small coven of three was large for most vampires. Only the Volturi and, briefly, Victoria's coven, who live in large groups, can threaten the Cullens. Yet it is only the Cullens, and a similar group in Alaska, the Denalis, who behave as a family. Laurent and other vampires find this behavior fascinating, even if they can't maintain a family themselves.[6] Many vampires recognize the strength the Cullens and Denalis draw from being a family. The Cullens' strength as a family is even threatening to the Volturi, who become uneasy, in *Breaking Dawn*, at the size and perceived strength of the Cullen family.

Love Is the Tie That Binds

The Twilight Saga's definition of family as a mutually supportive group based on love becomes crucial, especially when examined against the historical backdrops of the various periods its members come from. Family historians, who have studied family structures and their changes over time, have found that in most historical cultures, economic concerns and social status have been the primary motivating factors in the choice of spouses and the formation of families.[7] Parents and communities tended to encourage (or dictate) matches that were based on practical needs, such as access to land that one family wanted to add to its property, a generous dowry, or the social standing needed by one or both spouse's families, rather than privileging feelings of romantic love or sexual desire. During the medieval period, however, the idea that romantic love should be considered in choosing a marriage partner began to take hold.[8] The concept began to influence Europeans' ideas about marriage by the sixteenth century and has been growing in importance ever since.[9] Overall, the shift toward seeing marriage as a relationship based on companionship, mutual attraction, and romantic love gradually displaced the notion of marriage as an economic arrangement, although, as we will see with Rosalie's story, many men and women continued to take into account these more practical considerations well into the twentieth century.

A second change, which became established among the middle and upper classes over the course of the nineteenth century, was a shift away from seeing children as economic contributors to the family. Industrialization meant that, increasingly, children from more affluent families were no longer working on a family farm or outside of the home as wage-labor. Families that could afford to began to move children out of wage-earning positions and limited children's work in family businesses and on farms. By the mid-twentieth century, education rather than work had become the central focus of children's lives. The move away from what Demos calls the family as "a community of work" solidified the notion that love and caregiving formed the basis for the boundaries of a family.[10] The Cullens, without any kind of biological connection or economic necessity to bind them, are an excellent example of the modern idea that love makes a family.

In *New Moon* Alice explains to Bella that generally vampires can't live in large groups; in the rare cases when they do, like the Volturi, it is for the kinds of political and economic reasons that had determined upper-class marriage decisions for much of the Volturi's three thousand years on earth. The Twilight Saga is clear about its preference for the love-based family model and demonstrates that love creates the stronger family. In this respect the Twilight series clearly values modern marriages based on love over the tradition of choosing partners who would bring the most resources and other advantages to the prospective spouse and family, the motivation that the Volturi continue to have. In *Breaking Dawn*, Eleazar discusses a member of the Volturi guard, Carmen, who can break the bonds between people. He tells them that "anything weaker than the bond between partners is in danger" but then assures his family, the Denalis (the only other love-based vampire family), that "those are weaker bonds than in our family, though. Abstaining from human blood makes us more civilized—lets us form true bonds of love." (*Breaking Dawn*, 603.) Here Eleazar presents the logic that a family based on bonds of love rather than shared goals or economic interests is the stronger unit.[11]

Although the series champions the modern notion of a family bound by love, in other respects the families presented in positive terms in the Twilight Saga are not traditional in the sense used in the political discourse of conservative "family values" groups during the 1980s and 1990s and into the twenty-first century.[12] The term "traditional marriage" has been used by the conservative "family values" movement to refer to a married heterosexual couple, generally with biological children, living in a nuclear family household, preferably with a breadwinner father and a homemaker mother. But in many crucial ways I will discuss the successful families highlighted in the saga, the Cullens and the Quileute wolf pack, are intensely *non*traditional.

"Barren" Wives and the Kin We Choose: Families That Aren't Biological

Before Renesmee's arrival, the Cullens do not have the traditional legitimizing biological familial bonds, or (most likely) even the bond of legal adoption; instead, membership in their family is based in part on the fact that they are "others," and marginalized in society at large. In many ways this places the Cullens in much the same situation as the lesbian and gay kinship groups discussed in Kath Weston's *Family We Choose*, which examines various kinds of gay and lesbian families built through friendship, adoption, and romantic networks whose members are chosen as adults to join the family, rather than being limited to families formed by birth or marriage. It is the status of the members of these families as an "other" in a society, the necessity of keeping secrets from all of the "normal" people around them (passing for being straight in the case of gay households, or passing for being human in the case of the Cullens), that makes their belonging to these families of "others" so important. As Edward explains to Bella when he shows her the home he shares with his parents and four siblings, "It's the one place we never have to hide." (*Twilight*, 329.) Like some of the LGBT households Weston studies, the Cullens' chosen family is constructed as a family that consists solely of "others" who, by and large, are excluded from membership in other types of families because they are not human and are perceived as dangerous. Like many of the families studied by Weston, the Cullens aren't related to one another. With the exception of the siblings Leah and Seth Clearwater, there are no members of either the Cullens or the wolf pack who would be part of a biological nuclear family. While patrilineal ancestry is very important to the wolf pack, the Cullens have absolutely no members, until Renesmee, who are even distantly related biologically.

To be part of the Cullen family, live by their rules, and take part in their family-centered life was a conscious choice for every family member. It is important that Bella, by the beginning of *Eclipse*, comes to frame her decision to become a vampire as not solely motivated by her desire to spend an eternity with Edward but more generally by a desire to join the Cullen *family*. This is a logical extension of her decision in *New Moon* to go around Edward, who wants her to remain human, and pose the question of her fate to the entire Cullen family; she asks them to vote on whether she should be turned into a vampire. By asking them if they want her, she is not only asking whether they think she should become a vampire but more importantly, whether they want her to be part of their family. This becomes clear when Rosalie votes no, explaining that it is not that she does not want Bella for a sister but that she does not want to take being human from her. For Bella, becoming a vampire, an other, is thus presented as becoming part of a new family, based on otherness, choice, and nonbiological ties. Despite initially thinking of Alice as "not really" Edward's sister at the beginning of *New Moon*, by the end of *New Moon* and throughout the rest of the saga, Bella not only considers Alice to be Edward's sister but begins to think of her as her own sister as well, as much of a "real" sibling as Seth and Leah are to each other.

Yet historically, a family united by biological ties was seen as the only sort that was considered "real," fulfilling one of the essential functions assumed to be part of the American family: procreation. Even in times like the 1920s, when societal norms were more relaxed, many reformers drew a clear line between "childless marriages and the procreative family."[13] With only extremely rare exceptions, the vampires are not able to reproduce in this traditional sense.

Certainly "making" a new vampire can be thought of as a kind of reproduction, but traditional procreation, the conception of children, seems to be impossible for vampires at first. Even the attempt to create a substitute child, turning babies or toddlers into vampires, is absolutely forbidden. As a result, the immortal children become the ultimate taboo. For many of the Cullen women, and the sole female werewolf, this inability to procreate has a profound psychological impact. One of the primary reasons Rosalie discourages Bella from becoming a vampire, and why she in fact envies her, is Rosalie's strong desire to be a mother. While Esme seems relatively content with mothering Edward, Rosalie, Alice, Jasper, and Emmett as "substitutes," Rosalie wants to have a child—her own baby. This despair is echoed by Leah in *Breaking Dawn*, when she worries that she is "a genetic dead end," which leads her to sympathize with Rosalie and Bella, who are risking Bella's life so that she can have a baby. (*Breaking Dawn*, 317.)

In *History of the Wife*, Marilyn Yalom observes that "throughout the ancient world, the primary obligation of a wife was to produce offspring."[14] Women who could not have a child would be shamed and seen as "barren." Sometimes they were replaced with a second or third wife in polygamous societies, and they were often discarded by their husbands if they proved unable to have children. The historical association between marriage and procreation, and between womanhood and motherhood, is thus extremely powerful. Rosalie, who was turned during the Depression, grew up during a time when Americans were starting to have smaller families. But the link between marriage and childbearing was still unquestioned during her youth, and she clearly accepted that norm. Bella seems to not fully understand Rosalie's worldview. She has grown up in a very different culture in which choosing not to have children is an option, and during *her* youth families without children made up 62 percent of American households.[15] It makes sense then that Bella is willing to give up the idea of having a child in order to be with Edward, while for Rosalie losing the ability to have a child was a crushing blow.

While Bella's attitudes toward childbearing reflect her own moment in history, when she becomes pregnant, the book's treatment of this event begins to blur historical lines, and some characters even break from the roles that had previously defined them as "traditional." Bella's extremely dangerous pregnancy indeed could be part of the family history from a past century. By modern standards, pregnancy and childbirth before the twentieth century (and even up to World War II) often threatened the life of the mother. When Carlisle was turned in the mid-seventeenth century, women still frequently died as a result of childbirth. A wide variety of causes—from puerperal fever ("childbed fever") to babies stuck in breech position during labor—caused the death and injury of thousands of women during or shortly after labor in the London of Carlisle's youth. Hygienic and medical innovations introduced during the nineteenth and twentieth centuries eventually helped to reduce these risks. Lacking the benefit of some of today's methods and medications (or vampire venom), surgical interventions like caesarian sections would usually have killed the mother before the late nineteenth century and were done only to save the baby when the mother was presumed to be beyond saving. Even in Edward's youth, childbirth was still a relatively common cause of death. Rosalie alludes to this fact in *Breaking Dawn* when she says of the deaths of the mothers of children from vampire fathers that back then, "even the normal births went badly half the time." (*Breaking Dawn*, 303.) The fears about Bella's supernatural pregnancy are similar to the anxieties that Edward would have had if, as Bella imagines from time to time, she and Edward could have married and had children in 1918 as humans.[16]

The significant change in Bella and Rosalie's relationship after Bella becomes pregnant is consistent with the role that pregnancy played in women's relationships in earlier historical periods. While Edward sees the alliance between Rosalie and Bella as somewhat sinister, Carlisle, having been born in the seventeenth century, would have recognized it. Today the husband or father is often the primary support system for a pregnant woman, codified in the role of "birthing partner" in the hospital delivery room that has been popularized through birthing classes for middle-class couples. But before the transition to giving birth inside a hospital (a change introduced during the early and mid-twentieth century), it was usually a female relative who helped a woman in childbirth. This time together could become very important to both of the women involved. Historian Daniel Blake Smith observes that "women often developed close emotional attachments through the care they provided each other during childbirth and recovery."[17] Seen through Jacob's and Edward's eyes, Rosalie's commitment to seeing Bella's pregnancy through appears to be driven by a selfish desire for Bella's child and an indifference to Bella's safety. Although, even after the child is born, Bella and Rosalie continue to have a mutually supportive relationship. Seen through a historical lens, however, Rosalie was fulfilling what her normal role as the sister-in-law of a pregnant woman would have been in earlier periods, when even a normal pregnancy could be very dangerous.

Edward's reaction to the pregnancy, which he first proposes terminating, is hardly that of a modern "traditional" family conservative.

But his quick offer to essentially abort his and Bella's baby is *not* inconsistent with the attitudes of the culture he grew up in. Leslie Reagan's work on the period when abortion was illegal in America observed that during the end of the nineteenth century and the beginning of the twentieth century, when abortion had only recently become illegal, abortion continued to be an "open secret" accepted by many Americans as a birth control method.[18] Being party to an abortion would have been even less of a stretch for Carlisle, who had lived through the eighteenth and early nineteenth centuries, when abortions were legal under common law until quickening (defined as the stage of a pregnancy when the woman can feel the baby move).[19]

Historians have researched and documented the increasing availability of contraception and abortion after the mid-nineteenth century, as Americans began to try to limit the size of their families or avoid having children altogether. As in today's society, this trend met opposition from a "purity movement" and the American Medical Association, which sought to outlaw abortion.[20] By the time Edward was born at the turn of the century, however, the use of contraception or abortion (which was illegal in almost every state by this time) in order to limit family size had become quite common.[21] In fact at least one study of working-class clients of Margaret Sanger's birth control clinic in the late 1920s, just after Edward's turning, found that 20 percent of all pregnancies had been aborted.[22] While it was more common for boyfriends than husbands to be involved in their partners' abortions, many husbands did support their wives in having abortions and often for the very reasons that Edward wants Bella to have one: from a reasonable fear of the risk associated with childbirth.[23] While Bella's image of Edward's life is that of a sort of *Anne of Green Gables* innocence, in fact Edward's human life ended on the cusp of a set of radical social changes almost as important as those seen in the late twentieth century. During the 1920s, approaches to sex and relationships radically changed; contraception use became even more common, and adolescents had begun dating outside the home unsupervised by parents in the early 1900s.[24]

Twilight and the Nonnuclear Family

It is in its rejection of the nuclear family that the Twilight Saga presents families that are the most strikingly nontraditional. While historians once thought that Americans and Western Europeans mostly lived in extended families (with several generations in one household) and later shifted to nuclear families (with a mother, a father, and children living without other relatives), more recent research suggests that this was never the case; one historian has even referred to the idea of widespread extended families in the past as a "vulgar notion."[25] The nuclear family was the norm among Europeans who settled in the thirteen colonies (although there might be some exceptions in each community), and this has continued to be true throughout American history.[26] At the same time, however, some Native American cultures did not have the nuclear family as their fundamental household unit, a reality significant enough that the American legal system attempted to actively encourage, or even force, Native Americans to make the nuclear family the norm.[27] These subtleties become very important in the Twilight Saga, which emphasizes a move away from strictly nuclear family forms. For the Cullens, all of whom are white, the choice to live in an extended family household is a significant break from American tradition, a fully nontraditional choice. For the Quileute wolf pack, however, the move toward a largely extended family form can be understood as potentially a *return* to tradition.

Children are often seen as the center of the nuclear family. The introduction of Bella and Edward's daughter, Renesmee, in *Breaking Dawn* creates a long narrative sequence that goes back and forth concerning the possibility of their having a nuclear family. Ultimately, Renesmee serves to solidify the Cullens' choice of an extended family form, and therefore its break from the norm. At no point was the extended family common in most American communities, and the time when a child's birth signaled the extension, rather than the solidification, of a nuclear family predated any of the Cullens' lifetimes. When Bella first finds out she's pregnant, the possibility of Bella and Edward's forming a more traditional, biologically based, nuclear family first arises. However this image of "baby makes three" is quickly dashed when Edward announces his commitment to ending the pregnancy. While in utero, Renesmee affects various families in the story in unexpected ways. Initially she appears to divide families: she not only splits the Cullens between those who favor carrying the pregnancy to term (Rosalie, Emmett, and Esme) and those who do not (most notably Carlisle and Edward), but her existence also divides the wolf pack. As a result, Jacob claims his ancestral right to the role of Alpha and splits off from the main pack, which wants to kill Renesmee, and as a result Bella. At the same time, Renesmee's conception also leads to stronger ties between Bella and members of her new extended family, notably Rosalie, who stands with her against Edward.

While Renesmee appears to be the "missing piece" for Edward and Bella's own nuclear family, in the end her conception means that Edward and Bella will never form a fully separate household of their own. While this outcome appears possible for a moment—when Edward senses Renesmee's emotions while still a fetus and becomes committed to seeing the baby safely born—the moment that she is born, Renesemee in fact forestalls forever the possibility of a separate, isolated family unit when Jacob imprints on her, assuring an extended family structure. When Jacob imprints on Renesmee as an infant, his feelings are not at all romantic, avoiding any hints of pedophilia, but rather they consist of intense and absolute devotion to her. This imprinting derails any possibility of a "normal," three-person household and family life. Edward and Bella discuss moving away for a time, and despite the love of the Cullen family for Renesmee, particularly Rosalie, the Cullens have accepted that this might happen. But Jacob cannot stand to have Renesmee leave, and so tips off Bella's father, Charlie, to what is going on in order to make certain that Bella stays. This choice extends Renesmee's family from the vampire world to that of the wolf pack and human worlds as well.

As a child Renesmee functions to unite families and bring them together. This begins with Charlie, who quickly warms to the idea of being a grandfather and is charmed by the child at once. It is at this moment that Bella realizes with joy that she might have "my new family and some of my old as well." (*Breaking Dawn*, 517.) Bella's loving feelings for Jacob, which shifted from wanting him as a brother to seeing him as a romantic possibility, and which have caused them both so much pain, are now resolved into something else. Jacob is now, as Bella has insisted he was meant to be, part of her family, but with a new person to love, it no longer causes him or her pain. Jacob's imprinting on Renesmee also resolves the conflict within the wolf pack family and between them and the Cullens. The wolves could now never hurt, and in fact must protect, Renesmee, because "no wolf would ever intentionally destroy a brother" by hurting the object of their imprinting since "the pain of such a thing would be intolerable for the whole pack." (*Breaking Dawn*, 456.) Renesmee's birth thus creates an even larger extended family for the Cullens by including the pack as part of their kinship network, an alliance that might be further cemented by Charlie's involvement with Sue Clearwater.

The conclusion of the saga thus suggests that the nuclear family by itself is insufficient: when the Volturi come to destroy Renesmee and the Cullens, Bella and Edward know that they will not be able to protect Renesmee themselves. Even the Cullens as a unit cannot protect her; this challenge requires the joint effort of their entire extended family, including the wolves, the Denalis, and their friends. While Bella and Edward's unique powers play crucial roles, they need the support of the entire extended family in order to succeed. Bella even requires the Cullens' extended kinship and community network to discover and unlock her own powers. This large network of kin and allies who unite to resolve a crisis, and the renewal and establishing of new ties between them, indicates a historical tradition as old, or older, than Carlisle: a period when extended families and the community alliances that marriages formed were essential.

What *Is* a "Traditional" Family, Anyway?

The Twilight Saga includes many historically specific references, using an event like the American Civil War, for example, as the backdrop for a particular scene or character. But the series deals with the history of the family quite differently, mixing and blending aspects of family life from different periods together in ways that often don't reflect the lives of families in any particular historical time and place. The history of the family must be looked upon as a process rather than a single event, as the composition, work, and functions of the family changed over centuries. The definition of an "ideal" family in America has always been, and continues to be, in a state of flux. These changes are not necessarily "progress," and sometimes a pattern repeats itself. Carlisle has witnessed most of American history, and he must have observed the cyclical nature of some aspects of it. Historian Bert Adams refers to the Victorian era as the nuclear family's "period of greatest ascendancy," but at the same time, the number of households organized in this way peaked in absolute numbers during the 1950s and 1960s.[28] Although Bella often reflects on the fact that she and Edward quite literally are nearly from different centuries, in fact their worlds have some important historical similarities. Significant changes in dating and sexual mores occurred during the early twentieth century, coming to fruition in the 1920s, paralleling the changes in these areas that took place during the late twentieth century.[29] In some ways the family was in as much of a state of flux during Edward's youth as it is today.

The Twilight series sometimes incorporates historical features of traditional family life outside of the norm for the specific period it is discussing. The idea that marriage should be primarily based on love only gradually established itself in America and Europe after the eighteenth century. Indeed, as Marilyn Yalom has noted, "in the past, most marriages were affairs of the pocketbook rather than affairs of the heart."[30] Although the love match was always an important consideration in colonial American courtship, economic and social factors became less important over time; these changes occurred at different rates among different social groups, however. The lower classes generally accepted love as the primary motivation for marriage much earlier than upper classes and aristocracy in Europe and America, for whom issues of wealth and status played a bigger role.[31] These older, financially driven motives were very clear in Rosalie's ill-fated match to a rich man from a high-status family, who turned out to be violent and cruel. Here, too, the Twilight stories make use of history in a fashion that plays with what was really more typical for each historical period: when Rosalie became engaged in 1933, among Americans the love match was by far the most common and socially approved form of marriage. Thus, Rosalie's family's attempt to match her with a man of wealth and status was actually more appropriate to an earlier time. It was certainly plausible, however, given her family's social standing, the nation's economic status, and Rosalie's exceptional value (her stunning beauty) on the marriage market. Nonetheless, Edward's assertion that he would have married Bella in 1918 because he would have loved her was more typical of the attitudes of the period.

This combination of conflicting but historically accurate situations creates a kind of historical pastiche throughout the Twilight series. Bella and Edward's relationship can be seen as an example of this sort of historical collage, particularly their decision to marry. Bella clearly sees Edward's insistence that they marry, and wait to have sex until they do so, as traditional. She believes that they are too young to marry but tells herself that such a marriage would not have been unusual in Edward's time, nothing to remark on at all.

In fact, Edward's "traditional" values are more consistent with the values championed in the popular culture of the 1950s. In Edward's youth, middle-class couples actually married *later* in life then they did in the 1950s. In 1956, the median age at marriage among Americans was 20.1 years old for women and 22.5 years old for men. But in 1900, around the time that Edward was born, a typical bridegroom was about 26 years old, although brides (whose median age was 21.9 years in 1900) were somewhat younger. In 1920, Edward would still have been considered a rather young bridegroom, since the median age at marriage was 24.6 years old for men.[32] At no time in American history would 17 or 18 years old have been the "average" age of a bridegroom, and Edward would have been unusually young for his own generation. Had he been "that boy," as he claims, who would have married Bella at the age of seventeen, then he would have been bucking the trends of his culture nearly as much as she is doing in 2006. When Bella asks him, "Do you realize what century this is?" she attributes his desire to marry young to the period he comes from; in fact, even in 1918 it might have had more to do with his own personality.

The results of Bella and Edward's marriage also represent a pastiche of historical elements. While the wedding itself, styled to be reminiscent of 1918, appears to move the relationship toward the traditional family life that Bella associates with Edward's time, the two are not motivated by the usual historical motivations for marriage: economic reasons, social status, and procreation (which at the time Edward and Bella believed was impossible) but instead are motivated by love. The spectacle of their marriage (and the inclusion of the Denalis and Renée and Charlie) does allow the marriage to fulfill one of the traditional and unique roles of marriage in earlier historical periods, the acquisition of in-laws. Historian Stephanie Coontz has argued that this function of marriage was important because "marriage spoke to the needs of the larger group. It converted strangers into relatives and extended cooperative relations beyond the immediate family."[33] This was particularly true before "the notion of free choice and marriage for love triumph as a cultural ideal."[34] In Bella and Edward's marriage, then, two of the most essential elements of modern American marriage—choice and the love match—are combined, with a priority placed on the extended family, which has never been prevalent in American history.

Similarly, while the wedding itself points to the idea of Edward as traditional, the reality of their marriage has a thoroughly contemporary result, finally achieving equality between them. Throughout the Twilight Saga, Bella has been concerned that they were not truly equal; she has longed to "be partners, like Alice and Jasper." (*Eclipse*, 435.) When she becomes a vampire in *Breaking Dawn*, this aspiration is finally realized. The shift in their relationship to true equality, in which Bella no longer needs Edward to protect her, is particularly modern. This makes Bella and Edward's relationship a fascinating mix of historical elements: traditional views on premarital sex, a contemporary emphasis on equality between partners, and an endorsement of the quite ancient practice of living in extended family households.

This blurring of historical boundaries, or incorporating details from different periods into a historical collage, can be seen throughout the Cullen family. As Bella observes, Jasper is truly a partner with Alice, despite his having been turned during the Victorian era. Esme and Carlisle also seem to be relative equals, but Carlisle's role in the family can also be considered quite traditional because he is the moral center and leader of the family. This depiction of the father as the patriarch and keeper of the family's values is more consistent with the seventeenth century, in fact.[35] In many ways, Carlisle's rules end up creating an environment where the family itself becomes the keeper of traditional values. Edward must always demonstrate restraint around Bella, never taking their physical relationship beyond what even many conservative churches would sanction. If he were to lose control of himself, he could bite her; if they were to have sex, he fears he could injure her badly, even kill her, from just the slightest accident. Bella and Edward's abstinence, along with the constant need for self-monitoring and restraint, are intimately related to Carlisle's rules for their life.

Here again, while the biological families in the Twilight Saga often prove more or less ineffective, the nonbiological families of vampires and werewolves create effective moral centers. They provide guidance and rules to help the members of their family function in the context of their unique situation. Bella is perfectly content to thwart what she knows would be Charlie's will by allowing Edward to spend the night, but Edward would never think of defying Carlisle's sense of morality. While biological families thus have only a general influence over their children, the Cullen family provides clear and powerful moral guidance for its members. The behavior of every family member is governed by Carlisle's strict sense of ethics, since he insists on complete abstinence from drinking human blood.

The Cullens' adoption of Carlisle's moral code and the ability of the Cullen family to form bonds of true love through doing so are part of the reason that family can be seen as absolutely central to the Twilight Saga. Ideas about family and marriage have been important throughout American history, but definitions of the "normal" family, courtship, and marriage have been changing since the first European colonists landed, and they have varied across different social groups. For Bella, marriage makes sense only when she envisions herself and Edward on a porch swing together "wearing clothes from another kind of world. A world where it would surprise no one if I wore his ring on my finger. A simpler place, where love was defined in simpler ways. One plus one equals two." (*Eclipse*, 325.) However, what historians of the family, from Coontz to Cott, have all discovered was that there never was a simpler place or time when "one plus one equals two." The "simpler time" Edward came from balanced on the cusp of the 1920s, as American culture grappled with the image of the New Woman at the end of the nineteenth century; the 1920s were also marked by serious changes in courtship and sexual behavior, increased knowledge and availability of contraception and abortion, and concerns about the significant rise in divorce since the end of the nineteenth century.[36] The families formed in the Twilight novels negotiate this complex history, although the Quileutes do so in a way different from that of the Cullens, and defy all norms in American history by creating nonnuclear and largely nonbiological families that are not centered on procreation or childrearing.

Despite its emphasis on abstinence and marriage, the Twilight Saga should not be considered a traditional family values text. The complexity of the family history suggests that any household made up of members whose birth dates ranged from the seventeenth to the twenty-first century could never reflect the traditions of all of the historical periods and cultures that its members came from. Even adhering to the values of one particular point in time from the past does not necessarily result in behavior that we would now consider "traditional," as in Edward's willingness to abort Bella's baby before quickening, which indeed reflected the norms of his own youth.

Ultimately the Cullens' family life is a pastiche of the history of the American family, incorporating attributes that are contemporary, colonial, or just plain unusual, at least among European Americans.

While the Twilight series presents other aspects of history as a sequence of unique and specific events, Twilight's representation of families offers the reader a sense of living history. The Civil War belongs to the past, as does the Spanish influenza epidemic of 1918, or the Depression, but the history of the family is something that is happening still. Supposed "norms" like the prominence of a "nuclear family" household are not phenomena that necessarily ever reach a peak, a height from which they decline thereafter. Instead, each aspect of family life undergoes change and crisis over time. Although the personal history of each member of the Cullen family influences them even as they move forward; the story of their family never becomes a story about a single moment in the past. The same can be true for the role of history in our own discussions of modern families and marriages. For both the Cullens and many families today, history continues to exert its pull on the families and marriages that are formed in our own generation, influencing but not defining them. The Twilight Saga engages us in a timeless romance that allows us to question not only what a "traditional" romance and family mean to us today but also what we, like Bella, imagine when we think back to our favorite books and envision the traditions of the past.

Notes

1. Lev Grossman, "Stephenie Meyer: A New J. K. Rowling?" *Time*, April 24, 2008, online edition, 1–2, www.time.com/time/magazine/article/0,9171,1734838,00.html.

2. John Demos, *Past, Present, and Personal* (New York: Oxford Univ. Press, 1986), 25.

3. Stephanie Coontz, *The Way We Never Were: American Families and the Nostalgia Trap* (New York: Basic Books, 2000).

4. Nancy F. Cott, *Public Vows: A History of Marriage and the Nation* (Cambridge, MA: Harvard Univ. Press, 2000), 2529–2532.

5. I will not be discussing the Mormon family here, despite Stephenie Meyer's Mormonism, for two reasons. One, a discussion of Mormon family forms would require an examination of the Mormon religion, which I do not have space for in this particular work. Furthermore, in this chapter I am focusing entirely on elements inside the text, and while there are certainly Mormon overtones throughout the text, there are no explicitly Mormon characters.

6. Both Jasper's original coven, who routinely destroyed many of their own, and the Volturi sometimes have the word "family" applied to them, but it is clear that they do not behave in a cohesive way that protects each member.

7. Bert N. Adams, *The Family: A Sociological Interpretation* (San Diego: Harcourt Brace Jovanovich, 1986), 62.

8. Ibid., 62.

9. Stephanie Coontz, *Marriage, a History: From Obedience to Intimacy or How Love Conquered Marriage* (New York: Viking, 2005), 134–135.

10. Demos, *Past, Present, and Personal*, 28.

11. Here is a place where *Twilight* departs from the real past as it has been analyzed by historians. Stephanie Coontz, in *Marriage, a History*, comes to the conclusion that the move toward marriage based on love contributes to some of the systemic instabilities we see in marriage today, while perhaps improving the overall quality of some particular marriages.

12. I would argue that these groups remain very influential to this day, as Nancy Cott has demonstrated in her work.

13. Christopher Lasch, "Social Pathologists and the Socialization of Reproduction," in *The American Family in Social-Historical Perspective*, ed. Michael Gordon (New York: St. Martin's Press, 1983), 89.

14. Marilyn Yalom, *A History of the Wife* (New York: HarperCollins e-books, 2002), 112–114.

15. Cott, *Public Vows*, 2405–2408.

16. In fact, 1918 saw a spike in maternal deaths due to the Spanish influenza, which precipitated Carlisle's turning of Edward. Before this spike, maternal deaths were around 6 per 1,000 live births. Melissa Thomasson and Janet Treber, "From Home to Hospital: The Evolution of Childbirth in the United States," Miami University, Farmer School of Business, 38, www.sba.muohio.edu/thomasma/thomasson_and_treber.pdf.

17. Daniel Blake Smith, "Autonomy and Affection," in *The American Family in Social-Historical Perspective*, ed. Michael Gordon (New York: St Martin's Press, 1983), 211.

18. Leslie Reagan, *When Abortion Was a Crime: Women, Medicine, and Law in the United States, 1867–1973* (Berkeley: Univ. of California Press, 1997), 21. According to Reagan, in 1920 one medical commentator said that "the United States, tolerates abortion done within the bounds of discreet secrecy," 45.

19. Ibid., 8.

20. Yalom, *History of the Wife*, 5160–5162.

21. Ibid., 5246–5247.

22. Reagan, *When Abortion Was a Crime*, 23.

23. Ibid., 34, 38.

24. Yalom, *History of the Wife*, 5344–5347, and Adams, *The Family*, 73–74.

25. Daniel Scott Smith, "Parental Power and Marriage Patterns: An Analysis of Historical Trends in Hingham, Massachusetts," in *The American Family in Social-Historical Perspective*, ed. Michael Gordon (New York: St. Martin's Press, 1983), 265.

26. This is diminishing perhaps in practice, although its psychological importance persists in contemporary America.

27. Cott, *Public Vows*, 291–294, 320–321.

28. Adams, *The Family*, 69, and Yalom, *History of the Wife*, 6843–6844.

29. Coontz, *The Way We Never Were*, 184.

30. Yalom, *History of the Wife*, 129.

31. Ibid., 150–153.

32. U.S. Bureau of Census: "Estimated Median Age at First Marriage, by Sex: 1890–Present." internet release date September, 15, 2004, www.census.gov/population/socdemo/hh-fam/tabMS-2.pdf.

33. Coontz, *Marriage, a History*, 6.

34. Ibid., 7. Coontz dates this as the late eighteenth century, others as early as the sixteenth, although most would agree that a transition toward love and free choice of marriage partners was under way throughout this period.

35. Yalom, *History of the Wife*, 167–174.

36. Cott, *Public Vows*, 1260–1267. Although the rate of divorce was much lower than it is today, it had more than doubled between 1870 and 1900.

PART THREE

A World of Vampires

The Volturi and Beyond

The Sort of People Who Hired Michelangelo as Their Decorator

The Volturi as Renaissance Rulers

Birgit Wiedl

It is of the greatest importance in this world that a man should know himself, and the measure of his own strength and means; and he who knows that he has not a genius for fighting must learn how to govern by the arts of peace.

—*Niccolò Machiavelli*[1]

On July 14, 1564, the city of Florence saw a magnificent funeral held at the Basilica of San Lorenzo, the old and venerable church right at the center of the market area that was also the burial place of the city's most famous family: the Medici, whose wealth was rooted in banking.[2] Indeed, the spectacle would have been worthy of the city's ruler; yet it was not Cosimo de' Medici's burial that was being solemnized, nor *his* coffin that the Medici guards were escorting. In Cosimo's presence, innumerable people paid their last respects to another man who had shaped and dominated Florence perhaps almost as much as the Medici—Michelangelo di Lodovico Buonarroti Simoni, known to most by only his first name: Michelangelo.

In fact, Michelangelo had died at the age of eighty-nine almost six months earlier, in Rome. The Florentine ruler Cosimo de' Medici had his body moved and laid to rest in the church that had the strongest connection with the Medici in the public mind: San Lorenzo was not only the family's parish church and burial place, but it had been built on commission for another Cosimo, "Il Vecchio," the Elder, more than a century before. Michelangelo himself had designed the library and the Medici chapel within the vast complex of the church and the cloisters. Cosimo, soon to be the first grand duke of Tuscany, prided himself on being a great patron of the arts and continued the family tradition; Giorgio Vasari, Benvenuto Cellini, and Agnolo Bronzino are but three of the prestigious artists he promoted, and Florence was indebted to him for buildings as spectacular as the Uffizi and the Palazzo Pitti, with its huge Boboli Gardens.

Art patronage at that time was an essential characteristic of a member of the upper level of the social strata for a variety of reasons, including genuine interest in, and real love for, the arts. Yet Cosimo would not have been a true Medici—and, generally, child of his time—if his motives for honoring Michelangelo with so spectacular and flamboyant a funeral had not extended far beyond mere artistic considerations. His rule (while stable at the time of Michelangelo's funeral) had been, and would to a considerable extent always be, a constant struggle, dominated as much by warfare as by diplomatic twists and shrewd acting. Descending from the younger line of the family, he had seized power in Florence during a time of turmoil. Florence herself had suffered greatly from the aftereffects of the last "elder" Medici's assassination, while outside Florence, the war between Holy Roman Emperor Charles V and the French king Francis I was raging, with Cosimo firmly on the emperor's side. This support had earned him the hereditary title of duke of Florence (along with the de facto rule) in 1537, yet the need remained to assert his position, to publicly demonstrate that the younger line was as capable and worthy of the Florentines' loyalty as the elder had been.

Michelangelo was therefore the perfect person (or corpse) for Cosimo to use, in order to put his (Cosimo's) qualities on display: not only was Michelangelo the most famous artist of his time, he had worked for the family frequently and had even, in his youth, studied at the sculptors' school in Florence founded by Lorenzo "Il Magnifico," the Magnificent, de' Medici. Michelangelo had even lived in the Palazzo Medici at Lorenzo's invitation.[3] Michelangelo thus was part of the Medici's Golden Age. Cosimo's decision to honor Michelangelo was therefore much more than a demonstration of an undeniably profound understanding and appreciation of art and a master artist; it was first and foremost a political statement, a tie that bound Cosimo to the Florentine rulers of old, to the ones still vividly remembered by the public—Lorenzo the Magnificent and his grandfather Cosimo the Elder, the first de facto Medici ruler of Florence.[4]

Near-Royalty, Control, and Power Gained through Patronage

He it is who decides peace and war: he is king in all but name.

—*Pope Pius II, on Cosimo de' Medici*[5]

According to what the Cullens tell Bella Swan, the Volturi have ruled the Tuscan city of Volterra from time immemorial. "For three thousand years, since the time of the Etruscans," Alice reveals to Bella during their journey to save Edward, the Volturi have been ruling the city of Volterra in secret, but to the benefit of the humans in whose midst they dwell undetected. (*New Moon*, 430.) Alice's claim ignores the fact that the union of scattered Etruscan settlements into the town of *Velathri*, later called Volterra, actually occurred more than half a millennium later.[6] Yet the distinctive appearance and demeanor of the Volturi bring to mind not Roman magistrates nor medieval lords of towns (in the case of Volterra, the town was ruled by a bishop up until the twelfth century) but the powerful men (and women) of the Renaissance. The rulers that Aro, Caius, and Marcus most closely resemble were these Renaissance rulers, most notably the Medici of Florence, who achieved their goals by means of both peace and war, and later on inspired Machiavelli to write his own playbook. Indeed, the Medici, as much as the Volturi, probably could have given Machiavelli himself a few lessons.

We know next to nothing about Aro, Caius, and Marcus's rise to power, or about the means they resorted to in establishing and maintaining their hold on the city of Volterra, and it seems odd to compare a vampire family strongly focused on maintaining invisibility with the Italian Renaissance culture, which thrived on representation and public splendor. Yet in spite of that, there are similarities and differences in the way that the Volturi and the Medici wield their power, in patterns of political behavior that go far beyond patronage of the arts.

If we venture a guess and say that the Volturi's rule of Volterra was either acquired by force or came about so stealthily that no one actually realized it (apart from other vampires and ill-fated tourists), then the way they came to power differed greatly from the methods used by the Renaissance ruling families. Surprising as it may seem, many Northern and Central Italian cities were *communes* of the High Middle Ages, self-governing city-state republics based on partial democracy, not to be confused with "communes" as used in modern English-language contexts.[7] And yet, these (proto)democratic cities laid the groundwork for the rise of later ennobled families like the Medici. Most of the towns that were home to great families had risen to considerable power already as communes, and buildings like the Palazzo dei Priori, house of the city government, in Volterra, finished in 1246, bore witness to the self-confidence and pride of the citizenry. The city-states in Northern Italy were among the wealthiest in medieval Europe, their nonaristocratic merchant elite handling both trade and money-related business, while premodern industries (the wool industry of Florence; the alum, salt, and sulfur mines of Volterra; or the silk production of Lucca) provided a stable economic foundation for the towns. The increasing importance of mercenary soldiers allowed even smaller but wealthy cities to field considerable military forces, which meant that Renaissance politics and society developed against a backdrop of permanent warfare.[8]

From the fourteenth century onward, some of these cities declined and even came under the control of more successful neighboring communes, but the most powerful city-states continued to expand their influence and their realm. The rise of these cities was often interwoven with the coming to power of one or more particularly successful families—the Visconti and Sforza of the duchy of Milan, the Gonzaga, who turned the commune of Mantua into a duchy, the Este of the duchy of Ferrara, and, of course, the Medici of the republic of Florence. The origins of these families were varied. Some of them had roots among the medieval nobility, some claimed to be descended from ancient and grand ancestors, although none of these families claimed to go back as far as the Etruscan period, like the Volturi. Compared with a kinship network as impressive as that, families like the Sforza of Milan, who descended from the illegitimate son of a *condottiero*, a mercenary soldiers' leader, or the Medici, Florentine bankers with fairly recent rural roots, seem almost meek, yet they are typical examples of Renaissance rulers.

Perhaps the most widely known family, and certainly one of the most successful, was that of the Medici of Florence. They became the very model of Renaissance rulers, achieving, in the words of Pope Pius II, a position of "king in all but name."[9] In contrast to the Volturi though, whose rule remains unchallenged thanks to their invisibility, calling the Medici "rulers" of quattrocento (fifteenth-century) Florence is not only factually wrong but also contradicts the self-image they themselves had and promoted in public: that of leading citizens of a city-state republic. It was with and through the Republic of Florence, her offices and civic bodies, that the Medici accumulated and exerted their influence, and it was not simple "spin" when Cosimo the Elder wrote to Pope Pius II around 1460: "You write as if I weren't a private person but a prince . . . you do know how limited the power is of a simple citizen, in a state ruled by the people."[10] In spite of the fact that Cosimo cherished his image as a power broker who pulled the strings, Volturi-like invisibility and concealment were never an option for any of the grand Renaissance families who ruled towns like Florence, Milan, or even Volterra.

Cosimo used his family's great wealth to perfect the strategies that were the backbone of Florentine communal politics: the building up of a huge network of clientele by means of political and social patronage.[11] His descendants would pursue and expand his work, for patronage relationships (a bond between a powerful leader and a client who was often further down the social ladder) were meant as long-term relationships, binding together not individuals but families.[12] Patronage as a political and social tool was by no means an invention of the medieval Italian communes—classical Rome had operated on the basis of patronage networks. And the Volturi leaders' power had been based on patronage relationships for even longer, if we believe Alice's account.

The Medici and other Florentine banking families challenged the noble family Albizzi, the de facto rulers of Florence around 1400, by trying to gain the loyalty and support of as many citizens as possible. As a family that had only recently entered politics, the Medici particularly came to the aid of families of lower social standing or "new" families, who often had not already formed patronage relationships with the city's elite families. They used various methods to help their clients and assure themselves of their loyalty: easing their access to public office, bestowing dowries on the daughters of poorer families, assisting them in financial matters, acting as arbitrators and mediators, intervening on their behalf in the courts of law, and generally providing access to their network of kin, friends, and clients.[13] Good patron-client relationships were crucial to the smooth functioning of social life, politics, and government, and neither patron nor client could afford to neglect that: the client was obliged to honor his patron by demonstrating his loyalty if the patron called on him for a task or support, just as the patron was required to assist his network clients financially, legally, and socially.[14]

The aid and support between a patron and his clients was supposed to be mutual, with loyalty to the patron being the most important "contribution" from the client, thus allowing the patron to gain influence in many areas of society that he would otherwise not have access to.[15] Although many of these patron-client ties remained informal, they were "the real glue binding Renaissance society" and they closely resembled the ties that bind the Volturi together, and the relationships that Aro seeks to establish with as many vampires as possible around the world.[16] Just as Cosimo de' Medici chose his clients according to their usefulness for his family, Aro also picks his followers carefully and prudently. Jane and her brother, Alec, are good examples; they are the most cherished members of Aro's guard and were already chosen when they were still human, although we are never told what Aro saw in them before he turned them. Aro's main goal, as far as other vampires are concerned, is to gather them into his fold; he remains focused on this even when his colleagues are set on destroying those who, in their eyes, are threatening the very existence of all vampires.

Aro casts a carefully appraising look at the werewolf/shape-shifter pack during the Volturi's final confrontation with the Cullens in *Breaking Dawn*, even as they are growling at him, considering only how to use them to his benefit: "He's intrigued with the idea of guard dogs," Edward observes. (*Breaking Dawn*, 700.) Earlier, Edward had suspected Aro of delaying the company he sent to battle Victoria's army of newborns, because Edward thought Aro wanted to use Victoria's attack in order to diminish the Cullens' power (and numbers). In both instances, Aro shows himself to be capable of political machinations that even Niccolò Machiavelli, the grand master of political scheming in the Renaissance, would have been proud to call his own.

Family strength and loyalty, however, were the lifeblood of Renaissance Florentine society, and perhaps its highest ideal.[17] The Volturi also seem to operate on this medieval and Renaissance sense of the family as a group bound together by ties that go beyond the kinship of a biological family. The Volturi can rely on the powers of the vampire Chelsea, who wields her ability to strengthen the ties of relationships to the advantage of the Volturi, particularly Aro, and even compel other vampires to serve them willingly, but the Medici and their fellows had to put a lot more of effort into endearing themselves to their clients, and to the population of the town they controlled. It was, however, not merely an attempt to ingratiate himself with the *popolazzo*, the mob, when Lorenzo the Magnificent paid for, and participated in, feasts of the working-class people, hobnobbing with the workers to such an extent that he wrote bawdy carnival songs for them. Lorenzo's wife, Clarice Orsini, was motivated as much by politics as she was by personal concern when she appeared in person to support her peasant workers in court cases; Lorenzo's mother, a patron of orphanages and supporter of the poor herself, addressed her son as "a father to the poor."[18]

Displaying themselves publicly as patrons and supporters of the less fortunate was central to the self-image, and even the very identity, of the Medici and other ruling families of Renaissance Italy; in so doing, they presented themselves as the guarantors of justice, peace, and prosperity.[19] This is an image the Volturi cherish as well: "They have assumed the position of enforcing our rules," Alice tells Bella, and it seems that she is taking too narrow a view. (*New Moon*, 430.) They "clean up messes," guaranteeing if not peace, then at least survival for the rest of the vampires, and Jasper sums it up, "with respect, almost gratitude" in his voice: "If not for the Volturi, the rest of us would be quickly exposed." (*Eclipse*, 288.)

Like the Volturi, the Medici were also well suited to keeping the peace. At least, they played this role in their own eyes, yet also in the eyes of a good part of the population who had grown weary of the continuous warfare: the families vying for power within the city; wars against other city-states; war against the Pope, when Florence took the side of the Holy Roman Emperor; and a 1378 revolt of the Ciompi, the local wool beaters. It was a Medici, Salvestro di Alamanno, whose leadership helped to put an end to the revolt, and many citizens remained wary of the popolazzo for many decades to come.[20] The Medici maintained a balance of power, pacifying the populace while holding the other powerful families at bay, which earned them the trust of many who believed in their ability to maintain peace.

The generations of Medici who succeeded Salvestro di Alamanno followed this strategy, working painstakingly to build a reputation for being mediators who were not power-hungry, but rather known and appreciated for their wisdom and judgment while unifying the city and enhancing Florence's greater glory.[21] Unlike Machiavelli's ideal (and future) prince, the ideal of the early Renaissance rulers *was* to be rather loved rather than feared, like Aro wanting Carlisle to be his friend (again) even after they had almost fought a final battle. Charity and patronage blended together until these two virtues became almost indistinguishable, enabling families like the Medici, or the Volturi, to take credit for (and pride in) easing the social tensions, creating an era of harmony.[22]

Guarantors of peace and protectors of a way of life that seemed desirable, even crucial to most—this is precisely the image of themselves that the Volturi promulgate, and not without reason. "We owe the Volturi for our present way of life," Jasper explains when he tells Bella how the Volturi ended the threat that the vampire Benito has posed to the vampire world. (*Eclipse*, 287.) Jasper is repeating in more detail what Edward and Alice have already hinted at previously: the Volturi *were* the ones who took care of the vampires' safety, striving to eliminate every threat to their world, both from other vampires or from the outside world. Aro must have envied Cosimo the Elder the title the Florentines awarded him after his death: Pater Patriae, Father of the Fatherland, the ancient Roman honorific that reflected the great services that the bearer of the title had rendered to his country (or in Cosimo's case, his city-state); the title was carved on his tomb in the church of San Lorenzo, for everyone to see. It is hard to tell whether Aro would have taken more pride in the fact that he would never need a tomb himself, or whether he would have been tempted to give dying a try, just to acquire a title like that.

People You Wouldn't Want to Cross

A paradise inhabited by devils.

—*Agnolo Acciaiuoli*[23]

You didn't antagonize them unless you wanted to die.

—*Bella* (New Moon, 428)

Was Quattrocento Florence a paradise, then? Definitely not. *Uno paradiso habitato da diavoli*, "a paradise inhabited by devils," was the description offered by Agnolo Acciaiuoli, one of the leaders in a 1466 uprising against the Medici. "Cold and more cowardly than rabbits," he described them to Francesco Sforza, the Milanese duke and Florentine ally whom he sought to convince (in vain) that he would be a more desirable negotiating partner.[24] But Acciaiuoli and his coconspirators, who launched an attack against the Palazzo Medici in August of that year, had underestimated several factors: the Medici's acute radar for political tensions (the Medici, fully armed, were therefore waiting for their attackers); the value that the Milanese duke placed on his alliance with the Medici, which meant that he refused to switch allegiances; and, last but definitely not least, the trust that many citizens, patricians and popolazzo alike, put in the Medici (and the Medici alone) to maintain the city's peace. A large group of citizens had therefore gathered in front of the Medici's Palazzo to defend their patrons against the assailants. Yet after the failed revolt, the Medici—Piero and his son Lorenzo, the future Magnificent—neither hounded the escaped conspirators nor demanded the most serious penalty, execution, for the one who remained in Florence: Luca Pitti.[25] Pitti submitted himself to Piero's grace and was spared.[26]

Was this cowardice, as Edward claims the Volturi displayed? He accused them of being bullies, and thus cowards, when they walked away from the fight they had traveled so far for, after much posing. But it had gone down well with the population of Florence to see the anti-Medicean faction spared by Piero and Lorenzo; the rebelling families had, after all, many clients in the city who depended on them. The Medici had already achieved their goal, the reestablishing of peace and order. With a war against Venice looming and Francesco Sforza of Milan—the Medici's long-time ally—dead, the decision not to take drastic measures that would have further unsettled the city's ever-shaky balance of power was perhaps not the only, but definitely the wisest, option. It was the kind of outcome that Aro, too, decided to settle for.

It was, however, seriously unwise to challenge the Medici. Like other ruling Renaissance families, they were able soldiers, both in tactics and out in the field, and neither their position within Italian and European politics nor their grip on Florence remained unchallenged. Exiled from Florence four times in a mere 150 years, they knew better than to rest on their laurels even after they were made dukes of Florence in 1531 by the Holy Roman emperor Charles V and dukes of Tuscany by Pope Pius V. They remained vigilant even while members of the Medici clan were becoming popes, marrying the daughters and sisters of emperors or marrying off their own daughters to French kings. "We sat on our thrones and thought ourselves gods. We didn't notice for a long time that we were changing—almost petrifying," the last surviving members of the Romanian coven muse about their past. (*Breaking Dawn*, 631.) According to Niccolò Machiavelli, they had thus committed a fatal mistake. Machiavelli's *Il Principe*, "The Prince," had set new intellectual standards for the art of rule, and in it he noted that a ruler should "never in peaceful times stand idle," lest he lose his throne.[27]

The Medici, like the Volturi, knew how to strike and never hesitated when they considered action necessary. When facing a 1478 conspiracy to overthrow his dominant position within Florence, Lorenzo the Magnificent did not exercise the same leniency his father had shown against the 1466 rebellion, although—or perhaps because—the conspiracy stretched far beyond the walls of the city. Pope Sixtus IV, the archbishop of Pisa Francesco Salviati, his family of Florentine bankers, and their colleagues, the Pazzi family, were the main instigators of the conspiracy. They had prepared to strike both within Florence and outside, rallying their troops before the city wall. They failed, yet not before killing Lorenzo's younger brother, enraging the popolazzo by assassinating him right in the church during a Sunday mass.[28]

Even Aro and his guard could hardly have responded faster: the first wave of retribution executions was carried out by the Medici guards and the population while Lorenzo was suffering from a serious wound to his throat. The conspirators were either stabbed or hanged immediately, including Archbishop Salviati, and the Florentines roamed the city, seizing and killing everyone involved in the attack, cooling off only when they learned that Lorenzo had survived. Having regained his strength, Lorenzo resorted to the same drastic measures that the Volturi did when they learned about a threat: he pursued the remaining conspirators mercilessly, wiping out the entire Pazzi family in Florence and hunting all participants down across Italy.

He spared only two, both wisely chosen: Guglielmo Pazzi, who was married to Lorenzo's sister Bianca and fiercely loyal to Lorenzo thereafter, and the barely seventeen-year-old Cardinal Raffaele Riario, nephew of Sixtus IV, who was believed to be innocent of the charges. His ruthlessness secured Lorenzo's position to a degree unmatched in Florentine politics before, and his drastic response was echoed half a century later in 1537, when his younger relative and successor, Cosimo, who had just duped the Florentine Signoria, the leading families, into appointing him lord of the city, faced a rebellion from two leading local families, the Salviati and the Strozzi. He had all of the rebels beheaded after he had defeated them in a decisive battle, sparing no one. In cases of serious danger, both the Medici and the Volturi deemed it best to literally wipe the slate clean—the corpses of the Romanian coven, the Pazzi, the newborns of Benito, and the Salviati and the Strozzi all bear witness to this. But both Aro and Lorenzo possessed the cunning to spare just one or two enemies when they wiped out an opposing family (or coven), and like Lorenzo, Aro knew just who it would be useful to show "mercy" toward.

Although these rather randomly chosen incidents may be considered defensive actions, the Medici were well aware of the impression that a successful military action could make. In June 1472,

Lorenzo struck out against a city that had been under the de facto control of Florence for a few decades: Volterra. Several clashes over the right to exploit newly detected alum deposits—which, along with salt and sulfur, formed the main source of income for Volterra's human inhabitants—had already caused the Medici to tighten their grip on the city. In 1472, the outbreak of a revolt prompted Lorenzo to take the city by force; by his usual standards this was a highly undiplomatic and therefore rather untypical act of violence. The sacking of Volterra was actually more a diplomatic move within Florentine politics than the disposing of a threat; it served to consolidate his position within his regime and the city.[29] After the initial strike, Lorenzo hesitated to seek a completely military solution; instead, he was eager to tie the rebels to him through bonds of patronage and subservience, rather than executing them.

New loyal and subservient allies or dead enemies—the choice would not have been a hard one for Aro, either. To the very end of *Breaking Dawn*, he tries to convince Carlisle to join them; and even if the Cullens abhor the Volturi's methods, they themselves adapt and use similar means to protect themselves against Victoria's army of newborns, thus accepting the Volturi's model as the "way of the vampires." Even Garrett, the fierce revolutionary who challenges the Volturi's predominance and eventually decides to break with them, offers no alternative when the threat Joham (the father of several half-vampire children, including Nahuel) poses to the vampire world is revealed at the climax of *Breaking Dawn*. Instead, Garrett seems happy to let them deal with it, knowing that they would prevail and thus protect the rest of the vampire world. Acting against the Volturi's interests, or challenging them, remained a mortal risk.

"So *Medieval!*": Renaissance Art, the Artists, and the People Who Paid Them

"So medieval," Bella hears a shrill female voice exclaim, as a group of tourists are led into the Volturi's palace by the vampire Heidi, the mahogany-haired siren who goes fishing for food dressed in tight-fitting clothes. (*New Moon*, 482.) A true Renaissance ruler might indeed have felt a certain satisfaction at the unlucky fate awaiting anyone that ignorant and uncivilized; those who so profoundly misjudged the impression that the entry hall—or indeed any Renaissance piece of architecture should have on its visitors—that they thought it was *medieval*, perhaps deserved what they got.

From the early works of Filippo Brunelleschi in Florence, Donato Bramante's designs for the early Medici and the dukes of Milan, Michelangelo's St. Peter's Basilica in Rome, to the Mannerist buildings of Andrea Palladio that already anticipated the Baroque ideals, none of these examples of Renaissance architecture was meant to reflect features of medieval architecture, whether Romanesque or Gothic. *Renaissance*, French for "Rebirth," was used first in 1550 by the Italian artist Giorgio Vasari, one of Cosimo de' Medici's main artists, to describe the ideals of his time: the rebirth of classical aesthetics to achieve a new Italian art style that was a clear break from the "barbaric" Gothic of the Middle Ages.

Like his ancestors, Cosimo had been given an education in the arts, and like them, he had quickly learned to utilize the arts along with his political skills to ensure his family's hold over Florence, the public spectacle of Michelangelo's funeral being but one of his cleverly conceived maneuvers.[30] Seeing to an early education in the arts of the young Medici offspring had a long tradition, and Cosimo the Elder, from an earlier generation of the Medici family, had established himself as a connoisseur of the arts from the beginning. A "master of self-presentation," he picked his artists carefully in order to create and convey an image of himself for the public that, together with his other manifold talents, made him the "first man" of Florence even without holding a formal title or office.[31] In hiring the young Michelozzi to create the Palazzo Medici, he set a trend—the magnificent yet plain palace would serve as an archetype for rulers' palaces across Italy for decades to come, and those who had their residences built to resemble his were imitating more than just his home, acknowledging Cosimo himself as a role model.[32] At the same time, the palace announced the supremacy of the Medici over the other patrician families, most obviously by its sheer size and even more sublimely by its creative style, marking the Medici as being ahead of their rivals in every imaginable respect.[33]

Art patronage was not limited to objects designed only for family use: religious art was also commissioned quite often by Renaissance rulers. Rulers like the Medici particularly liked to promote their "family saints," a method even the Volturi weren't above using. The Volturi acted straightforwardly in pushing aside the real patron of Volterra, the sixth-century bishop Giusto (Justus), who (as the legend goes) did in fact save the city's population from barbarian siege; he was set aside as the patron of Volterra in favor of the Volturi's own "saint," Marcus. The choice of the name Marcus is somewhat peculiar, since the Catholic church does indeed acknowledge three saints of that name, with Marcus the Evangelist being the most popular one, yet none of them is the patron of any area within Tuscany—to the contrary, Marcus the Evangelist is the patron of one of the greatest rivals of the Tuscan cities (Volterra among them), the Republic of Venice.

The Medici had to resort to more contrived methods of promoting "their" saints than the Volturi did, however. The Medici's family church of San Lorenzo served as the stage for many a show (like Michelangelo's funeral), and Cosimo the Elder used the family's patron saints, Cosmas and Damian, to introduce the Medici identity to a broader public. Not only did art appear all over the city featuring saints who had been previously unknown, but the identification of the saints not only with martyrs but (saintly) doctors—*medici* in Italian—allowed creators of both scholarly treatises and popular culture to associate the two, suggesting that the ills and problems of the city were best entrusted to the Medici.[34] It would, however, miss the point entirely to attempt to pry apart the various reasons for ecclesiastical patronage—genuine religious feelings, pursuit of political interests, dynastic schemes and family obligations, fulfillment of civic duties—because for Renaissance patrons, these were not competing motivations but rather formed a single entity, an amalgamation of all these agendas.[35]

During the Renaissance, being a connoisseur of the arts (and letting everyone know via extensive patronage) became an increasingly crucial aspect of the upper classes' self-conception and self-image.[36] This included an involvement with the artists that went far beyond mere commissioning of art pieces. A close relationship, like that of Michelangelo and Lorenzo Il Magnifico, which bordered on friendship, enhanced both the reputation of the artist and the ruler.[37] The lives of artists and their patrons were inseparably intertwined; illustrious artists cultivated close relationships with the (wealthy) courts of rulers as much as the noted members of famous families coveted the acquaintance of gifted artists, priding themselves on the "discovery" of new talents. Being the court artisan of a Renaissance ruler often amounted to more than mere financial advantages; it meant being included in the wider *familias*, the clan, of the respective family and thus could secure the future of the artist's entire family. Niccolò Michelozzi, son of Cosimo's favorite architect, who had obviously not inherited his father's artistic talents or interests, became Lorenzo's secretary and one of his closest confidants. Even when they were not that closely attached to one family, artists were often involved in matters that went far beyond the scope of their actual commissions; they even acted as spies and diplomats. Michelangelo, for example, was sent to Rome to Pope Julius II by the Florentine Signoria as an "ambassador of the Republic" in 1506; other artists served as messengers for a variety of purposes, including the negotiating of peace treaties and marriage contracts.[38]

Cultural sophistication and patronage were not limited to the visual arts. Literature, particularly poetry, was not only supported and paid for by Renaissance patrons, it was a branch of art they themselves practiced. Music was another field that Renaissance rulers emphasized, and some skill in music was expected of every person who hoped to get ahead in the Renaissance courts: at the Sforza court in Milan, a center of Renaissance music, a young Leonardo da Vinci was particularly celebrated for his skillful handling of the lyre (a small harp).[39] It was Leonardo who, as a promising young artist just finishing his studies in Florence, was chosen by Lorenzo Il Magnifico as a messenger to secure peace with the Milanese duke Ludovico.[40] The present Lorenzo had him deliver to the Milanese duke was of exceptional quality and beauty, complimenting Ludovico's musical talents: a silver lyre, crafted in the shape of a horse's head by Leonardo himself.[41]

One might argue that there are hardly any parallels between the two clans discussed in this chapter: the magnificent, publicity-loving Medici, who celebrated themselves with lavish, bombastic feasts and strove to extend their influence ever further across the whole of Tuscany and to Rome and France; and the secretive, secluded Volturi, who control their city of Volterra by use of extremely clandestine methods. From the limited information we gather throughout the Twilight Saga, the main goal of the Volturi is to keep the existence of vampires a secret under all circumstances and at all costs. Hence, since the population of Volterra (with the exception of randomly chosen, and particularly unlucky, tourists) had to remain ignorant of their city's rulers' true nature, even their mere existence—save one Saint Marcus—what use would art patronage serve for these rulers? They might, like the Medici, provide their subjects with many beautiful things to gaze at, with statues, edifices, and meticulously designed gardens for them to enjoy (although we do not hear about this). But the secretive Volturi would not gain any admiration from their own populace, the vampires, for their artistic expertise, and so the display of their splendor and glory would come to nothing at the end of the day.

Yet, let us return to Bella's first encounter with the Volturi. She is at the Cullens' home, and after a sightseeing tour through the house, Edward shares with her the story of Carlisle, the vampire hunter's son. When he reaches the part of Carlisle's life spent in Italy, there is no mention of rigid rule keepers or ruthless royalty with a serious penchant for control. The first thing that strikes Bella is their tranquil appearance; the first information Edward gives her about the Volturi, before even telling her their names, is that they are "civilized" and "educated." She learns that Carlisle was impressed by their "refinement" and gets to know that "Solimena was greatly inspired" by the Volturi. (*Twilight*, 340–341.) The information that

Francesco Solimena (1657–1747), one of the great Italian artists of the Baroque era, master of the chiaroscuro style and artist to rulers and noblemen across Europe, "often painted them as gods" seems to be most crucial—in spite of the fact that Solimena seems a surprising choice, since he hardly ever left the town of Naples, and the depiction of gods was not a specialty of his.

Be that as it may: even if Edward is (as it is his habit) allowing his desire to protect Bella to rule him, and thus avoids revealing too much in order to not spook Bella, it is telling that he chooses those particular words to characterize the Volturi: "nighttime patrons of the arts." This is the phrase that Bella recalls later when the Volturi, now called by their "family name," come up again in their conversation about vampiric suicide. The Volturi are indeed patrons, although the audience they are performing for, and ruling, is not the same as that targeted by the Medici. The Medici sought to impress and cultivate support among their own townspeople, their duchy of Tuscany, and, eventually, the whole of Europe, while the Volturi hide themselves from the rest of Volterra and the world. But despite the carefully maintained ignorance of the Volterra population, those who are meant to know—their own kind—do indeed know, and other vampires see the Volturi as they want to be seen. Just like the Medici, the Volturi maintain their reputation and image where it is most important to them: among their own networks of clients, and across the vampire world at large.

Notes

1. Niccolò Macchiavelli, *The Life of Castruccio Castracani of Lucca*, from the online edition, www.fordham.edu/halsall/basis/machiavelli-prince.html#LIFE%20OF%20CASTRUCCIO.

2. Henk Th. van Veen, *Cosimo I de' Medici and His Self-Representation in Florentine Art and Culture*, trans. Andrew McCormick (Cambridge, Eng.: Cambridge Univ. Press, 2006), 177–183; Cristina Acidini Luchinat, "Michelangelo and the Medici," in *The Medici, Michelangelo, and the Art of Late Renaissance Florence*, ed. Cristina Acidini Luchinat, in conjunction with the Detroit Institute of Arts (New Haven, CT: Yale Univ. Press, 2002), 9.

3. Alan P. Darr, "The Medici and the Legacy of Michelangelo in Late Renaissance Florence: An Introduction," in *The Medici, Michelangelo, and the Art of Late Renaissance Florence*, 1; Francis William Kent, *Lorenzo de' Medici & the Art of Magnificence* (Baltimore: Johns Hopkins Univ. Press, 2004), 8–9.

4. Paola Tinagli, "The identity of the prince: Cosimo de' Medici, Giorgio Vasari and the *Ragionamenti*," in *Fashioning Identities in Renaissance Art*, ed. Mary Rogers (Aldershot and Burlington, Eng.: Ashgate, 2000), 192.

5. The famous statement Pope Pius II made about Cosimo the Elder, "Political questions are settled in his house. The man he chooses holds office. . . . He it is who decides peace and war and controls of laws. . . . He is King in all but name," is here quoted after Niall Ferguson, *The Ascent of Money. A Financial History of the World* (London: Penguin Press, 2008), 44–45.

6. Stephan Steingräber: *Volterra. Etruskisches und mittelalterliches Juwel im Herzen der Toscana* (Mainz, Ger.: Zabern, 2002).

7. Philip Jones, *The Italian City-State: From Commune to Signoria* (Oxford: Clarendon Press, 1997), 333–334.

8. Generally, see the basic works by Peter Burke, *The Renaissance* (Basingstoke, Eng.: Macmillan, 1987), *The European Renaissance: Centres and Peripheries* (Oxford: Blackwell, 1998), and particularly *The Italian Renaissance: Culture and Society in Italy* 2nd ed., rev. (1972; Princeton, NJ: Princeton Univ. Press, 1999), here quoted by use of the German translation by Reinhard Kaiser that was based on the slightly revised edition of 1974 (Berlin: Wagenbach, 1984). With particular regard to Florence, see Gene Adam Brucker, *Renaissance Florence: Society, Culture, and Religion* (Goldbach, Ger.: Keip, 1994).

9. Ferguson, *The Ascent of Money*, 44–45 (emphasis added).

10. John R. Hale, *Florence and the Medici: The Pattern of Control* (London: Thames and Hudson, 1977), here quoted after the translation into German by Grete and Karl-Eberhard Felten, *Die Medici und Florenz: Die Kunst der Macht* (Stuttgart and Zurich: Belsen Verlag, 1979), 50.

11. Ronald Weissman, "Taking Patronage Seriously: Mediterranean Values and Renaissance Society," in *Patronage, Art, and Society in Renaissance Italy*, ed. Francis William Kent and Patricia Simons (Oxford/Canberra: Oxford Univ. Press/Clarendon Press, 1987), 25.

12. Still valid is the study by Dale Kent, *The Rise of the Medici: Factions in Florence 1426–1434* (Oxford: Oxford Univ. Press, 1978).

13. On the "blurring" of these often indistinguishable groups, see the contributions in *Patronage, Art, and Society in Renaissance Italy* by Weissman, "Taking Patronage Seriously," 35–36, and Guy Fitch Lytle, "Friendship and Patronage in Renaissance Europe," 46–61.

14. Margery A. Ganz, "Perceived Insults and Their Consequences: Acciaiuoli, Neroni, and Medici Relationships in the 1460s," in *Society and Individual in Renaissance Florence*, ed. William J. Connell (Berkeley: Univ. of California Press, 2002), 155.

15. Francis William Kent, "'Un paradiso habitato da diavoli': Ties of Loyalty and Patronage in the Society of Medicean Florence," in *Le radici cristiane di Firenze*, ed. Anna Benvenuti Papi, Francesco Bandini, Elena Giannarelli, and Ada Gunnella, Storia saggistica 1 (Florence: Alinea, 1994), 183–210.

16. Weissman, "Taking Patronage Seriously," 27.

17. Dale Kent, *Cosimo De' Medici and the Florentine Renaissance: The Patron's Oeuvre* (New Haven, CT: Yale Univ. Press, 2000), 11.

18. Francis William Kent, "'Be Rather Loved than Feared': Class Relations in Quattrocento Florence," in *Society and Individual in Renaissance Florence*, ed. William J. Connell (Berkeley: Univ. of California Press, 2002), 30–37.

19. Lorenz Böninger, "Politics, Trade and Toleration in Renaissance Florence: Lorenzo de' Medici and the Besalú Brothers" *I Tatti Studies* 9 (2001): 139–169, presents the intriguing example of Lorenzo in the role of an arbiter in "international" financial matters, with insights into his self-image.

20. Kent, "Class Relations," 15–16; Francis William Kent, "Palaces, Politics and Society in Fifteenth-Century Florence," *I Tatti Studies* 2 (1987): 54–57.

21. Kent, *Lorenzo de' Medici*, 2.

22. Kent, "*Class Relations*," 47.

23. Kent, "Palaces, Politics and Society," 63.

24. Ganz, "Perceived Insults and Their Consequences," p. 158.

25. Francis William Kent, *Lorenzo De' Medici and the Art of Magnificence* (Baltimore: Johns Hopkins Univ. Press, 2006); Miles J. Unger, *Magnifico: The Brilliant Life and Violent Times of Lorenzo de Medici* (New York: Simon and Schuster 2008).

26. Hale, *Florence and the Medici*, 59–60.

27. Niccolò Machiavelli, *Il Principe*, chap. 14. Of the various online versions, the following was used: www.dustylibrary.com/philosophy/19-the-prince-nicolo-machiavelli.html.

28. Lauro Martines, *April Blood: Florence and the Plot Against the Medici* (Oxford: Oxford Univ. Press, 2003); Marcello Simonetta, *The Montefeltro Conspiracy: A Renaissance Mystery Decoded* (New York: Doubleday, 2008).

29. Kent, *Lorenzo de' Medici*, 48–51.

30. Darr, "The Medici and the Legacy of Michelangelo," 3–4; Van Veen, *Cosimo I*, 177–178, also points out the parallels between the honors carried out for Brunelleschi in 1477 and those originally planned for Michelangelo.

31. Kent, *Cosimo De' Medici*, 16.

32. It has been disputed whether the Palazzo Medici was originally designed by Brunelleschi and only executed under Michelozzo. See Kent, *Cosimo De' Medici*, 228–229. On Cosimo as a role model, see Kent, "Palaces, Politics and Society," 53–56.

33. Kent, *Cosimo De' Medici*, 225.

34. Hale, *Florence and the Medici*, 38; Kent, *Cosimo De' Medici*, 142.

35. Kent, *Cosimo De' Medici*, 131–132.

36. Jill Burke, "Patronage and Identity in Renaissance Florence: The Case of S. Maria a Lecceto," in *Fashioning Identities in Renaissance Art*, 51–62.

37. Kent, *Lorenzo de' Medici*, 57.

38. Francis Ames-Lewis, *The Intellectual Life of the Early Renaissance Artist* (New Haven, CT: Yale Univ. Press, 2000), 64–66.

39. Ibid., 61.

40. Paolo Rossi, *The Birth of Modern Science* (Oxford: Blackwell Publishing, 2001), 33.

41. Ames-Lewis, *The Intellectual Life*, 65–66; Paul A. Merkley and Lora L. M. Merkley, *Music and Patronage in the Sforza Court*, Studi sulla storia della musica in Lombardia, vol. 3 (Turnhout, Belgium: Brepols, 1999), chap. 10.

"Where Do the Cullens Fit In?"

Vampires in European Folklore, Science, and Fiction

Eveline Brugger

> "As the legend goes, a Christian missionary, a Father Marcus—Marcus of the Volturi, in fact—drove all the vampires from Volterra fifteen hundred years ago. The story claims he was martyred in Romania, still trying to drive away the vampire scourge. Of course that's nonsense—he's never left the city. But that's where some of the superstitions about things like crosses and garlic come from. Father Marcus used them so successfully. And vampires don't trouble Volterra, so they must work."
>
> —*Alice Cullen* (New Moon, *440–441*)

Twilight vampires go way back, as this quote from Alice Cullen's explanation to Bella Swan seems to prove. Fifteen hundred years ago, the mysterious, powerful Volturi established themselves as vampire hunters in Volterra, an Italian city that they had already ruled for one and a half millennia at that point. By doing so, they were not only able to hide their true nature from the population, they even managed to raise one of their own, Marcus of the Volturi, to the status of sainthood. An impressive achievement, especially if one considers the fact that in the year 500, no one in Italy or anywhere else in Western Europe had ever even heard the word *vampire*.

It is a natural reflex to ascribe great age to well-known myths that, from our point of view, have been around forever. A closer look at the development of European vampire folklore is therefore bound to lead to surprising discoveries, because it turns out that in fact, the vampire as we know him from today's popular culture is a latecomer to the established circle of things that go bump in the night. The term *vampire* itself didn't enter the vocabulary of western European languages until the first half of the eighteenth century—which means that St. Marcus's claim to have driven the vampires away from Volterra would have been met with blank stares for about twelve hundred years.[1]

But what of Romania, where our vampire saint was said to have been martyred? In *Breaking Dawn*, we learn of the Romanian coven of vampires, which was once the most powerful group within the whole vampire world until the Volturi overthrew its rule. The members of this mighty coven never bothered with hiding their true nature and let the people of Romania know that they were vampires. So, is Romania the true homeland of European vampires, before they began to carve their blood-red career through the jugulars of the entire European continent?

Surprisingly, the answer is no. Although Romania, or more precisely the historical province of Transylvania, is famed as the original breeding ground of European vampire myths, it owes this reputation to a Victorian novelist who had never set foot on the territory he was about to make (in)famous: Bram Stoker, author of *Dracula*. It was only through his novel, first published in 1897, that legends about the fearsome yet historical fifteenth-century Wallachian prince Vlad III the Impaler were linked with (more Slavic than Romanian) vampire lore, thus fusing folklore with a real, but totally unrelated, historical person to create the character of the vampire

Count Dracula.[2] By the time the novel was published, the "real" vampire hunts were long past—although not for nearly as long as Alice tells Bella in *New Moon*.

So where do the Volturi and the Cullens fit into this confusing mixture of fact, folklore, and fiction? To answer that question, we'll need to take a closer look at the development of vampires as we know them today.

Demonic Creatures with a Taste for Blood and Corpses That Won't Stay Put

> These vampires were corpses, who went out of their graves at night to suck the blood of the living.
>
> —*Voltaire, "Vampires"*[3]

This is the definition offered by the French philosopher Voltaire in his essay *Vampires*, published in 1764. Voltaire treated the topic with all of the biting sarcasm that an enlightened thinker could muster, but his definition remains valid today. Modern pop culture has produced many different kinds of vampires, but the two descriptive terms "living corpse" and "blood drinker" seem to be the attributes shared by all. This wasn't always the case, though; if one takes a closer look at our vampires' ancestors and relatives all over the world, one finds creatures that possess only one of the two traits without necessarily also possessing the other. Bella reads up on a few such species when she does her Internet research on vampires in *Twilight*; she refers to them as vampires, but none of these particular species actually fit both criteria of our definition.

Legends of blood-drinking creatures are abundant worldwide; almost every culture has developed them at some point in the past, and some of them can be traced back over millennia. Not all of these creatures were believed to have physical bodies: some were spirits or ghosts, others demons, some even gods; they could appear in the shape of a person or an animal, but they were usually supernatural beings from the start, not humans who had somehow been "turned." Many of them were flesh-eaters as well as blood-drinkers, and some preferred a particular kind of human prey, such as babies or young men.

Then there are the so-called revenants ("those who return"), the bodies of humans who—for some reason—can't rest peacefully in their graves and return to a kind of life-in-death, often to frighten or even harm the living. Revenant myths are common enough as well, although they are generally limited to areas where earth burials instead of cremation are the norm. These revenants aren't to be confused with ghosts—ghosts are merely the spiritual essence of the dead, although they can be dangerous to the living as well.[4] Revenants are dead people who rise from the grave in the flesh and can physically interact with humans, sometimes to the point of having sexual relations with them.

Fear of the dead returning seems to have been common since prehistoric times, since there is archaeological evidence of measures taken to prevent such an occurrence; yet the legends of undead bodies that have been preserved in writing don't go back as far as the stories of blood-drinkers.[5] Still, the revenant myth had greater influence on the development of the modern vampire than the legends of blood-drinkers; revenant myths from various regions of Central and Eastern Europe were especially influential in shaping the concept of vampires during the eighteenth century.

Romanian folklore had the *moroi* and *strigoi*, who sometimes drank blood and greatly influenced the development of the classic vampire, although strigoi could be living persons as well and were often linked to witchcraft.[6] Incidentally, the term *nosferatu*, which Bram Stoker's *Dracula* made popular, doesn't seem to be Romanian in origin and doesn't appear in any European revenant legends.[7]

Slavic folk belief, varying significantly from region to region, included many different kinds of undead revenants and many ways in which a living person could become one; premature or violent death was a risk, as well as improper burial. Ill-fated signs at birth (such as teeth in the newborn's mouth) could also be an indication that this person was likely to rise again from the grave. Children born out of wedlock and children who died before baptism were in danger, just like mothers who died in childbed. It was especially southern Slavic revenants who were said to leave their tombs at night, usually but not exclusively in physical form, and torment the living before returning to their graves. They weren't necessarily immortal, and blood-drinking was not a prominent feature although it was sometimes mentioned. Southern Slavic folktales mentioned revenants who were able to father children with living women, especially with their own widows. The term *vampire* itself is Slavic as well, although there is some debate about its origins.[8]

German revenant myths included the Wiedergänger ("those who walk again"), dead bodies who left their graves and sometimes sat on top of a sleeping person to suffocate them, and the Nachzehrer, a term that can mean both "those who devour after (their deaths)" and "those who pull (others) after them." Nachzehrer were restless corpses of a different kind: the body of a Nachzehrer stayed in the grave but made itself known by sucking or smacking sounds. Although it didn't physically attack the living, it was still lethal to them because it had the ability to suck the life force out of living creatures until they died. If the grave of a Nachzehrer was opened, it would often turn out that it had chewed on its shroud or even started gnawing at its own corpse, making it appear fatter and healthier than it had ever been in life.[9]

Remedies against these undead infestations included the destruction of the corpse (by dismembering or burning it), driving stakes or nails through various body parts (thus pinning it to the earth so that it couldn't rise again), and putting heavy stones on top of the grave. Religious measures included holy water, exorcism, and—if improper burial had been the cause—the performing of the correct rites. Several plants were believed to ward off the undead, garlic being the most prominent among them. German Nachzehrer could be rendered harmless by pouring poppy seeds into the coffin; allegedly, the creature would then have to count them at a rate of one grain per night before it could turn its attention to the living.

It is difficult to say how far back all of these myths go and how much they changed over time, because they were mostly passed down by oral tradition; there are few written accounts on the topic until the seventeenth century. Some elements may predate the spread of Christianity, although Christian ideas about souls, the afterlife, and satanic possession strongly influenced the development of the legends. Ironically, it was during the period of the Enlightenment, the eighteenth-century movement that began as a rejection of superstition and irrational belief, that the European vampire finally made his "official" debut in written sources.

Vampire Hunters and Vampire Science during the "Century of Light"

Vampire hunters are mentioned several times in the Twilight Saga. Yet, apart from Carlisle's father (who believed "in the reality of evil" so strongly that he went after vampires decades before they even became known in England) and his pitchfork-wielding posse, the people doing the hunting are usually other vampires or—like Carlisle—at least vampires-to-be. This idea would have come as a shock to the men who set out to stop the virtual plague of vampires that was spreading in the Balkan territories during the first half of the eighteenth century.

This "epidemic of vampirism" took place in territories that had only recently been taken from the Ottoman Turks by the Austrian Habsburg rulers, especially in Serbia. War, epidemics, and the not always peaceful mix of different cultures may have contributed to the general climate of fear and insecurity that helped the panic spread. Austrian army forces that were occupying the territory reported the local rumors of revenants that terrorized whole villages, and of exhumed bodies that showed no sign of decay. German-speaking scientists, doctors, and theologians started investigating and analyzing the topic; the results were published in newspapers, treatises, and books, thus introducing the "vampire"—both the word and the concept—to the Western European public.

These documents aren't horror stories, but they breathe the spirit of the Enlightenment, a movement that sought logical explanations for allegedly supernatural phenomena. Works like Michael Ranft's *Tractat von dem Kauen und Schmatzen der Todten in Gräbern* (Treatise on the chewing and smacking of the dead in [their] graves) blamed the chemical composition of certain soils for the fact that some corpses wouldn't decompose, although he expressed his belief that it was indeed possible for a dead body to maintain a "vegetative life force" for a certain amount of time.[10] Instead of resolving the question, the main accomplishment of such works was to fan the flames of public fascination. Emperor Charles VI himself sent delegates to investigate the matter in the affected areas, and the results of these investigations in turn caused more books to be written on the topic.[11]

So what was actually going on in Serbia and its neighboring territories? The most famous cases of suspected vampires concerned men returning from their graves to harass their relatives and neighbors. They allegedly choked people in their sleep, causing them to die within a few days, and drank the blood of the cattle, which put everyone who later ate the meat at risk of becoming vampires themselves.

Those early vampires utterly lacked the glamour and sex appeal of their literary successors: when the investigators opened the graves, they found bodies that showed no sign of decay but were bloated and smeared with blood. When their skin was pierced, they produced groaning sounds (most likely from the gases that had caused the swelling, which were now escaping). All this was taken as proof of their vampiric qualities by the local population, even though the investigators believed in natural causes.[12] It was only in 1755 that the emperor's daughter and successor, Maria Theresia, forbade the exhuming and desecrating of "undead" corpses.[13]

By that time, all of Europe had become familiar with vampires, and the scholarly debate—about the question whether vampires could be real, and how the strange phenomena that had been so well documented by the investigators could be explained—had been going strong since the 1730s.[14] In addition to scientific and philosophical questions, the matter posed theological problems as well: Augustin Calmet, one of France's leading theologians, published a detailed analysis of the existing material on vampires and reminded his readers that only God and his saints had the power to raise the dead.[15] Even Pope Benedict XIV found it necessary to denounce the belief in vampires as superstition in 1749.[16]

The debate went on for several decades, but then died down fairly quickly during the second half of the eighteenth century. Folk belief in vampires survived, and singular "executions" of suspicious corpses were documented into the early twentieth century, but overall, interest in "real" vampires was fading.[17] Except for a few latecomers like the British occultist Montague Summers, whose extensive research on vampires—which Bella stumbles upon in her own online research—in the first decades of the twentieth century was driven by his conviction that vampires really existed (and whose last name was reputedly chosen for their heroine by the creators of *Buffy the Vampire Slayer*), scholars dismissed the topic.[18] Yet vampires didn't fade back into obscurity, quite the contrary: instead of scientists, it was now writers who kept the undead alive. Toward the end of the eighteenth century, romantic authors began taking an interest in the subject, which meant that the disgusting walking corpses Europe had known until then were due for a drastic makeover.

Sexing Up a Myth: From European Vampire Literature to Pop Culture Vamps

Just as the first scientific works on vampires were written by German-speaking scholars, German authors were the first to introduce the vampire into fiction. The very first German vampire poem, Heinrich August Ossenfelder's "Der Vampir" (The vampire), is almost a crossover between the two genres, because it was commissioned in 1748 by the editor of a popular scientific journal to reflect the theme of an article on the vampire reports.[19]

Ossenfelder's vampire is still pretty close to his folkloristic roots, but this earliest piece of vampire fiction already presents the most important aspect of the literary revenant: the dark seducer. In Ossenfelder's poem, the vampire is a metaphor for the forceful seduction of an unwilling girl. Half a century later, Johann Wolfgang von Goethe reversed the gender roles in his poem "Die Braut von

Korinth" (The bride of Corinth), in which an undead girl pays a nighttime visit to the young man she was supposed to marry. Both poems also deal with the topic of religion, and although their approaches are different, both Ossenfelder's and Goethe's revenants rebel against the Christian faith, which they defy by their very existence.[20]

Still, the literary vampire was never much more than an experiment for German authors; it was in the hands of British romantic writers that he really came into his own. During the same year as Goethe's "Bride of Corinth," in 1797, vampires first appeared in English literature in Robert Southey's epic poem *Thalaba the Destroyer*.[21] However, the real breakthrough of the British vampire happened not in poetry, but prose: in 1819, John Polidori published his short story "The Vampyre," which was later thought to have been written by Polidori's famous employer, Lord Byron. Polidori's story introduced the vampire Lord Ruthven, a sinister, haughty aristocrat of remarkable intelligence, charm, and physical beauty. In Lord Ruthven's character, the dark seducer is fully developed—he preys on the innocent, winning them over with the sheer hypnotizing force of his presence.[22]

"The Vampyre" led to the development of an entire genre—a genre that produced literary works of all levels of quality, from the trashy gothic tales of *Varney the Vampire* (1845–1847) to Sheridan Le Fanu's novella *Carmilla* (1872), the finely crafted portrayal of a female vampire with strong lesbian overtones.[23] Different as all of these vampires are from one another, they have hardly anything in common with their forerunners in European folklore; appearances aside, what also sets them apart from the revenants of old is a much stronger interest in the drinking of blood. Blood is what keeps these vampires strong and beautiful, and after the middle of the nineteenth century, it also becomes the source of their immortality (a quality that is hardly ever mentioned in folk belief). "The blood is the life," as Bram Stoker puts it in the most famous of all vampire novels, *Dracula*.

Dracula, first published in 1897, established the literary vampire once and for all as the replacement of the old revenant myths.

Although some features of Stoker's vampire count can be traced back to the folktales, they're changed almost beyond recognition. It was Dracula, the elegant, mysterious Prince of Darkness, who subsequently set the path for the further development of the vampire genre, culminating in modern pop culture with its huge variety of blood-drinkers. Thus, the Victorian obsession with the mesmerizing combination of sex, blood, and death has been kept alive—or should we say undead?—until the present.

In his literary reincarnation, the European vampire has conquered the world. Thanks to the international nature of modern media, with their huge market for translated movies and books, Dracula's offspring count among the most familiar monsters all around the globe; in many cases, they even replaced, or at least strongly influenced, preexisting myths of blood-sucking and/or undead creatures. Beyond the field of literature, it was mostly vampire movies that brought about this international success; Dracula's silver screen incarnations from Bela Lugosi and Christopher Lee to Gary Oldman have kept the count's allure alive during a time when fewer and fewer readers find themselves able to stomach Stoker's original novel.

Vampires have made their way onto the stage as well. From the early plays that defined Dracula's "typical" look long before Bela Lugosi first donned the famous cape, to recent European musical adaptations, vampires have kept theatergoers in their thrall. Vampires appear in popular TV series, whether they are lead characters as in *Buffy* or *True Blood*, or guest appearances on the *X Files* and even in such unexpected places as *Baywatch*. Together with the still-booming genre of vampire literature, the (blood)suckers are basically everywhere.

With greater numbers comes greater diversity, so it is hardly surprising that each new adaptation of the topic comes up with its own specific take on the nature and qualities of vampires. Still, there are features that are so widely known by now that they have to be acknowledged, even if it's only to ridicule them as being utterly off the mark. For example, the vampire Louis from Anne Rice's *Interview with the Vampire* mocks the idea that vampires can be killed by staking them through the heart as peasant superstition (which is actually correct, since the belief can be traced back to the Eastern European vampire panic of the eighteenth century); however, staking is the standard way of killing vampires for Buffy the Vampire Slayer.

In *Buffy*, vampires also display an aversion to crosses and holy water, thus perpetuating the old Christian influence on European vampire myths within a secular American setting. Many other popular vampires are completely untroubled by Christian symbols of any kind, whether their human selves came from a Christian background or not. The matter lent itself to parody as well: in Roman Polanski's satirical movie *Dance of the Vampires* (1967), a barmaid tries to ward off the Jewish innkeeper-turned-vampire with a cross, to which he replies with a chuckle, "Oy vey, have you got the wrong vampire."

Another trait, the vampire's aversion to sunlight, is still one of the most common vampiric qualities in modern vampire fiction. This is all the more interesting because it is an extremely late addition to common vampire lore. While the vampires of European folklore were believed to walk during the night because the dark was their natural element, there is no mention of the belief that light would harm them, and even Bram Stoker's *Dracula* mentions only that the vampire's powers are weaker during the daylight hours, but not that daylight would kill him.[24] The concept that a vampire will crumble into dust when he's hit by the rays of the sun was introduced by F. W. Murnau's silent-movie classic *Nosferatu* in 1922, but it quickly became a standard feature in later vampire movies and literature alike. Besides light, many pop culture vampires are also vulnerable to fire, a weakness that originated in the old folk myths: burning was considered the safest way to destroy a revenant, because it combined the utter destruction of the troublesome undead body with the cleansing qualities of the flames.

Apart from an aversion to sunlight and fire, the drinking of blood and eternal life are still the most typical qualities of vampires. In addition, vampires have also held on to their seductive sex appeal, which may be the main reason for their ongoing success. Their ethical nature, however, is open to broad interpretation—besides the soulless monster of folklore and the sophisticated predator of early vampire literature, the modern vampire can also be a tortured creature whose human conscience rebels against his predatory nature, or who finds himself unable to bear his eternal, unchanging existence.[25] In the Twilight novels, Edward Cullen's struggle to overcome his "monstrous" nature is a good example of this ongoing trend in vampire fiction—which finally brings us back to the question this chapter opened with.

So, Where *Do* the Cullens Fit In?

It is always a tricky endeavor to "fit" a fairly modern concept into a historical setting. If the author doesn't have a firm grasp of historical details, errors are almost unavoidable, and the Twilight series is certainly no exception to that rule. Edward's tale of how Carlisle became a vampire in the middle of the seventeenth century is a very typical example—according to Carlisle, vampires were hunted and burned in England during Cromwell's rule, more than half a century before the word *vampire* even entered the English language. Going even further, the "ancient" vampire from the sewers who attacks Carlisle speaks Latin, insinuating that he existed since antiquity, when Latin was last used as a spoken language. However, ancient Rome knew no more of vampires than did seventeenth-century England: Greco-Roman mythology featured quite different sorts of blood-drinkers, like Empusa, the demonic daughter of the goddess Hecate, or Lamia, the ex-lover of Zeus, who drank the blood of children, and the *striges*, birdlike creatures of the night who feasted on human flesh and blood.[26]

Premature vampirism isn't the only problem that Edward's account of Carlisle's early life is suffering from, though. The claim that "time wasn't marked as accurately then" is utterly ludicrous, especially since it is allegedly coming from the son of a pastor, a man of education; for starters, the date of Carlisle's baptism would have been recorded in a church register, so he would know exactly when he was born. The common punishment for witchcraft in early modern

England wasn't burning, but hanging, and it wasn't carried out by mobs, but by courts. Hiding in the London sewers would have been tricky during the seventeenth century, because London's sewage system dates from the mid-nineteenth century; before that, open drains, culverted river branches, and cesspits were in use. Finally, Carlisle would hardly have had a chance to hide under "rotting potatoes" in a London cellar in the 1760s, given that potatoes were still a rare exotic curiosity at the time—the first potatoes had been brought to England from the New World only a few decades earlier and were cultivated in botanic gardens, but not yet as a source of food.

Historical nitpicking aside, though, how do the Cullens and their kind fit into the overall concept of vampirism, either with the "real" vampires of early modern European folklore or with the fictional undead from books and movies?

If we go by Voltaire's classical definition that was mentioned previously, we're in the clear—Twilight vampires are undead humans who feed on blood. They also live forever, which is probably the most distinctive feature of the literary vampire, and possess the supernatural beauty and strength that is typical of this species. The primary danger they face is the most traditional one: fire. Still, their overall makeup is rather peculiar as far as the commonly accepted idea of vampires is concerned.

Twilight vampires are not only frozen in time and therefore unchanging like most vampires from literature, they are basically moving marble statues, since their bodies are hard and cold like stone. All fluids in their bodies have been replaced by venom, a liquid that is apparently responsible for their vampiric qualities since it can infect victims who are bitten and turns them into vampires themselves. The idea of vampirism as a contagious infection goes back to the old folk beliefs and is widespread in literature as well, but the venom introduces a new element. Also, while many vampires are cold to the touch, the idea that they are hard as stone sets Twilight vampires apart from their fellow undead, not to mention the fact that it creates a lot of practical problems, since Twilight vampires regularly touch humans and can even father children with human mothers. This last detail is not such an uncommon feature in itself: the idea that revenants can father children is an established part of southern Slavic vampire folklore, and vampire fiction knows of vampire-human hybrids as well as of children whose parents are both vampires.[27]

Even more remarkable is the appearance of Twilight vampires: not only are they pale like most vampires in fiction (as opposed to the ruddy corpses that eighteenth-century vampire hunters dug up), they also give off a scent that is appealing to humans, which is a rather peculiar ability for creatures who are basically corpses. They don't sport the fangs that have been a standard feature for the trashier part of the genre ever since the "penny dreadful" novels from the middle of the nineteenth century, but they still feed on blood exclusively. The nature of their diet is reflected in their eye color: their eyes are red if they feed on human blood, golden if they feed on animals, and black if they're hungry.

These color-coded eyes also define their moral qualities: evil vampires drink human blood, good vampires are "vegetarians," which—ironically—means that they live exclusively on animals. This concept isn't new, although it's only in modern literature that the killing of animals was considered a morally acceptable alternative for vampires (like Louis in *Interview with the Vampire*, who lives on rats for a while because he doesn't want to kill humans). Folk belief knew of animal-eating vampires as well, but they were feared no less for it: first, because the death of their cattle posed a huge threat to rural populations who depended on their animals, and second, because it was believed that anyone who ate the meat of these animals would also be turned into a vampire.

Another significant deviation from "standard" vampires is the effect that sunlight has on Twilight vampires: not only is it harmless to them, it even accentuates their beauty because it makes them sparkle like crystals. This is an unparalleled quality—Montague Summers only mentions the Bulgarian legend that a newly risen vampire makes its presence known at night by giving off sparks "like those from a flint and steel," which is most likely unrelated to Twilight vampires, given their highly flammable nature.[28]

Speaking of flammable, one of the most striking differences between the Twilight series and other vampire romances is the nature of Edward and Bella's relationship. Ever since Lord Ruthven's appearance in literature in 1819, it was the vampire who picked out his or her human prey, who followed and seduced the victim. Modern vampire fiction has often changed the intention of the vampire. It's no longer (just) the blood that the vampire is after; it may also be sexual attraction and/or a true romantic interest, but the undead seducer still uses his or her dangerous appeal to win over the human, often against the victim's better judgment. Edward and Bella start out rather traditionally, with Bella falling for Edward's dark charms and Edward beginning to stalk her, but it soon turns out that their roles have been reversed: it is Bella, the mortal girl, who tries to overcome Edward's resistance to her erotic advances. Edward is the vampire, but it's Bella who is the vamp, the woman who does her best to overcome her chosen partner's willpower and seduce him. Thus, the dynamics between hunter and prey have fundamentally shifted; the classic connection between Eros and Thanatos, sexual attraction and death, that is the basis of the vampire's erotic appeal has been broken. This reflects Meyer's statement that her "books are about life, not death—love, not lust," but it goes against the grain of the entire vampire genre, which has been firmly based on the figure of the dark seducer ever since Ossenfelder's poem in 1748.[29]

With all of these striking deviations from the genre's most typical features, it is all the more remarkable that the Twilight Saga doesn't attempt to establish its own vampire mythology, as other authors—such as Anne Rice in her Vampire Chronicles—have done. Bella learns about vampires on a need-to-know basis, and even though there is some background information that goes a long way back in time (such as the Volturi's three-thousand-year-long rule over Volterra), the underlying mythological questions are never addressed. There is no vampiric "creation myth," not even in *Breaking Dawn*, the book that greatly expands Twilight vampire lore with the birth of Renesmee and Bella's own transformation into a vampire. As readers, we never learn why Twilight vampires are the way they are and what made them so different from all the vampires we knew before.

So Where Does That Leave Us?

Since vampires don't exist in the first place, it's not much of a conclusion to say that Twilight vampires are fictional. It *is* valid, however, to conclude that vampire history and lore as they are presented in the Twilight series are almost entirely fictional, because not only do they contradict most European vampire myths, they also don't correlate with general historical events from ancient times to the modern period. Carlisle's anachronistic hunts of Latin-speaking vampires in the London sewers are a good example, but far from the only one. People in Romania didn't believe in vampires fifteen hundred years ago, mostly due to the fact that the Slavs, among whom the European vampire myth originated, hadn't even settled yet in the territories that make up today's Romania.[30] The Italian legends of *Stregoni benefici* that Bella discovers during her Internet research don't exist—Italy never developed any kind of vampire folklore beyond the Roman legends of blood-drinkers, and besides, there was never folk belief in "good vampires" anywhere since vampires were considered unnatural and dangerous by their very nature. Finally, although the city of Volterra does exist, its real patron saint is St. Justus, whose holiday is celebrated on June 5; the real St. Marcus Day is April 25, and it commemorates the author of one of the four gospels, not a vampire hunter.

Of course, it's not necessary to ground a work of fantasy literature in historical fact; most classic vampire novels don't bother with it either. What's probably more interesting is to note that Twilight vampires also don't have all that much in common with their fictional cousins throughout literature from Carmilla to Lestat; neither is there a lot that connects them to popular movie or TV vampires, be it Christopher Lee's Dracula or Spike from *Buffy the Vampire Slayer*. Therefore, Bella's question "Could the Cullens be vampires?" (*Twilight*, 138) was probably best answered by Alice in *New Moon*, when she told Bella, "We Cullens are unique in more ways than you know." (*New Moon*, 428.)

Notes

1. The term is Slavic in origin; its first known use in a German text dates from 1725. The English and French versions of the word are derived from the German form *Vampyr* (modern spelling: *Vampir*). Norbert Borrmann, *Vampirismus oder die Sehnsucht nach Unsterblichkeit* (Munich: Diederichs, 1998), 13.

2. Raymond T. Mcnally and Radu Florescu, *in Search of Dracula: The History of Dracula and Vampires* (Boston: Houghton Mifflin Company, 1994).

3. Voltaire, "Vampires," in *A Philosophical Dictionary from the French of M. de Voltaire*, vol. 6 (London: John and Henry L. Hunt, 1824), 304.

4. Christa A. Tuczay, "'. . . swem er den tôt getuot, dem sûgents ûz daz warme bluot'. Wiedergänger, Blutsauger und Dracula in deutschen Texten des Mittelalters," in *Poetische Wiedergänger. Deutschsprachige Vampirismus-Diskurse vom Mittelalter bis zur Gegenwart*, ed. Julia Bertschik and Christa A. Tuczay (Tübingen, Ger.: Francke Verlag, 2005), 61ff.

5. Annett Stülzebach, "Vampir- und Wiedergängererscheinungen aus volkskundlicher und archäologischer Sicht," *Concilium medii aevi* 1 (1998): 105–113.

6. Claude Leconteux, *Die Geschichte der Vampire. Metamorphose eines Mythos*, trans. Harald Ehrhardt (Düsseldorf and Zürich: Artemis and Winkler, 2001), 111–113.

7. Patrick Johnson, "Count Dracula and the Folkloric Vampire: Thirteen Comparisons," *Journal of Dracula Studies*, no. 3 (2001), blooferland.com/drc/images/03Johnson.rtf.

8. Elena E. Levkievskaja, "La mythologie slave: problèmes de répartition dialectale (une étude de cas: le vampire)," *Cahiers slaves*1 (September 1997), www.recherches-slaves.paris4.sorbonne.fr/Cahier1/Levkievskaja.htm.

9. Hanns Bächtold-Stäubli and Eduard Hoffmann-Krayer, eds., *Handwörterbuch des deutschen Aberglaubens*, vol. 6 (Berlin: Walter de Gruyter, 1987), 812–823; vol. 9 (Berlin: Walter de Gruyter, 1987), 570–578.

10. Michael Ranft, *Tractat von dem Kauen und Schmatzen der Todten in Gräbern, worin die wahre Beschaffenheit derer Hungarischen Vampyrs und Blut-Sauger gezeigt, auch alle von dieser Materie bißher zum Vorschein gekommene Schrifften recensiret werden* (Leipzig: Teubners Buchladen, 1734), http://commons.wikimedia.org/wiki/Tractat_von_dem_Kauen_und_Schmatzen_der_Todten_in_Gr%C3%A4bern.

11. Hans Meurer, "1732—Die Wiedergeburt des Vampirs in der Neuzeit," in *Draculas Wiederkehr*, ed. Thomas Le Blanc, Clemens Ruthner, and Bettina Twrsnick, vol. 35 of *Schriftenreihe und Materialien der Phantastischen Bibliothek Wetzlar* (Wetzlar, Ger.: Förderkreis Phantastik in Wetzlar, 2003), 192.

12. Peter Mario Kreuter, "Vom 'üblen Geist' zum 'Vampier': Die Darstellung des Vampirs in den Berichten österreichischer Militärärzte zwischen 1725–1756," in *Poetische Wiedergänger: Deutschsprachige Vampirismus-Diskurse vom Mittelalter bis zur Gegenwart*, ed. Julia Bertschik and Christa A. Tuczay (Tübingen, Ger.: Francke Verlag, 2005), 113–128.

13. Gábor Klaniczay, "Historische Hintergründe: Der Aufstieg der Vampire im Habsburgerreich des 18. Jahrhunderts," in *Poetische Wiedergänger. Deutschsprachige Vampirismus-Diskurse vom Mittelalter bis zur Gegenwart*, ed. Julia Bertschik and Christa A. Tuczay (Tübingen, Ger.: Francke Verlag, 2005), 86.

14. For a compilation of these sources see Klaus Hamberger, *Mortuus non mordet: Dokumente zum Vampirismus 1689–1791* (Vienna: Turia and Kant, 1992).

15. Dom Augustin Calmet, "Dissertation sur les vampires, les revenants en corps, les excommuniés, les oupires ou vampires, brucolaques etc.," ed. Roland Villeneuve (Grenoble: Editions Jérôme Million, 1998).

16. Klaniczay, "Historische Hintergründe," 103.

17. Clemens Ruthner, "Sexualität Macht Tod/t. Prolegomena zu einer Literaturgeschichte des Vampirismus," *Kakanien Revisited* (13/4/2002), www.kakanien.ac.at/beitr/fallstudie/CRuthner1.pdf, 6.

18. Montague Summers, *The Vampire: His Kith and Kin* (London: Routledge and Kegan Paul, 1928); Montague Summers, *The Vampire in Europe* (London: Routledge and Kegan Paul, 1929).

19. Heide Crawford, "The Cultural-Historical Origins of the Literary Vampire in Germany," *Journal of Dracula Studies* 7 (2005), http://blooferland.com/drc/images/07Heide.rtf.

20. Ruthner, "Sexualität Macht Tod/t," 14ff.

21. Marco Frenschowski, "Vampire in Mythologie und Folklore," in *Draculas Wiederkehr*, ed. Thomas Le Blanc, Clemens Ruthner, and Bettina Twrsnick, vol. 35 of *Schriftenreihe und Materialien der Phantastischen Bibliothek Wetzlar* (Wetzlar, Ger.: Förderkreis Phantastik in Wetzlar, 2003), 53.

22. Wayne Bartlett and Flavia Idriceanu, *Legends of Blood: The Vampire in History and Myth* (Phoenix Mill, Eng.: Sutton Publishing, 2005), 30ff.

23. Bartlett and Idriceanu, *Legends of Blood*, 33; Frenschowski, "Vampire in Mythologie und Folklore," 54.

24. Johnson, "Count Dracula and the Folkloric Vampire," chap. 9.

25. Borrmann, *Vampirismus*, 90–93.

26. Frenschowski, "Vampire in Mythologie und Folklore," 36–38.

27. Interestingly, in Serbian folk belief, vampire-human hybrids had the ability to see and kill vampires. Levkievskaja, "La mythologie slave."

28. Summers, *The Vampire in Europe*, 317. The information that vampires are highly flammable is given on Stephenie Meyer's official Web site in the FAQ category for *Breaking Dawn*: http://stepheniemeyer.com/bd_faq.html.

29. "Will New Bestseller 'Eclipse' Harry Potter?" www.abcnews.go.com/WN/story?id=3499052.

30. Romania in itself is not a Slavic country, given that the Romanian language derives from the Latin; therefore, the blood-drinking *strigoi* of Romanian folklore go back to the *striges* of ancient Rome.

Getting Younger Every Decade

Being a Teen Vampire during the Twentieth Century

Kat Burkhart

"How old are you?"
"Seventeen," he answered promptly.
"And how long have you been seventeen?"
"A while."

—*Bella and Edward (*Twilight*, 185)*

As the Cullen family moved around the world over the course of the twentieth century, decades passed, and individual family members were given choices as to what roles to play in each new community. Although Esme and Carlisle Cullen both appear to be young, claiming to be in their mid- to late twenties or sometimes in their late thirties, they would have been considered adults, no matter where the family lived. However, Edward, Rosalie, Emmett, Alice, and Jasper, the "children" of the Cullen family, were "frozen in time" during their late teens. As a result, they could have played a variety of roles in different settings, and their experiences as teenagers must have changed quite a bit over the course of the twentieth century. The primary goal of the Cullen family is to remain inconspicuous, to blend in with the local human population, and to act appropriately for the circumstances and the decade. In different locations and at different time periods, the roles changed as a result for each of the Cullens; and as teenage vampires, their experiences—including the family roles they played, whether as "siblings" or openly married couples—would have reflected changes in the lives of American teenagers throughout the twentieth century.

Most of the Cullen family members became vampires in the first few decades of the twentieth century. The exceptions were Jasper, who was turned during the American Civil War and Carlisle, turned just before Cromwell's rule in seventeenth-century England. All members of the family were considered adults, or nearly adults, during their human lives; but in twenty-first-century America, Edward, Rosalie, Emmett, Alice, and Jasper now "play" at being modern teenagers without the responsibilities of work or children. They do not always live together, sometimes choosing to travel or to attend college. Because they must remain inconspicuous, they must move frequently, before their neighbors notice that they are not aging. "Sometimes they [Rosalie and Emmett] live separately from us, as a married couple. But the younger we pretend to be, the longer we can stay in any given place," Edward explains to Bella Swan. (*Twilight*, 289.)

When these teens were human, their lives were very different from the modern life they share with Bella. Jasper might have attended school during the 1860s, but a boy in that period was just as likely to have to make his own living by the age of sixteen. In the last half of the nineteenth century, only about half of all eligible students were enrolled in school, since school attendance was not mandatory for children under a certain age, as it is today.[1] Older boys would have been expected to work, to join the military, or perhaps (if they came from very well-off families) to go on to college. Teenage girls from middle-strata families were expected to help their mothers with housekeeping until they got married, but working-class girls (like their brothers) were expected to get a job and contribute toward their own support. Many became domestic servants in the homes of better-off families. In the late nineteenth and early twentieth centuries, high school was thus a luxury some students could not afford, and many left school after completing the eighth grade, since their families needed them to contribute to the household income by either taking a job, working on the family farm or (if they were girls) in the household, helping with younger siblings, or doing chores. The beginning of the twentieth century brought sustained increases in school enrollment for all children, however. The overall enrollment rate of school-age children and teens reached 51 percent in 1900 and increased to 75 percent by 1940.[2] As the decades passed, therefore, the Cullen teens would have increasingly been expected to attend high school, or perhaps college, wherever they moved in the United States.

As greater numbers of students enrolled in high school, and as more and more colleges began to accept female students, teenagers' lives, and the lives of the Cullen family, changed as well. The expectations and responsibilities of teenagers were altered over time due to greatly increased life expectancy, increased secondary school enrollment for both genders, and delayed marriage. During the century when the Cullens created their family, life expectancy at birth increased from forty-six to seventy-five years for men and from forty-eight to eighty years for women.[3] For many people in the United States around 1900, by the age of seventeen (when Edward was turned), they had already lived one-third of their lives. Over the course of the century this changed, however, and so the Cullens increasingly would have appeared to the humans around them as part of the younger segment of the population as a whole.

Dramatic changes also took place in women's roles and their level of education over the course of the century. In the late 1800s and early 1900s few women expected to attend college or have independent careers of their own, although working-class women usually added to their households' incomes by doing menial labor, and farm wives contributed enormously to the economies of rural communities. Many households thus depended on women's financial contributions, but the ideal presented in American popular culture of this period was that of the stay-at-home middle-class mother, who devoted herself to housework and childrearing. Rosalie fits this role as a member of the middle class, though this powerful norm was the reality only for a minority of the more affluent families. Rosalie and Esme sought to define themselves through this traditional nurturing female role of wife and mother, even decades later when Bella met them. Both very much wanted to be mothers, and they grieved because that option was taken from them.

During wartime or other hard times, teens often took control of their lives by dropping out of school to help support the family by working, leaving the family—giving them one less mouth to feed—or enlisting in the military.[4] Edward and Jasper, born during turbulent times, were considered by many to be adults at the time they changed. Both were excited and eager to become soldiers and ready to assume adult responsibilities. Jasper left his family to strike out on his own, never to be heard from again: "When I was human, I lived in Houston, Texas. I was almost seventeen when I joined the Confederate Army in 1861. I lied to the recruiters and told them I was twenty. I was tall enough to get away with it." (*Eclipse*, 292.) For over a year Jasper thrived in the military, quickly rising through the ranks to become "the youngest Major in Texas," but from his tales, one can guess that he was not considered typical even when he was human.

What Is a Teenager?

> Only a teenage boy would agree to this: deceiving both our parents while repairing dangerous vehicles using money meant for my college education.
>
> He didn't see anything wrong with that picture.
>
> —*Bella (*New Moon, *136)*

Today, the teen or adolescent years are seen as a time of transition between dependence and independence. A hundred years ago, this transition was often very swift and hardly noticeable.[5] By the late twentieth century, however, the teen lifestyle had expanded to become a stage of life that lasted for many years; it usually included high school attendance and the pursuit of many diverse interests, including popular music, dating, emerging technologies, fashion, and establishing one's own identity. For many twentieth-century teens, sports and other games became a primary focus of their leisure time, as well. For some, the teen years were also a time of experimenting with drinking, sex, and drugs; this sort of experimentation had characterized earlier generations, as well, but late-twentieth-century popular culture was more accepting of such behavior, and thus it tended to take place more openly in many social circles.

Obviously, the Cullen family members do not eat or drink human food (unless they have to), play high school sports, or show any interest in dating humans (except for Edward). They do, however, enjoy fast cars, fashionable clothes, cutting-edge technology, music, and games. At the prom with Bella, Edward demonstrates that he is an excellent dancer, as are Alice and Jasper, and Rosalie and Emmett. Though they do not find their high school academic curriculum very challenging, the Cullen teens seem to enjoy the life of a teenager and all the fun that goes with it.

What the Kids Today Are Listening To

Edward loves a wide variety of music. He is a talented pianist and keeps an enormous music collection in his room; he mentions music often and even composes pieces for the piano. Edward frequently plays music in his car, shares some of his musical interests with Bella, and composes a lullaby that he sings or hums regularly for her. When Bella sees Edward's room for the first time, she sees modern media; there are no vinyl albums in his collection. Edward, like the rest of the Cullen family, enjoys the latest technology and appreciates a state-of-the-art sound system. In *New Moon* Edward's siblings even buy Bella a new stereo for her truck, so that she will also have a modern sound system.

Decades are often defined by the music and dance popular during a particular era. From jazz and ragtime to swing and rock and roll, teens have been early devotees of the new sounds and the dances that accompany the new music. The Lindy, the jitterbug, and the Charleston—popular dances in the 1920s, 1930s, and 1940s—all caused the adults in charge to wonder about the morality and appropriateness of the dances.[6] Music was increasingly available on the radio, in record shops, in jukeboxes, and in clubs. The widespread availability of records in the 1950s, augmented by television and radio and the debut of rock and roll, meant that this decade was marked by huge changes in musical tastes, and the generational tensions that accompanied them.[7] No wonder Edward enjoyed the music of the fifties: "'Music in the fifties was good. Much better than the sixties, or the seventies, ugh!' He shuddered. 'The eighties were bearable.'" (*Twilight*, 286.)

With a radio in every home and every car, the Cullen family would have been able to hear a variety of music, news, and sports programming without going outside, and they probably would have enjoyed many sports broadcasts, particularly baseball. One imagines every Cullen house with at least one radio, though very possibly many, so that each member of the household could listen to his or her own choice of programming. And they probably listened to more than just music; they would have been interested in news, sports, and weather as well. Radio would have been a connection to the outside human world. The Cullen family could isolate themselves, but to remain inconspicuous they would need to be connected to current events.

Dracula and the Drive-in Movie

Movie theaters became popular all over the United States during the 1920s, and because films were often shown at night, the Cullen family could easily enjoy this form of entertainment. By the time Edward felt comfortable enough to be around humans without killing them, he thus would have had new choices of entertainment. Before the spread of television sets after World War II, private home consumption of popular culture was limited to the radio and the printed page, and in order to see any sort of "show" (whether live or filmed), families had to go out in public. The most famous vampire movie of all time came out in 1931, starring Bela Lugosi as *Dracula*. Bela Lugosi's performance as Count Dracula lent a sense of sophistication and aristocracy to the vampire image in popular culture.[8] The Cullens might have gone to see the movie *Dracula*, if only to understand the current public image of the vampire; one can imagine the conversations they had among themselves afterward.

Clark Gable, born in 1901, the same year as Edward, starred in many movies that the Cullen family might have seen in the theater during the years between the two world wars. *It Happened One Night*, *Gone with the Wind*, *Call of the Wild*, and *Mutiny on the Bounty* were all great successes and would have been part of the conversation around town.[9]

The advent of the drive-in movie probably allowed the Cullens to look the part of typical teens. Going to a drive-in movie, which would of course play only after dark, would be a great way to avoid contact with humans but still interact in a way. Low-budget science fiction movies became quite popular during the fifties. One can imagine Edward, perhaps with Rosalie and Emmett, or perhaps alone at the drive-in, watching *I Was a Teenage Werewolf* or *Invasion of the Body Snatchers*.[10]

Teens generally embrace new technology and tend to be very adaptive. The Cullen family uses technology to its advantage and probably has a unique perspective on how changing technology affects social structures and values. Some twentieth-century technological advances had a major impact on the general teenage population but were of little consequence to our vampire family. The availability of birth control pills, for example, brought about many changes in American culture and family structure that people are still debating today, but that development would have had little impact on the Cullens' day-to-day existence. The invention and common use of tinted windows in automobiles were probably more important to them than any chemical or food-related inventions, since it allowed them to drive on sunny days without sparkling.

Television

The first television in the United States was unveiled at the World's Fair in New York City in 1939. One can imagine that the Cullen family, then consisting only of Carlisle, Esme, and Edward, would have greatly enjoyed the newfangled device and bought one of the very first sets for home use. Unable to attend outdoor daytime functions or even be seen outside, the Cullen family might have missed out on a great deal of information during the first half of the twentieth century, but the arrival of television would have changed the situation. Radio broadcasts (available starting in the 1920s) were very helpful but were limited in scope. To blend in and to learn something about their community, the Cullens may have subscribed to the local papers. The advent of television must have broadened their sources of information considerably; the Cullen family could now see what was happening in different parts of the country without leaving home or traveling during the daytime. In the early days of television they probably gathered around the set just as human families of the day did to watch popular programs. In the late 1950s daytime dramas might have entertained them, as well as evening programs such as *Alfred Hitchcock Presents*.[11]

Modern cable and satellite television (available after the 1970s), with hundreds of channels available twenty-four hours a day, could keep the Cullen family entertained indoors for long periods of time. They could also play board games and cards, but playing games of chance or strategy with Alice and/or Edward would offer limited amusement. They may have tried video games as well, though with perfect recall, reflexes and no need to sleep, they might get bored with them quickly.

Automobiles

The availability of the automobile, which improved steadily in terms of speed and available options throughout the century, was probably a boon to the Cullen family; they could explore the world without attracting attention or coming into direct contact with humans. Like their homes, which they changed often to avoid notice, the Cullens would have had to buy new models regularly in order to blend in. There are no vintage cars in the Cullen garage; they all enjoy speed too much to keep antique cars. One would imagine, however, that they would always have the fastest cars available. Many of the cars in the Cullen garage are ostentatious; they make an effort to blend in by purchasing up-to-date ones, but their cars are a hobby and a point of pride for them.

The automobile existed during Edward's human lifetime, but he probably would not have had his own car, as he does by the time he meets Bella. As humans, Rosalie and Emmett were also probably familiar with them but they probably didn't own one (although their parents might have). Rosalie contradicts the stereotype that only boys are interested in cars, and she is constantly tuning and fixing up the Cullen family cars, including her own BMW. Her hobby represents a small rebellion against the norms for girls of her youth: in 1933, the odds would have been slim that she ever would have been under a car, working on one and enjoying it.

Throughout the twentieth century, teens have been captivated by the automobile and the freedom it represents. Jacob Black and Bella, both modern teens, are highly conscious of the independence that comes with having a car, though neither drives a new car, because their families cannot afford it; Jacob builds his own car throughout *Twilight* and *New Moon* for just that reason. Bella's first priority when she moves to Forks is to get her own car so that her father doesn't have to drive her around.

Going Steady, Dating, and Teen Marriage

Marriage before the age of twenty, common in the nineteenth century (although never the typical age for marriage in any period of American history), has become a much-debated topic in recent decades, as reflected in Bella's own struggles with this question. Before college or other skill-based training became an expected part of girls' education after World War I, many girls did marry in their teens with the blessings of their parents and their communities, although such brides were still below the median age for marriage for women of this period. Census data shows that during the first half of the twentieth century, the median age for brides fell between twenty and twenty-one years of age, but teen brides weren't unheard of. Rosalie, for example, had planned to marry young and have a family, a goal that ended at the hands of her fiancé and his friends. Bella has a late-twentieth-century expectation that marriage should come after she finishes her education, although ironically, she does end up marrying Edward at the age of eighteen.

Rosalie lays out this generational difference for Bella, describing expectations that were actually old-fashioned (and realistic only for those from affluent families) even back in the 1930s: "I lived in a different world than you do, Bella. My human world was a much simpler place. It was nineteen thirty-three. I was eighteen, and I was beautiful. My life was perfect." (*Eclipse*, 154.) "It was a different time. I was the same age as you, but I was ready for it all. I yearned for my own little baby. I wanted my own house and a husband who would kiss me when he got home from work—just like Vera. Only I had a very different house in mind." (*Eclipse*, 156.)

In 1933, marriage was considered the most desirable option for a girl from a small-town middle-class family like Rosalie's, especially if she could marry someone above her family's middle-class social station. Bella, on the other hand, is embarrassed to be a teen bride, having been raised with the idea that teen marriage is not something to be proud of. Edward shares his own perspective on marriage with her, based on his human memories and feelings, and she begins to understand how much things have changed over the decades. Edward's feelings about getting married at eighteen "for love" are more understandable to Bella, once she considers and tries to understand his perspective. Compared to others in his generation, however, Edward was probably a bit old-fashioned even when he was human, since teenage grooms were even less typical than teen brides, when he was young.

Bella has always been the caregiver—especially of her mother—but even with her nurturing instincts, she does not plan on having a husband and children at such a young age. Bella is shocked and stunned to find out that one of Jacob's older sisters, hardly older than herself, is married: "Married. Wow. I was stunned. The twins were only a little over a year older than I was." (*Twilight*, 120.) In *Twilight*, she begins to examine her own feelings about marriage, though she never envisions herself a teen bride. "I'm not that girl, Edward. The one who gets married right out of high school like some small-town hick who got knocked up by her boyfriend!" Do you know what people would think? Do you realize what century this is? People don't just get married at eighteen! Not smart people, not responsible, mature people! I wasn't going to be that girl! That's not who I am." (*Eclipse*, 276.) But Edward truly believes that it is reasonable to marry at age eighteen for love. "I was that boy, who would have—as soon as I discovered that you were what I was looking for—gotten down on one knee and endeavored to secure your hand." (*Eclipse*, 277.) If he had done so, however, Edward would have been a very young bridegroom, even for his own generation, but Bella seems unaware of this.

Rosalie and Emmett, a "newlywed" couple for at least a decade, would have been hard-pressed to describe themselves in any other terms; but since they were both born in 1915, this probably seemed "natural" to them. In the early years of their marriage, Rosalie and Emmett probably did not leave the house often, and so they had little worry about blending in. During the 1930s and 1940s, a married couple their age would still have caused little comment, anyway. Edward seems to accept it as normal, as well, commenting dryly that "I suppose we'll have to go to their wedding in a few years, *again*." (*Twilight*, 289.) Sometimes Rosalie and Emmett live as a married couple and travel on extended honeymoons. But as time passed, a teen marriage would have become increasingly conspicuous, which explains why Rosalie and Emmett, by the late twentieth century, begin to present themselves as foster siblings who are romantically involved.

The roles that each vampire plays within the family (as sibling, adopted child, or spouse) therefore change over time, reflecting changes in social expectations regarding teen marriage, along with what the Cullens find convenient in each new community. Edward has played the role of Esme's brother as well as her son, for example. When we are first introduced to the Cullen family, the public story is that Jasper and Rosalie are twins. By the late twentieth century, a teen marriage between Alice and Jasper would have been less socially acceptable, apparently, than presenting them to the people of Forks as romantically involved teenagers under the same roof. The same is apparently true of Rosalie and Emmett, who put on great displays of affection; both couples would have created much more gossip in previous decades, when it would have been easier to simply present them as teenage married couples.

Eager Human Soldiers or Draft-Dodging Vampires?

War was often presented in Victorian and early-twentieth-century culture as the true test of manhood, and Edward was excited about going to war; indeed, he told Bella later that he'd dreamed of becoming a soldier. Although a small percentage of the soldiers in the Civil War were drafted, military conscription was first used on a broad scale in 1917 and would have been the talk of all young men of Edward's generation. The Selective Service System, created to administer the draft in World War I, registered 2,810,296 inductions (draftees) between September 1917 and November 1918.[12] Edward had hoped to be one of these soldiers, but influenza put a stop to this dream and opened the door to immortality instead. Edward never achieved his human dream of becoming a soldier, but as the decades passed, he would watch generation after generation of his peers go off to war. Though Edward would technically never reach the age of eighteen, the draft and military service would have been a topic of discussion at schools and in cities and towns across the country. Over the course of the twentieth century, Edward must have watched the young men around him go off to war and return, time and again, always aware that he could never join them. Over 10 million young men were drafted for World War II, then just over 1.5 million for the Korean War.[13] Edward would have known classmates who were drafted or who volunteered to fight in each war.

Even if the Cullen men did not socialize much with humans, there might have been talk about why Edward and Emmett were not being drafted or were choosing not to serve. Because their primary goal was to avoid attracting attention, the need to avoid the draft would have created a problem, especially during the Korean and Vietnam Wars. After Jasper and Alice joined the Cullen family, the United States drafted 1.8 million men for the Vietnam War.[14] Talk about the young male Cullens might have begun again, especially if they were living in smaller, rural communities at the time. During that period it might have even been wise for the Cullen family, like many others who wished to avoid the draft, to move north to Canada or Alaska. Over the decades, the Cullens spent a great deal of time with the Denalis. Indeed, they might have been living in Alaska when it officially entered the Union as the forty-ninth state on January 3, 1959.

What *Is* an Adult, After All?

What makes someone an adult? This subject has been debated for decades, if not centuries. When Bella and Jacob meet as human teens, they discuss and debate in a lighthearted way their responsibilities and skills:

> Sure, but, considering the difference in maturity between guys and girls, don't you have to count that in dog years? What does that make me, about twelve years older? (*New Moon*, 146.)
>
> We bantered like that till Hoquiam, still arguing over the correct formula to determine age—I lost two more years because I didn't know how to change a tire, but gained one back for being in charge of the bookkeeping at my house. By the time we got back to La Push, I was twenty-three and he was thirty—he was definitely weighting skills in his favor. (*New Moon*, 147.)

Bella's and Jacob's ideas about what made an "adult" were both rooted in their own time and place: back when Edward was born, in 1901, a young woman might well have done the bookkeeping for a family business. But few would have known how to change an automobile tire.

When Edward and the rest of the Cullen family had been growing up, however, their human definitions of what it meant to be an adult might have included someone able to take over the family business or farm, to support a household, or to defend one's country by going to war. None of these roles occurred to Jacob or Bella in their debates over "adult" skills; at least, they certainly weren't the first traits that came to mind for teenagers in their culture. But definitions of adulthood changed over time. Rosalie originally saw adulthood defined as motherhood, marriage, and the ability to run her own house. Jasper was able to leave everything and everyone he knew to join the army. Carlisle is the father figure of the vampire family, although his chronological age is not much older than the others. He is respected and deferred to because of his wisdom and patience. Carlisle understands who he is and what he and his family stand for. In the Twilight series, adulthood is defined in multiple ways: by legal age, by skills, and by the willingness to sacrifice oneself for others. But each character's definition of what it means to be "adult" reflects the values of the period he or she grew up in.

Bella: Born in the Wrong Century?

> "I was a very different person from my mother. Someone thoughtful and cautious. The responsible one, the grownup. That's how I saw myself. That was the person I knew".
>
> —*Bella* (Eclipse, 45)

Bella doesn't see herself as a typical teenager, at least not for her own generation. Her mother describes her as an old soul: "My mom always says I was born thirty-five years old and that I get more middle-aged every year." (*Twilight*, 106.) Bella handles responsibility well, cooks, does the housework and the grocery shopping for herself and Charlie, and is in charge of paying the bills.

She does not date and has never had a boyfriend. Bella is horrified that she ends up attending the prom and is not interested in fashion, makeup, movies, or much music. She drives an old truck, has an old computer, and does not carry a cell phone. Much of this is due to her financial situation, but even when she marries Edward and has access to money, she uses the cell phone only on occasion. Bella feels that she does not fit in well with normal humans and enjoys feeling part of both the Cullen family and the werewolf pack.

Her sense of social awkwardness is clear: "I couldn't let myself think about that. Not if I was going to have to act human for the next several hours." (*Eclipse*, 365.) Perhaps ironically, Bella, still human, has trouble acting like a regular teen and looks to the Cullens for cues on how to behave. Alice acts much more like a typical teen girl than Bella and constantly tries to encourage Bella to join in normal teen activities.

The Twilight Saga is full of teenagers acting as adults. The fate of the world sometimes rests on their shoulders, and they confront horrors and trials both alone and together, without the benefit of adults in authority. Charlie and Billy are prime examples of adults who mean well and who are good parents, but who are not able to do what is needed to keep everyone safe. "I would have tried to protect you too, if I'd had known how," Charlie confesses to Bella. (*Breaking Dawn*, 512.)

Leaving the Decades Behind, or When in Rome . . .

> "You will soon be leaving time behind altogether. So why should the transitory customs of one local culture affect the decision so much?"
>
> —*Edward* (Eclipse, 277–278)

Edward was born in Chicago in 1901. By the time the Cullen family met Alice and Jasper in the late fifties or early sixties, Edward had been "living" for about fifty years and seen two world wars, the flu pandemic that left him at death's door, and the Great Depression. The Depression may not have seemed so bad to the Cullen family, since they do not eat, sleep, or need shelter, but Edward surely noted its effects on the humans around him. Other vampires might not concern themselves with human events, being nomadic, but the Cullen family makes a concerted effort to blend in and would have felt a connection with the local humans of that era.

Having been "alive" for more than sixty years, one would imagine during the social protest movements of the 1960s that Edward might identify more with the grandparents of his teenage "peers" than with his fellow students, if he attended high school or college during that period. By that time he had witnessed the inception of automobile culture, the early days of human-powered flight, and the beginnings of space exploration. Edward, Rosalie, Jasper, Alice, and Emmett all observed the social upheaval associated with the New Deal, the civil rights movement, the rise and fall of the Berlin Wall, and the assassination of an American president. A great deal has happened during their "lifetimes" and yet they are able to act like teens of the day, not the wise old souls they have become.

For the Cullen family, human rites of passage become a way to pass the time. Alice in particular, having no memories of her human life, remembers all of these rites of passage only as a vampire. For her, proms, graduations, and weddings are all opportunities for fun. This may be one of the reasons she wants them for Bella as a human: she has the opportunity to live vicariously through Bella. Bella observes, "Probably Alice had done this on purpose, to force me into the center of attention—a place she thought I should enjoy more. She was forever trying to make me be human the way she thought humans should be." (*Eclipse*, 368.) Alice missed all of the typical human milestones as a teen. She has no memory of her human years because of her treatment in the asylum: "A hundred years earlier and she would have been burned at the stake for her visions. In the nineteen-twenties it was the asylum and the shock treatments." (*Twilight*, 448.)

With Bella as their connection to the modern era, the Cullens seem to have involved themselves to a greater extent in high school life than in previous years. The Cullen teens attend the Forks High School prom along with all of the human teens, although this would be Edward's first formal dance with a romantic interest. Having Bella around also gives Alice an excuse to throw a graduation party and invite most of their fellow students.

Part of the fun of the Twilight Saga is watching a nearly 110-year-old vampire—who has been masquerading as a teen for many decades—actually *become* a modern teenager when he falls in love with Bella. In *Twilight,* Edward considers his fellow classmates to be children, and he even refers to Jacob as a child, which perplexes Bella, because on the surface, Edward and Jacob are not far apart in age. In *Midnight Sun* the reader comes to understand Edward's perspective as he ponders his life and his relationship to others and the fact that he is the only single Cullen, brooding that "some days it was harder than others to live with three sets of perfectly matched lovers. This was one of them. Maybe they would all be happier without me hanging around, ill tempered and belligerent as the old man I should be by now." (*Midnight Sun,* 56.) Through the entire series Edward behaves more and more like a young man in love, which he is. By the end of the saga, it is no longer an act: he has become, once again, a young man. Together, he and Bella can now be teen vampires in love.

Notes

1. Taken from chapter 1 of *120 Years of American Education: A Statistical Portrait,* ed. Tom Snyder (Washington, DC: National Center for Education Statistics, 1993), http://nces.ed.gov/naal/lit_history.asp.

2. Ibid.

3. Centers for Disease Control and Prevention—Your Online Source for Credible Health information, www.cdc.gov/nchs/data/hus/hus08.pdf#026.

4. Lucy Rollin, *Twentieth-Century Teen Culture by the Decades: A Reference Guide* (Westport, CT: Greenwood Press, 1999), 82.

5. Ibid., 1.

6. Ibid., 92, 107

7. Ibid., 180–181

8. Ephraim Katz, *The Film Encyclopedia,* 5th ed., revised by Fred Klein and Ronald Dean Nolen (New York: HarperCollins Publishers, 2005), 879.

9. Ibid., 520
10. Rollin, *Twentieth-Century Teen Culture,* 187.
11. Ibid., 188.
12. Katz, *Film Encyclopedia*, 652–653.
13. Selective Service System Web site, www.sss.gov/induct.htm.
14. Ibid.
15. Ibid.

The Forks High School Faculty

Eveline Brugger is a lecturer at the University of Vienna, Austria, and an instructor at the Viennese Institute for Economic Promotion. She specializes in medieval Central European history and archival sciences. Thanks to her work in dusty old archives, she is no stranger to creatures who lurk in dark corners, although she is quite chagrined that she has yet to encounter one who sparkles.

Kat Burkhart is the Curator at the Carnegie Museum in Crawfordsville, Indiana, and the current president of the Association of Indiana Museums. She specializes in integrating popular culture into interdisciplinary museum exhibits and programs and could really use Alice's help with her closet.

Kristin Burnett is an Assistant Professor in the Department of History at Lakehead University in Thunder Bay, Ontario. Her research examines the health work of Aboriginal and non-Aboriginal women in the Prairie West. She does not find cold hard marble men attractive, especially the ones that creep through her window and stare at her all night.

Sara Buttsworth teaches in the history department at the University of Auckland, New Zealand. She recently coedited and contributed to *Restaging War in the Western World: Noncombatant Experiences 1890–Today* (2009), and is now involved in a project on representations of Nazism in postwar popular culture. Sara's research into princesses has led her to wonder about the correct cocktail apparel to accompany hunting with bare hands—and teeth.

Kate Cochran is an Assistant Professor of English and Director of the English Licensure Program at the University of Southern Mississippi, where she teaches courses in southern literature and English education. Her recent interest in pop culture vampires led her to write articles on the HBO series *True Blood*, as well as on the Twilight Saga. It's entirely possible that she is watching you from the tree outside your bedroom window.

Catherine Coker is an Assistant Professor of Library Science at Texas A&M University and the Coordinator of Research Services at Cushing Memorial Library and Archives. Her research focuses on the work and depictions of women in science fiction and fantasy. She is sometimes thought to be a vampire but has never (to anyone's knowledge, at least) sparkled in the sunlight.

Andrea Robertson Cremer is an Assistant Professor of History at Macalester College in St. Paul, Minnesota. She spends her days discussing the intersection of religion, sex, and violence in the early modern world. When she's not focused on Puritans, warfare, and witches, she's authoring children's literature—except the same themes show up in her fiction, too, hmm. Her debut novel *Nightshade* will be published by Philomel (Penguin) in fall 2010. She admits that if Jasper asked nicely, which of course he would, she'd let him bite her.

Elizabeth Baird Hardy, author of *Milton, Spenser, and the Chronicles of Narnia: Literary Sources for the C. S. Lewis Novels* (McFarland, 2007), is a senior instructor of English at Mayland Community College, where she was selected as the 2006 Outstanding Faculty member. She has had great success using the Twilight Saga with her students and in literary discussions. Hardy also teaches Appalachian culture and is a storyteller, historic interpreter, and frequent collaborator with her husband, award-winning author and historian Michael C. Hardy. When they and their two children aren't donning multiple layers of clothing to portray an 1860s family, they live on a foggy forest mountainside in the same corner of Appalachia

Emmett once called home and where one might just catch a glimpse of a bear.

Judith Leggatt is an Associate Professor and chair of the English Department at Lakehead University in Thunder Bay, Ontario. Her published papers include work on Lee Maracle, Thomas King, trickster poetics, Salman Rushdie, Charlotte Brontë, and postcolonial pedagogy. She is currently working on a larger project on Native science fiction. She prefers her vampires not to sparkle and thinks the Twilight Saga would be more interesting if told from Leah's point of view.

Janice Liedl is an Associate Professor of History at Laurentian University in Sudbury, Ontario. Her major scholarship deals with sixteenth-century English history and the Norse presence in North America. She's able to pass off her firsthand knowledge of these subjects as historical research, as long as she stays out of direct sunlight.

Grace Loiacono is a graduate student in Library Science and Information Studies and is writing a memoir of her life that is currently six volumes long. She is also investigating properties in Alaska large enough to house her entire coven.

Laura Loiacono is pursuing a graduate degree in English and plans to complete as many other degrees as she can find time for. She can usually be found indoors when the sun is out or engaging in a friendly game of baseball during a storm.

Kyra Glass von der Osten is a doctoral student at the University of Wisconsin, Madison's Media and Cultural Studies program. Her research centers on the portrayal of family, religion, and sexuality in popular film and television. She prefers to teach at night, since that's when the most interesting lessons are learned.

Nancy R. Reagin is a Professor of History and Women's and Gender Studies at Pace University in New York. She has published several books and a number of articles on modern German history, although she likes teaching even more. Her recent research has focused on the history of literary fan communities in Germany and the United States. She rooted for Team Jacob long past the point where any reasonable person would have given up, and thinks that cliff-diving should be an Olympic sport.

Birgit Wiedl is a lecturer at the University of Salzburg, Austria. She specializes in late medieval and early modern European history, with an emphasis on economics and urban history. Despite her obsession with people who have been dead for a long time, she is rather sure that she herself is not undead, even if the red eyes that stare out of her mirror on Monday mornings frequently give her cause to reconsider that.

Index

Alice Foresaw All of This

abortion, 192, 20, 67
Acciaiuoli, Agnolo, 216
Adams, Bert, 196
Adams, James Eli, 12
age issues
  adulthood and, 257–258
  Bella and, 246, 249, 253, 254, 257–259, 260
  conscription and, 256–257
  courtship and, 73
  dating and marriage, 253–256
  expectations and, 245–248
  rites of passage and, 259–261
  technology and, 249–253
  teenage lifestyle and, 248–249
Alamanno, Salvestro di, 214–215
Albizzi family, 212
Alec, 213
American Civil War, 89–91, 248, 256
  Appalachia and, 116
  camp life and, 95–98
  combat and, 98–99
  depression and, 102–104
  families and, 195–196
  male archetypes and, 165, 166–168, 173–174, 179–180
  promotion and, 99–102
  recruitment for, 91–95
American Dream (Cullen), 53
Anderson, Kim, 41
Anne of Green Gables (Montgomery), 10, 73–74, 192
Appalachia, 106–107
  family loyalty and, 122–123
  fatalism and, 121–122
  history of, 107–109
  humor and, 117–118
  industrialization and, 109–111, 115, 116
  isolation and, 114–115
  self-improvement and, 119–120
  stereotypes of, 111–114, 116–117, 118–119
  traditionalism and, 123–125
Aro, 54, 57, 210, 213, 215, 217–219
asylums, 127–132
  commitment to, 132–137
  therapies used by, 137–143
Austen, Jane, 15, 16–18, 71, 72, 183

Beauty and the Beast (film), 64, 65
Behringer, Wolfgang, 153, 157
Belle *(Beauty and the Beast)*, 64, 65
Benedict XIV, Pope, 233–234

Benito, 215
Bennet, Elizabeth *(Pride and Prejudice)*, 16–18, 71
Biggers, Jeff, 111
Black, Billy, 33, 35, 36–37, 78, 185, 259
Black, Jacob
  age issues and, 253, 255, 257–258
  courtship and, 75, 78
  fairy tales and, 58–59, 62–63, 64
  families and, 185, 191, 194–195
  imaginary history and, 22
  treaties and, 26–44
Blethlen, Tyler H., 108
Blue Ridge Folklife (Olsen), 113
"Body of an American, The" (Dos Passos), 11
Bow, Clara, 60–61
"Braut von Korinth, Die" (von Goethe), 234–235
Brinckle, Adriana P., 132
Brontë, Charlotte, 15, 16, 18–20, 84, 128, 130
Brontë, Emily, 15, 16, 20–23, 71–72, 183
Brugger, Eveline, 153
Buffy the Vampire Slayer, 236, 237
Byron, Lord (George Gordon), 14

Cabins in the Laurel (Sheppard), 112–113
Caius, 54, 57, 210
Calmet, Augustin, 233
Calvinism, 121
Carmen, 187
Carmilla (Le Fanu), 235
Carraway, Nick *(The Great Gatsby)*, 12
Cashman, Sean Dennis, 10–11
Catholicism, 150, 152
Charles I, King of England, 150–151
Charles II, King of England, 157
Charles V, Holy Roman Emperor, 208, 217
Charles VI, Holy Roman Emperor, 233
Charlotte, 94, 104, 172
Chelsea, 58, 214
Cherokee, 107–108
chess, 97–98, 117
Chettle, Henry, 150
childbearing, 187–192, 198, 248
Christianity Not Mysterious (Toland), 159
Church of England, 150
Cinderella (film), 62
Cinderella myth, 51, 59–60
Clearwater, Leah, 41, 188
Clearwater, Seth, 188
Clearwater, Sue, 195
Confirmation and Discovery of Witchcraft (Stearne), 154
conscription, 92, 103, 256–257
Coontz, Stephanie, 198
Cosmas (Medici family patron saint), 221
Cott, Nancy, 184
Cotton, Henry, 140
courtship rituals, 1, 70, 84–85, 196
  age issues and, 253–256
  in early twentieth century, 74–77
  gender roles and, 77–79, 246–248, 253–256 (*See also* women)
  influence of time period and, 80–84
  romance and, 71–74
  See also families
Cowley, Malcolm, 11, 12
Cromwell, Oliver, 151
Crowley, Tyler, 14, 15
Cullen, Alice, 2, 15, 43
  age issues and, 245, 246, 259, 260
  Civil War and, 95, 97, 104
  clairvoyance of, 127–128, 132–137, 138, 140–142, 168, 260
  fairy tales and, 66
  families and, 186–187, 189, 199
  male archetypes and, 173, 174–179
  vampire folklore and, 227, 242
  Volturi and, 209, 215
Cullen, Carlisle, 39
  age issues and, 245
  Appalachia and, 107–108, 119, 122, 124
  courtship and, 78

fairy tales and, 51, 53–54, 55, 60, 61, 62, 66
families and, 190–191, 194, 196, 199
Jasper and, 90
male archetypes and, 173, 176
vampire folklore and, 238, 242
Volturi and, 215, 219, 223
witch hunts and, 145–161
Cullen, Edward
abandonment by, 165, 175
age issues and, 245, 246, 248, 249–251, 254, 255, 256, 261
Alice and, 127
Carlisle and, 146, 148, 157–161
courtship and, 1, 70–85
Emmett and, 116–117, 120, 121
fairy tales and, 51–52, 55–56, 60, 65, 66
families and, 182–201
imaginary history and, 7–24
male archetypes and, 164, 165, 168, 169–170, 172, 175, 177, 178
treaties and, 27, 35–36, 41
vampire folklore and, 238, 241
Volturi and, 209, 213, 215, 223
Cullen, Emmett McCarty
age issues and, 245, 246, 249, 255–256, 260
Appalachian roots of, 106–111
Civil War and, 97
fairy tales and, 56
families and, 122–123, 189, 194
fatalism and, 121–122
humor and, 117–118
isolation and, 114–115
male archetypes and, 171, 173, 175–176
self-improvement and, 119–120
as stereotype, 111–114, 116–117, 118–119
traditionalism and, 123–125
Cullen, Esme, 60, 61, 78, 119
age issues and, 245, 248
families and, 189, 194, 199
male archetypes and, 173, 176
Cullen, Jim, 53
Cullen, Pastor, 146–150, 151–153, 156–158
Cullen, Renesmee, 43–44, 74, 149, 187–192, 193–195

Dance of the Vampires (Polanski), 237
Darcy, Fitzwilliam *(Pride and Prejudice)*, 15, 16–18, 71, 72
da Vinci, Leonardo, 222–223
Davis, William C., 100
Dawes Act, 42–43
daylight, 237, 240
Declaration of Independence, 53
Deism, 159–160
Demetri, 116, 121
Demonology (James I), 156
Demos, John, 184
Denalis, 187, 195, 257
Discovery of Witches, The (Hopkins), 154
Disney, Walt, 61
Dos Passos, John, 11
Dracula, Count *(Dracula)*, 229, 236, 251
Dracula (film), 251
Dracula (Stoker), 228–229, 230, 235–236
"Dreaming with Adam" (Garrett), 9
Dwyer, Phil, 49
Dwyer, Renée, 49, 64, 185, 248, 254

Earnshaw, Catherine *(Wuthering Heights)*, 21–23, 71–72
Eco, Umberto, 1
Egg and I, The, 113
Eleazar, 187
Emily, 35
England
English Civil War, 146, 150–152
Restoration, 157
witch hunts in, 145–161
Enlightenment, 159, 232
Essay Concerning Toleration (Locke), 159
Eyre, Jane *(Jane Eyre)*, 18, 84

Fairfax, William, 152
fairy tales, 47–48, 66–67
  American Dream and, 50, 52–59
  as "survival tales with hope," 48–52, 66
  Twilight references to, 59–66
families, 182–184, 186, 193–195
  extended, 193–195
  kinship groups and, 187–192
  love-based marriage and, 185–187, 196–197, 254
  loyalty and, 122–123, 213–214
  loyalty and male archetypes, 164, 168
  traditional, 184–185, 195–201
fangs, 240
Faulkner, William, 11
Fawkes, Guy "Guido," 150
feminism, 64, 183. *See also* women
fire, 237, 240
Fitzgerald, F. Scott, 12, 81
folklore, 227–229
  Appalachia and, 107
  Cullen family and, 238–242
  European legends of vampires, 228, 229–232, 237, 240, 242
  popular culture vampires and, 234–238
  vampire hunters and, 232–234
  See also literary history
Forks, Washington, 65, 77, 107, 184–185
Francis I, King of France

Gable, Clark, 251
Galileo, 159
Garrett, 56–57, 219
Garrett, George, 9, 23
Gatlinburg, Tennessee, 107, 108, 113, 115, 119
gender roles, age issues and, 246–248, 253–256. *See also* women
Gifford, George, 154
Gilbert, Sandra M., 14
Grant, Ulysses S., 102
Great Depression, 61, 63, 260
Great Gatsby, The (Fitzgerald), 12
Gubar, Susan, 14

Hale, Jasper, 2, 89–91, 93
  age issues and, 245, 246, 248, 249, 256, 260
  Civil War and, 95–104
  Emmett and, 116
  families and, 189, 199
  male archetypes and, 163–180
Hale, Rosalie, 60
  age issues and, 245, 246, 248, 249, 254, 255–256, 260
  Appalachia and, 123
  Emmett and, 112–113, 115
  fairy tales and, 56
  families and, 186, 189, 190, 194, 197
  male archetypes and, 176, 178
Harmon, Alexandra, 32
Heathcliff *(Wuthering Heights)*, 15, 16, 20–23, 71–72
Heidi, 219–220
Hemingway, Ernest, 11–12, 81
Herbert, Edward, 159
Hillyer, Jane, 138
History of the Wife (Yalom), 189–190
Hopkins, Matthew, 145, 153–156, 158

imaginary history, 7–8, 23–24
  Byronic hero image and, 14–16
  Darcy *(Pride and Prejudice)* and, 15, 16–18
  defined, 8–10
  Heathcliff *(Wuthering Heights)* and, 15, 16, 20–23
  Rochester *(Jane Eyre)* and, 15, 16, 18–20
  Victorian gentleman image and, 12–14
  World War I and, 10–12
immortality, 239
imprinting, 43, 194–195
Interview with the Vampire (Rice), 236–237, 240, 241
Irina, 39
It, 60–61

James, 15, 95, 121, 140, 143, 185
James I, King of England, 156
Jane, 58, 213
Jane Eyre (Charlotte Brontë), 15, 16, 18–20, 84, 128, 130
Jenkins, Henry, 80
Jillson, Cal, 55
Joham, 219
Jones, Loyal, 122
Julius II, Pope, 222

Kephart, Horace, 113–114, 118–119
Killer Angels, The (Shaara), 102
Kirkbride, Thomas, 129

Lamb, Lady Caroline, 14
Lancaster, Edith, 136
La Push, Washington, 37–39
Laud, William (archbishop of London), 151
Laurent, 38, 40, 185
Lee, Kate, 138
Lee, Robert E., 102
Le Fanu, Sheridan, 235
Life of Johnny Reb, The (Wiley), 97
Lincoln, Abraham, 91, 102
literary history
  courtship and, 71–74
  Dracula (Stoker) and, 235–236
  male archetypes and, 167
  See also folklore; imaginary history; *individual titles of books*
Locke, John, 159
Louis *(Interview with the Vampire)*, 236–237, 240
Lucy, 94
Lugosi, Bela, 236, 251

Machiavelli, Niccolò, 213, 217
male archetypes, 163–165, 179–180
  American Civil War and, 165, 166–168, 173–174, 179–180
  desertion and, 174–179
  violence and, 168–174
Marcus, 54, 57, 210, 221, 228
Marcus the Evangelist, 221, 223
Maria, 94, 101–102, 104, 173
Maria Theresia, Empress of Austria, 233
marriage
  age issues and, 197–198, 253–256
  courtship and, 76–79
  divorce and, 184–185
  fairy tales and, 66–67
  love-based, 185–187, 196–197, 254
  "traditional," 187
Mason, Bertha *(Jane Eyre)*, 16, 18, 19, 128, 130
McCall, Lenore, 141
McClellan, George, 102
McLean Asylum, 136
Medici, Bianca de, 218
Medici, Cosimo de, 207–209
Medici, Cosimo "Il Vecchio" (the Elder) de, 208, 211–213, 215, 218, 220–221
Medici, Lorenzo "Il Magnifico" de, 209, 214, 216–219, 222–223
Medici, Piero de, 216
Medici family, 207–209
  challenges to, 216–219
  patronage and, 210–215, 219–224
Meyer, Stephenie, 9, 11, 23–24, 241
Michelangelo, 208–209, 221, 222
Michelozzi, Niccolò, 220, 222
Mickey Finns, 139
Montgomery, L. M., 10, 73–74, 192
moral treatment movement, 129–130
Morganroth, Chris, III, 36
moroi, 230
Murnau, F. W., 237

Nachzehrer, 231
Nahuel, 15, 219
Native Americans, 26–28
  American Dream and, 58
  contemporary treaty conflicts and, 39–44
  indigenous identity and, 28–37
  treaties and rogue entities, 37–39
Nazareth Sanatorium, 133

Nettie, 94
nosferatu, 230
Nosferatu (Murnau), 237

Obama, Barack, 51
Obi, Doctor, 37
Ogle, Martha Jane Huskey, 108
Olsen, Ted, 113
Orr, Linda, 8
Orsini, Clarice, 214
Ossenfelder, Heinrich August, 234, 241
Our Southern Highlanders (Kephart), 113–114

Past, Present, and Personal (Demos), 184
Payne, Tommy, 34
Perrault, Charles, 48, 60
Peter, 94, 104, 172
Phillips, Mary, 154
Pi Beta Phi School, 119
Pinel, Phillipe, 129
Pius II, Pope, 211–212
Pius V, Pope, 217
Polanski, Roman, 237
popolazzo, 214–215
post-traumatic stress disorder (PTSD), 102–104
Powell, W. L., 38
Pretty Woman, 59
Pride and Prejudice (Austen), 15, 16–18, 71, 72
"princess culture," 52
Principe, Il (Macchiavelli), 217
Priory, 136
Public Vows (Cott), 184
Pullen, Dan, 37–39
Puritans, 53, 55, 151, 153
"purity movement," 192

Quakers, 55
Quileute Nation, 26–28
  contemporary treaty conflicts and, 39–44
  General Allotment Act (Dawes Act) and, 42–43
  Pullen and, 37–39
  Quinault River Treaty, 30
  Treaty of Olympia, 27, 30, 33
  See also Black, Jacob; Native Americans
Quinault River Treaty, 30

Ranft, Michael, 232–233
Rapunzel, 60
Rathbone, Jackson, 163
reading, 80, 97–98
Reagan, Leslie, 192
religion. *See* Native Americans; *individual names of religions and rulers*
Renaissance rulers, 207–209
  challenges to, 216–219
  patronage and, 209–215, 219–224
reproduction, 187–192, 198, 248
revenant myths, 230, 235, 237, 240
"Revenge of Literature" (Orr), 8
Revere, Paul, 56–57
Rialto Beach, 39–44
Riario, Cardinal Raffaele, 218
Rice, Anne, 236–237, 240, 241
Robertson, James R., 92
Rochester, Edward *(Jane Eyre),* 15, 16, 18–20, 84, 128, 130
Romeo and Juliet (Shakespeare), 71, 183
Rose, 173
Rosenfeld, Gavriel, 8
Royce, 63
Royster, Charles, 174, 180
Russell, Alice Bingham, 136–137
Ruthven, Lord, 241

Sakel, Manfred, 141
Salviati, Francesco (archbishop of Pisa), 218
Sanger, Margaret, 192
schizophrenia, 135, 142, 143
Second Beach, 39–44
Sevierville, Tennessee, 108
sexuality
  abstinence, 182–184

courtship and, 76–77, 79
families and, 191–192, 196, 197
reproduction and, 187–192, 198, 248
vampire folklore and, 237–238, 241
See also families; marriage
Sforza, Francesco, 216
Shaara, Michael, 102
Shakespeare, William, 71, 183
Sharpe, James, 157
Sheppard, Muriel Earley, 112–113
Sherman, William, 173–174
Shirley, Anne, 73
Sixtus IV, Pope, 217, 218
slavery, 33, 166
Sleeping Beauty, 61, 62–63
Slotkin, Richard, 166
Smith, Daniel Blake, 191
Snow White and the Seven Dwarfs (film), 60–62
Snow White (character), 60–61
Soldier's Pay (Faulkner), 11
Solimena, Francesco, 223–224
Southey, Robert, 235
sports, 97, 117, 120
staking, 237
Stanley, Jessica, 17
Stearne, John, 154–155, 158
Stein, Gertrude, 11
Stevens, Isaac I., 29–30
Still, James, 106
Stoker, Bram, 228–229, 230, 235–236
Stone, Elizabeth T., 136
strigoi, 230, 238, 240
Summers, Montague, 234, 240
Sun Also Rises, The (Hemingway), 11–12
sunlight, 237, 240
Swan, Bella
age issues and, 246, 249, 253, 254, 257–259, 260
Alice and, 127, 133–134, 140
courtship and, 1, 70–85
Emmett and, 112, 115, 118, 119, 121
fairy tales and, 48–67
families and, 182–201
imaginary history and, 7–24
Jasper and, 98
male archetypes and, 164, 171, 172, 175–176, 178–180
treaties and, 26–44
vampire folklore and, 229, 234, 241, 242
Volturi and, 209, 219–220, 223–224
witch hunts and, 146–147, 158
Swan, Charlie, 35, 78, 119, 120, 123
age issues and, 259
fairy tales and, 49, 56, 64–65
families and, 185, 194–195
imaginary history and, 12, 13

Talbout, John, 140
Tanya, 172
Thalaba the Destroyer (Southey), 235
Tillotson, Kenneth, 140
Toland, John, 159
Tractat von dem Kauen und Schmatzen der Todten in Gräbern (Ranft), 232–233
Trail of Tears, 108
Transylvania, 228
treaty negotiation, 26–28
Appalachia and, 107–109
contemporary conflicts and, 39–44
indigenous identity and, 28–37
rogue entities and, 37–39
Treaty of Olympia, 27, 30, 33
Tulloch, John, 80
Twilight (film), 1, 48, 64, 163

Uley, Sam, 31, 32, 33, 35, 40–41, 42
Upton, Jonika, 133

"Vampir, Der" (Ossenfelder), 234
vampires, 52–53, 228
Appalachian people compared to, 112
characteristics of, 237, 239, 240
legends about blood, 229, 230, 235, 238, 239
"newborn," 3, 41, 66, 101, 127, 171, 177, 178
vampire hunters, 232–234

vampires (*continued*)
"vegetarian" lifestyle of, 21, 164–165, 173, 240
witch hunts and, 153
See also folklore; literary history
Vampires (Voltaire), 229
Vasari, Giorgio, 220
venom, 122, 239
Victoria, 15, 38, 39, 40, 60, 101, 171, 173, 185, 213
Vlad III "the Impaler," Prince of Wallachia, 228
Voltaire, 229, 239
Volterra, Italy, 209, 210–211, 219, 221, 223, 227–228, 242
Volturi, 2
Carlisle Cullen and, 149
challenges to, 216–219
Emmett Cullen and, 120, 121, 124
fairy tales and, 54, 57
families and, 185, 186–187, 195
imaginary history and, 15
male archetypes and, 176
patronage and, 209–215
treaties and, 38, 40
vampire folklore and, 227–229, 238–242
von Goethe, Johann Wolfgang, 234–235

Walt Disney Company, 52, 61–62, 63–64, 65. *See also individual names of characters and films*
Watauga Association, 107–108
"Why Do We Ask 'What If?' (Rosenfeld), 8
Wiley, Bell, 97
Williams, Michael, 110, 118
Wilson, Margaret Isobel, 140
Wilson, Woodrow, 10
Winn, J. Emmett, 59
witch hunts, 145–146, 158–160
Hopkins and, 145, 153–156
Restoration and, 157–158
seventeenth-century London and, 146–153
vampire folklore and, 238–239
women
American Dream and, 51, 58
Civil War and, 91–95
commitment of, to asylums, 132–137
courtship and, 74–77, 81, 83, 84–85
fairy tales and, 60, 64
feminism and, 64, 183
witch hunts and, 154
Wooten, Bayard, 112–113
Working Girl, 59
World War I, 10–12, 73, 81, 256
World War II, 64, 256
writers, Appalachia and, 112–114
Wuthering Heights (Emily Brontë), 15, 16, 20–23, 71–72, 183

Yalom, Marilyn, 189–190, 196